God and Ethics

God and Ethics

Editor

David Baggett

Basel • Beijing • Wuhan • Barcelona • Belgrade • Novi Sad • Cluj • Manchester

Editor
David Baggett
Philosophy
Houston Christian University
Houston, TX, USA

Editorial Office
MDPI
St. Alban-Anlage 66
4052 Basel, Switzerland

This is a reprint of articles from the Special Issue published online in the open access journal *Religions* (ISSN 2077-1444) (available at: https://www.mdpi.com/journal/religions/special_issues/A00AZSX32V).

For citation purposes, cite each article independently as indicated on the article page online and as indicated below:

Lastname, Firstname, Firstname Lastname, and Firstname Lastname. Article Title. *Journal Name* **Year**, *Volume Number*, Page Range.

ISBN 978-3-0365-9222-0 (Hbk)
ISBN 978-3-0365-9223-7 (PDF)
doi.org/10.3390/books978-3-0365-9223-7

Cover image courtesy of Chad Greiter

Contents

Preface

The relationship between God and ethics has been a topic of perennial interest to thinkers from a number of disciplines and has received renewed attention more recently in light of the resurgence of interest in theistic ethics and variants of the moral argument. This Special Issue provides a deep dive into several aspects of this rich discussion.

David Baggett
Editor

Editorial

God and Ethics

David Baggett

Department of Philosophy, School of Christian Thought Apologetics, Houston Christian University, Houston, TX 77074, USA; dbaggett@hbu.edu

This unique and rich volume is the culmination of a Special Issue of *Religions* with a focus on "God and Ethics", a topic both rich with historical significance and of special contemporary importance in light of the recent resurgence of interest in this branch of natural and philosophical theology, philosophy of religion, and religious epistemology. Suggested themes for the Special Issue include whether or not the evidence furnished by various aspects of ethics points in the direction of God and, if so, in what fashion; discussions of obstacles in the way of theistic ethics; and challenges in making the best sense of ethics apart from theism.

It was suggested in the original call for papers that the nature of the adduced moral evidence might cover (but was not limited to) intrinsic human value, binding moral obligations, moral knowledge, moral transformation, the category of evil, issues associated with reconciling moral reasoning and prudential reasoning, and the historical discussion of moral atheology or the moral argument. Matters of the roles of reason and emotion in moral epistemology, the nature of potential dependence relations of morality on God, and what a sufficiently robust moral theology looks like are all topics for investigation that are rife with potential.

The ten contributions that passed muster by surviving peer review did not disappoint, and they now comprise this collection, making for an exciting contribution to the literature. We are deeply grateful to all the excellent contributors and all the good folks at *Religions* for everything they did to make this volume possible.

William Lane Craig starts with his article entitled "Is God's Moral Perfection Reducible to His Love"? Defenders of the *identity thesis* maintain that God's moral perfection is reducible to and identical to God's love, but Craig argues that this thesis overlooks the fact that, biblically, God's righteousness comprises both God's love and justice. Moreover, Craig argues that divine justice is, in some significant measure, retributive in nature. This is especially evident in God's eschatological punishment of the wicked, which can only be justified on retributive grounds. Such a retributive punishment cannot be attributed to love but is the just desert of the wicked.

Kevin Kinghorn replies directly to Craig's piece with an article of his own: "God's Moral Perfection as His Beneficent Love. Comment on Craig (2023). Is God's Moral Perfection Reducible to His Love?" Craig had insisted that Kinghorn was wrong in reducing God's moral goodness to his beneficent aim of drawing all people to himself. For Craig, God's moral goodness, best conceived in terms of righteousness, must also include God's retributive justice toward the wicked, who deserve the punishment they receive. Kinghorn's response is that Craig's argument rests on two assumptions about value, neither of which, he argues, Christian theists have good reason to affirm.

After that, we shift gears and devote several chapters to works of critical scrutiny by secular thinkers, starting with J. P. Moreland's "A Critical Assessment of Shafer-Landau's Ethical Non-Naturalism". Moreland first specifies the nature of two versions of naturalism and argues that one is embraced ubiquitously—more importantly, should be embraced—by contemporary naturalists. He does so because, if he is right about this, there will be a significant burden of proof for Shafer-Landau to meet. In Moreland's view, that burden

Citation: Baggett, David. 2023. God and Ethics. *Religions* 14: 1290. https://doi.org/10.3390/rel14101290

Received: 28 September 2023
Accepted: 6 October 2023
Published: 13 October 2023

is strong enough to justify the claim that a critic's epistemic task is merely to provide undercutting defeaters for Shafer-Landau's position and not to proffer rebutting defeaters, although Moreland attempts to supply both. After presenting a crucial characterization of contemporary naturalism followed by a critique of naturalist emergent properties, Moreland states and critiques Shafer-Landau's ontology and does the same for his epistemology. Both are evaluated with a particular focus on their plausibility to support Shafer-Landau's ethical non-naturalism.

Then, this is followed by Adam Lloyd Johnson's "Is It Morally Permissible for Some People to Rape and Murder? Responding to Erik Wielenberg's Argument that Divine Command Theory Fails to Explain How Psychopaths Have Moral Obligations". Atheist moral philosopher Wielenberg recently argued that Divine Command Theory is implausible as an explanation of objective morality because it fails to explain how psychopaths have moral obligations. In this chapter, Johnson explains that everyone agrees the consciences of psychopaths do not work as they should, but there is disagreement among experts as to whether (a) the consciences of psychopaths *do not* inform them of right and wrong or (b) the consciences of psychopaths *do* inform them of these things but merely do not generate the appropriate moral emotions.

Johnson argues that, based on psychological research, a strong case can be made for (b), and thus, under DCT, psychopaths do have moral obligations because their consciences inform them of what is right from wrong and that they should do what is right. He also argues that even if (a) is true, God can and does make psychopaths aware of what is right and wrong and that they should do what is right using other means such as rationality, society, parents, culture, direct verbal commands, etc. So, even if (a) is true, psychopaths still have moral obligations under DCT because they do know right from wrong, and they should do what is right. Lastly, Johnson turns the tables on Wielenberg and points out that his theory is even worse than DCT when it comes to providing an explanation for the moral rights and obligations of psychopaths.

Christopher R. Pruett extends this discussion of Wielenberg and the issues of psychopathy in his piece called "Divine Command Theory, Robust Normative Realism, and the Argument from Psychopathy: A Reply to Erik Wielenberg". Again, Wielenberg's fascinating *argument from psychopathy* from moral psychology against Divine Command Theory (DCT) focuses on the pathology known as psychopathy—a perennial interest for those concerned with abnormal and moral psychology. The strength of the argument is that it forces the Divine Command Theorist to maintain that there are some human beings who have no moral obligations yet still do evil actions. This, he argues, is an implausible thesis. Therefore, DCT is false. In this chapter, Pruett defends DCT and argues that there is good reason to be neutral or skeptical with regard to whether psychopaths have moral obligations and, to the degree that they do, whether they are able to grasp morality in a way consistent with DCT. Furthermore, if the argument does present a serious problem for DCT, then it does so for Wielenberg's own view, Robust Normative Realism (RNR), just as much as for DCT.

In "Theological Utilitarianism, Supervenience, and Intrinsic Value", Matthew Alexander Flannagan criticizes a different aspect of Wielenberg's work, namely the notion that robust realism can account for the "common-sense moral belief" that "some things distinct from God are intrinsically good". In contrast, Wielenberg argues that theological stateism cannot account for this belief. Hence, robust realism has a theoretical advantage over all forms of theological stateism. Flannagan replies by pointing out that Wielenberg distinguishes between R- and D-supervenience. The coherence of Wielenberg's robust realism depends on this distinction. Flannagan argues that this distinction undermines Shafer-Landau's critique of theological stateism by making three points. First, once we utilize the distinction between R- and D-supervenience, Wielenberg's argument for the incompatibility of theological stateism and intrinsic value fails. Second, theological stateism is compatible with intrinsic value. A historical example of theological utilitarianism, expounded by thinkers George Berkeley and William Paley, shows that someone can accept that moral properties simultaneously R-supervene on God's will and D-supervene on the natural properties of actions. Third, robust realism and theological stateism are in the same boat regarding intrinsic value once we distinguish between R- and D-supervenience.

Next, in "The Secular Moral Project and the Moral Argument for God: A Brief Synopsis History", Dale Eugene Kratt provides an overview of the history of what he calls the secular moral project by providing a synopsis of the history of the moral argument for God's existence and the various historical processes that have contributed to the secularization of ethics. Kratt argues that three key thinkers propelled the secular moral project forward from the middle of the 19th century to the 20th: John Stuart Mill, whose ethical thinking in *Utilitarianism* served as the background to all late 19th century secular ethical thinking; Henry Sidgwick, who, in the *Methods*, indisputably established the secular autonomy of ethics as a distinctive discipline (metaethics); and G. E. Moore, whose work, *Principia Ethica*, stood at the forefront of virtually all secular metaethical debates concerning naturalism and non-naturalism in the first half of the 20th century. Although secular metaethics continues to be the dominant ethical view of the academy, it is shown that theistic metaethics is a strong reemerging position in the early 21st century.

In "Might Beauty Bolster the Moral Argument for God?" David Baggett discusses the moral argument from a different angle. John Hare argues that Kant, in his *Third Critique*, offers an aesthetic argument for God's existence that shares premises with his famous moral argument. Karl Ameriks demurs, expressing skepticism that this is so. In this chapter, Baggett stakes out an intermediate position, arguing that the resources of Kant provide ingredients for an aesthetic argument but one that is distinctly less than a transcendental argument for God or an entailment relation. Regardless of whether the argument is best thought of as abductive in nature, a C-inductive argument, or a Pascalian natural sign, prospects for its effective formulation are strong. And such an argument, for its resonances with the moral argument(s), can work well in tandem with it (them), a fact not surprising at all if Kant was right that beauty—in accordance with an ancient Greek tradition—exists in close organic relation to the good. More generally, Baggett argues that the sea change in Kant's studies over the last decade or so should help us see that Kant is an ally, rather than foe, to aesthetic theodicists.

In the penultimate chapter, Martin Jakobsen's "A Christological Critique of Divine Command Theory" revisits DCT by presenting a theological critique of Divine Command Theory. First, he argues that this theory does not qualify as a Christian moral theory because it lacks connections to central parts of Christian theology, such as Christology. This does not imply that the theory is wrong, nor that it is inconsistent with Christianity, only that it is not Christian as such. Second, he argues that DCT does not fit well with the New Testament's vision of the moral life in which conforming to the image of Christ has precedence over adherence to the law. This argument, he argues, implies that the Christian ethicist should look elsewhere for a metaethical theory. He instead argues in favor of a moral theory of imitation, in which the moral life consists of imitating God, the prime exemplar of goodness, which is made possible via an imitation of Christ.

Finally, Brandon Rickabaugh's chapter follows: "Normative Reasons, Epistemic Autonomy, and Accountability to God". According to many, human autonomy is necessary for moral action and yet incompatible with being morally accountable to God's divine commands. By issuing commands that ground normative facts, God demands our accountability without understanding our normative reasons for moral action, which vitiates human autonomy. Rickabaugh calls this the *Autonomy Objection to Theism* (AOT) and argues that there is an unexplored connection between models of normative reason and AOT and that any plausible AOT must be stated in terms of an adequate model of normative reason. There are two broad metaethical categories for models of normative reason: anti-realist and realist views. He defends the thesis that both anti-realism and realism about normative reasons fail to support AOT using a dilemma. If the AOT defender adopts anti-realism for normative reasons (subjectivism and constructivism), AOT loses its force. However, if the AOT defender adopts moral realism, they face the same problem as the theist, as normative fact constrains autonomy. Consequently, AOT is a problem for all moral realists, including non-theists, such as Russ Shafer-Landau, David Enoch, and Erik Wielenberg, among others

Conflicts of Interest: The author declares no conflict of interest.

 religions

 MDPI

Article

Is God's Moral Perfection Reducible to His Love?

William Lane Craig

Department of Philosophy, Houston Christian University, Houston, TX 77074, USA; wcraig@hbu.edu

Abstract: Defenders of the identity thesis maintain that God's moral perfection is reducible to and identical to His love. Unfortunately, this thesis overlooks the fact that, biblically, God's righteousness comprises both His love and justice. Moreover, divine justice is, in some significant measure, retributive in nature. This is especially evident in God's eschatological punishment of the wicked, which can be justified only on retributive grounds. Such a retributive punishment cannot be attributed to love but is the just desert of the wicked.

Keywords: moral perfection; retributive justice; divine love; identity thesis; punishment; consequentialist justice

Citation: Craig, William Lane. 2023. Is God's Moral Perfection Reducible to His Love?. *Religions* 14: 140. https://doi.org/10.3390/rel14020140

Academic Editors: David Baggett and Joseph Rivera

Received: 30 November 2022
Revised: 27 December 2022
Accepted: 9 January 2023
Published: 20 January 2023

Believers in the monotheistic tradition have always held that God is perfectly good, and Christian theologians have thought of God as the fount of all varieties of goodness, whether moral, metaphysical, esthetic, or any other. Here, my primary interest is in God's moral goodness from a Christian perspective. Obviously, God, as a being worthy of worship, possesses moral attributes. A being that is very good but morally imperfect might be worthy of admiration or respect, but only a being that is morally perfect could be worthy of worship.[1] Indeed, perfect being theology entails, by definition, that God is morally perfect since to be morally imperfect or morally flawed is inconsistent with perfection. Hence, God must be perfectly good.

An important question arises in connection with God's perfect goodness; namely, what is the content of God's perfect goodness? In order to answer this question, let us first look to the biblical data concerning divine goodness.

1. Biblical Data Concerning Divine Goodness

The Bible ascribes to God a wealth of moral properties, including holiness, righteousness, love, grace, mercy, long-suffering, loving kindness, and faithfulness.[2] We might think that the goodness of God is a general moral property designating God's moral perfection and comprising His righteousness, love, grace, mercy, and long-suffering,[3] but, biblically speaking, this would be, in fact, incorrect. Rather, as John Feinberg explains, the Hebrew words for goodness *tôb/tûb* have, like the English word, a breadth of meanings: (1) practical, economic, or material blessing; (2) abstract properties such as desirability, pleasantness, and beauty; (3) quality or expense; (4) moral goodness; and (5) *eudaimonia* (the "good life") (Feinberg 2001, p. 366). When the biblical authors speak of God's goodness, what they typically have in mind is not God's moral goodness but God's beneficence or generosity. Thus the Psalms are filled with grateful praises for the goodness of the LORD (Ps 34.8a; 100. 5; 106.1; 107.1; 118.1, 29; 135.3; 145.7, 9; cf. I Chron 16.34; II Chron 5.13; 7.3). Feinberg concludes, "When we look at the biblical concept of divine goodness, one major idea stands out. It is that God is concerned about the well-being of his creatures and does things to promote it. Of course, God is interested in doing what is morally good and right, but biblical writers capture that idea by referring to his *righteousness* and *holiness*" (Feinberg 2001, p. 366; my emphasis). Since our interest is in God's moral goodness, we are, therefore, better advised to look more closely at the biblical data concerning God's righteousness, rather than His goodness.

The Hebrew word *ṣedeq* (righteousness) and the Greek expression *dikaiosynē theou* (the righteousness of God) are Janus-faced terms used to denote, among other things, God's moral character.[4] That is to say, God's righteousness in Scripture looks in two directions, as it were, covering both God's love and His justice.[5] Feinberg observes that there is a wealth of biblical material concerning the righteousness of God. Words deriving from the root *ṣedeq* occur 523 times in the OT. The nominal forms fall mainly into three groups: legal righteousness (123 times), ethical righteousness (114 times), and correctness (26 times). The NT has 92 examples of the noun *dikaiosynē*, 39 of the verb *dikaioō* (to justify or reckon righteous), 81 of the adjective *dikaios* (just or righteous), ten of the noun *dikaiōma* (ordinance or sentence of justification), and five of the adverb *dikaiōs* (justly or righteously) (Morris 1983, p. 181).

In recent decades, a debate about the expression *dikaiosynē theou* has arisen as a result of the so-called "new perspective on Paul," some proponents of which construe God's righteousness to be His covenant faithfulness. This construal is not itself new but goes back to German theologians like Hermann Cremer in the late 19th century.[6] Cremer believed that the righteousness of God is not a normative concept but rather a relational concept involving persons. He claimed that God's righteousness has only to do with God's saving activity. Cremer did not deny that God's salvation of the righteous entails His punishment of the wicked, but he insisted that God's righteousness finds expression only in His saving action. Proponents of the new perspective followed Cremer in thinking God's righteousness to be a relational, not a normative, concept, and they identified it with God's being faithful to His covenant people.

The claim here seems to be implausible on the face of it, for it amounts to nothing less than the claim that teams of English translators, not to mention non-English translators, have for generations actually mistranslated the expression *dikaiosynē theou*, since the English word "righteousness" does not mean *faithfulness*.[7] Proponents of the new perspective would have us believe that the meaning of NT Greek *dik-* words, under the influence of the LXX, were fundamentally changed so as to introduce covenantal ideas not present in extra-biblical Greek. The Hebrew word *ṣedeq* (also, in effect, mistranslated by "righteousness") is also said not to express a normative concept like *moral goodness* but rather a relational concept like *faithful to*.

The implausibility of the new perspective's reductionism is perhaps best seen by asking what Paul holds the opposite of righteousness, that is, unrighteousness, to be.[8] It is not unfaithfulness, but wickedness and ungodliness (Rom 1.18) or lawlessness (II Cor 6.14). Faithlessness is one of a litany of sins listed by Paul, resulting in God's just condemnation (Rom 1.29-31; 2.2). Righteousness is a broad moral property that entails faithfulness since to break one's word is wrong but is not reducible to it. As Mark Seifrid puts it, "All 'covenant-keeping' is righteous behavior, but not all righteous behavior is 'covenant-keeping.' It is misleading, therefore, to speak of 'God's righteousness' as his 'covenant-faithfulness.'" (Seifrid 2001, p. 424). Seifrid points out that righteousness language in the OT has primarily to do with God's role as the Judge and Ruler of creation. As such, it is normative, having to do with God's establishing the correct moral order in the world. It takes on a positive or salvific sense because biblical writers expect God to intervene to reinstate the correct order when it is usurped by evil in the world. It takes on a negative or punitive sense because biblical writers expect the reinstatement of correct order to involve the punishment of the wicked. As Seifrid so aptly puts it, "Retribution remains on the 'backside' of divine acts of righteousness".[9] So while there are 64 instances of God's saving righteousness in the OT, Seifrid counts as well 15 cases in which God's righteousness is conceived in retributive or punitive terms (Exod 9.27; Ps 7.10; 7.12; 11.5-7; 50.6; Is 1.27; 5.15-16; 10.22; 28.17; Lam 1.18; II Chron 12.1-6; Neh 9.33; Dan 9.7; 9.14; 9.16). God's righteousness comprises both aspects.[10]

Fortunately, proponents of the new perspective have now backed away from the overly simplistic, one-sided conception of God's righteousness. For example, J. D. G. Dunn, in response to his critics, acknowledges that the Hebrew concept of righteousness cannot be reduced to covenant faithfulness or salvation. The righteousness language in the Hebrew Scriptures also involves punitive divine justice, according to which righteousness is "understood as measured by a norm, right order, or that which is morally right", with the qualification that "the norm is not seen as some abstract ideal. .., but rather as a norm concretised in relation" between God and creatures.[11] So when we come to Romans, "That God's righteousness towards the peoples he has created includes wrath and judgment as well as faithfulness and salvation is clearly implicit in the sequences Rom. 1.16–18 and 3.3–6"(Dunn 2008, pp. 64–65).

The righteousness of God, therefore, seems to be the relevant biblical concept for God's moral perfection and comprises both His love and justice. On the one hand, the Scriptures famously assert that "God is love" (I Jn 4.8) and even ascribe relationships of love to the eternal Trinitarian persons (Jn 3.35; 14.31; 17.22–26). At the same time, the Scriptures are replete with references to God's hatred of sin, jealousy, wrath, and vengeance, which are manifestations of His justice.[12]

2. The Content of God's Moral Character

A number of contemporary philosophical theologians sought to reduce the content of God's moral character to His *agape* love. Jordan Wessling dubbed this claim the Identity Thesis. The thesis is that "God's love is identical to His moral goodness", such that "God possesses no moral attribute that is not essentially and most fundamentally a matter of love".[13] This superficially appealing thesis seems to be the lingering vestige of classical liberal theology, which eschewed the justice and wrath of God in favor of His love. Despite the eclipse of classical liberal theology in the early twentieth century, it has become almost an axiom among contemporary theologians that God does not need to be reconciled to sinners; the entire obstacle lies on our side. It is said that because the NT authors use *katalassō* (reconcile) and its cognates only with respect to human beings, not God, we may infer that God does not need to be reconciled to humanity, but only humanity to a welcoming God. Our hearts need to be changed so that our hostility to God evaporates and we embrace His love. However, such an argument from silence overlooks the abundant scriptural testimony to God's justice and wrath, which may demand satisfaction and propitiation.[14] In contrast to classical liberal theology, neo-liberal theology, if we may coin a term, affirms God's wrath but sees it wholly as a manifestation of His love aimed at the reformation of sinners.

Wessling adduces two lines of New Testament evidence in support of the Identity Thesis. First, Jesus, as well as various New Testament authors, teaches that love fulfills the law. Second, Jesus, as well as certain biblical authors, ground this completed human ethic of love in God's nature. These considerations do not, however, bear the theological freight that Wessling would lay upon them. The appeal to Jesus' aphorism about love's fulfilling the law's positive demands overlooks what those who break the law are said to deserve, which is punitive justice. That the law reflects God's loving character most certainly does not imply that God's righteousness does not comprise justice as well as love or that His justice is reducible to His love.

We have seen that, biblically speaking, justice, as well as love, belongs to God's righteousness. But what sort of justice is this? Theories of justice may be broadly classified as either *retributive* or *consequentialist*. Retributive theories of justice hold that punishment is justified because the guilty deserve to be punished. Consequentialist theories of justice hold that punishment is justified because of the extrinsic goods that may be realized thereby, such as deterrence of crime, sequestration of dangerous persons, and reformation of wrongdoers. Retributive theories are often said to be retrospective, imposing punishment for crimes committed, whereas consequentialist theories are prospective, aiming to prevent crimes from being committed.

Retributivism may be further distinguished as either positive or negative. While negative retributivism holds that the innocent should not be punished because they do not deserve it, the essence of retributive justice lies in positive retributivism, which holds that the guilty should be punished because they deserve it. What distinguishes retributivism as a theory of justice is the positive thesis that the punishment of the guilty is an intrinsic good because the guilty deserve it. The intrinsic goodness of punishment of the guilty does not preclude that there are also extrinsic goods that might be achieved by giving people their just deserts. But what ultimately justifies punishment is that it is the just desert of the guilty.

In the Bible, God is described as a positive retributivist "who will by no means clear the guilty" (Exod 34.7). In the biblical view, the wicked deserve punishment (Rom 1.32; Heb 10.29), and the Bible ascribes to God retribution (Heb. *gemûl* Is 59.18; *neqamah* Jer 50.15; 51.6; Grk. *ekdikēsis* Rom 11.9; *avtapodoma* Rom 12.19) for sins so that God's justice must be in some significant measure retributive.[15] The God of the Bible is not just a benevolent father figure but, as Hugo Grotius emphasized in his critique of Faustus Socinus, God is the impartial Ruler and Judge of the creation, responsible for maintaining its moral order (Grotius 1889, II).

Indeed, it is plausible, I think, that retributive justice belongs essentially to God. The more central and prominent an attribute is in the biblical picture of God, the stronger the case for taking it to be an essential attribute of God rather than accidental to Him. It is hard to think of an attribute more central and prominent in the biblical picture of God than His righteousness, which comprises His justice. "Shall not the Judge of all the earth do right?" (Gen 18.25). "Is there injustice (*adikia*) on God's part? By no means!" (Rom 9.14). It would have been inconceivable to the biblical authors that God might act unjustly.

Kevin Kinghorn, like Socinus, disputes that retributive justice belongs to God's essence. For God, existing alone, sans creation, would not exhibit retributive justice in intra-Trinitarian relationships: "because the Father, Son, and Holy Spirit could never wrong one another, retributive justice would never be operative" (Kinghorn and Travis 2019, p. 30). He concludes, "God's attribute of justice is not essential to God's nature in the way that his attribute of love is essential. God's justice is only needed in the world (such as ours) where there are imperfections and shortages. God's essential nature is therefore not just"(Kinghorn and Travis 2019, p. 35). But this objection is misconceived. God can have the property of giving every person his due without the existence of created persons. Moreover, God sans creation exhibits negative retributive justice among the persons of the Trinity in that He does not punish the innocent. Kinghorn is right that, sans creation, God is not wrathful, just as He is not wrathful in possible worlds in which created persons never sin, so that wrath is not an essential property of God.[16] But God, though wrathless, is in such circumstances still essentially righteous and perfectly just.

In any case, in relation to created persons, the God of the Bible exhibits retributive justice. Wessling notwithstanding, there is no *prima facie* incompatibility between God's valuing the flourishing of people and valuing friendship with them, even though He sentences them to their just desert with no expectation of reform. Retributivism is perfectly compatible with God's ongoing love for those He punishes, even the damned in hell, just as it is possible for a judge to personally love and forgive someone brought before his bar, even as he declares him guilty and sentences him to severe punishment. God can personally will the good of sinners and desire their union with Him without waiving the demands of retributive justice. In short, God's giving the guilty their just desert does not preclude His loving them.

During the first half of the twentieth century, under the influence of psychologists and social scientists, retributive theories of justice were frowned upon in favor of consequentialist theories. Fortunately, there has been, over the past half-century or so, a renaissance of theories of retributive justice, accompanied by a fading of consequentialist theories,[17] so that the Christian theologian working within the mainstream position need not be diverted by the need to justify a retributive theory of justice.

It is striking that proponents of the Identity Thesis tend to endorse, explicitly or implicitly, a consequentialist theory of divine justice; for they insist that God's sole purpose in punishing wrongdoers is reformative rather than retributive. So, for example, Kinghorn says that God's administration of justice will ultimately be for the same reason that we need rules of law in the first place, namely, the "benevolent goal that people flourish".[18] In response to Arthur Holmes' critique of Christian consequentialism, Kinghorn does not address the shortcomings of consequentialist theories of justice but simply doubles down in affirming a sort of Christian utilitarianism.[19] He appeals to God to direct our efforts to ensure that acts of beneficence are also equitable, which only pushes the problem upstairs, so to speak. Does God direct His acts in accordance with justice? Kinghorn responds, "I find no reason for thinking that justice must be added … to God's love in order to give God's actions direction" (Kinghorn and Travis 2019, p. 78). Given a consequentialist theory of justice, God's love suffices to motivate His harsh treatment of sinners aimed at their reformation. Kinghorn declares, "God's expressions of wrath are not vindictive or emotional outbursts aimed at the punishment of unrighteous people as an ultimate goal"(Kinghorn and Travis 2019, pp. 142–43). This characterization of retributivism is, of course, a straw man since the retributivist would agree that God's expressions of wrath are not vindictive or emotional outbursts but may nonetheless be aimed at the punishment of unrighteous people as the ultimate goal. God's wrath is an affective expression of God's retributive justice so that the issue is not ultimately wrath but the nature of God's justice.[20] Kinghorn's endorsement of consequentialism is clearly in view when he affirms, "Expressions of divine wrath must … be for the ultimate, benevolent purpose God has of drawing people into relationship with himself, thereby bringing fullness of life to them".[21]

Not only is pure consequentialism at odds with the biblical view of divine justice, but consequentialism seems, in any case, ill-suited to serve as the justification for divine punishment because God's judgment is described in the Bible as ultimately eschatological. The ungodly are "storing up wrath" for themselves for God's final day of judgment (Rom 2.5). The punishment imposed at that point could seemingly serve no other purpose than retribution.[22] For all hope of reform is gone. But the damned are punished nonetheless because they deserve it. God, in effect, carries out what Kant deemed to be necessary for a just society about to dissolve: to execute any prisoners condemned to death (Kant 1999, p. 140).

Wessling defends God's ongoing punishment of the damned aimed at persuading them "to start down the path of spiritual transformation" but only at the admitted expense that one "is willing to allow for post-mortem opportunities for salvation in hell," (Wessling 2021, p. 152) a consoling but unbiblical view (Mt 25.46; II Thess 1.9). Moreover, Wessling's view either must deny God's omniscience so that He continues to pursue a pointless action that only perpetuates suffering or, in effect, transforms hell into purgatory and results in *apokatastasis*, the restoration of all things, a universalistic doctrine that is both unbiblical and condemned by the Church.[23]

No universalist, Kinghorn struggles to justify God's punishment of the damned on consequentialist grounds as an act of His benevolence aimed at their reformation. He recognizes that "We can use our God-given freedom to place ourselves eternally under God's wrath by decisively rejecting his offer to participate in the fellowship of self-giving love" (Kinghorn and Travis 2019, p. 148). Indeed, at some point, the opportunity for repentance will be gone: "the time for possible repentance will have passed" (Kinghorn and Travis 2019, p. 150). So why does God continue to punish people beyond that point? Kinghorn's answer seems to be: He does not. "For those in hell, God does not persist in pressing on them the truth about themselves," which Kinghorn interprets as the essence of divine wrath.[24] With no consequentialist justification for punishment, God ceases to punish the damned in hell, though they may (mistakenly) think themselves to be under God's wrath.[25] Rather, He simply leaves them alone. Hell, then, is not a punishment for sin, rather, "Hell is just a natural consequence of life apart from God"(Kinghorn and Travis 2019, p. 145). Citing Peter Geach to the effect that "God does allow men to sin; and misery is the natural, not the arbitrarily inflicted, consequence of sin to the sinner," (Geach 1977, p. 138) Kinghorn claims that "The alternative to Geach's position is to suggest that there is something of value, something good, about God devising an extra form of punishment for people in hell, over and beyond what they are naturally experiencing apart from him"(Kinghorn and Travis 2019, pp. 145–46). This is a misunderstanding of the retributivist position. The alternative to Geach's position is that the harsh treatment is not arbitrarily inflicted by God but justly inflicted and, therefore, something of value, something good. The punishment need not be something over and above the damned's being eternally separated from God; rather, that separation is their just desert.

Wessling calls Geach's position "the *natural consequences view*"(Wessling 2021, p. 151). It must not be confused with a consequentialist view of divine justice. On consequentialism, God does punish the damned in hell for their sin with a view toward some extrinsic benefit. But on the natural consequences view, hell is not a punishment of sin flowing from divine justice but simply a natural consequence of sin. Curiously, Kinghorn offers no biblical justification for so remarkable a thesis as the claim that hell is not divine punishment for sin. To the contrary, Wessling points out that the natural consequences view "certainly does not sit well" with texts like I Cor 11.27–31; II Pet 2. 1–16; Rev 16), which speak of divine wrath, judgment, condemnation, and punishment.[26] In any case, on Kinghorn's natural consequences view, it remains mysterious why God does not simply annihilate the damned and put them out of their misery rather than allowing them to suffer interminably and undeservedly what Kinghorn calls *"the worst possible situation for humans"*.[27]

In general, the natural consequences view of God's response to sin is biblically inadequate.[28]

Certainly, sin is regarded in the Scriptures as self-destructive in its consequences, but God's response to sin is not reducible to permitting sin's natural consequences. Rather God imposes justly deserved punishments in response to sin. Already in the story of the fall in Gen 3, the words "you shall surely die" (*môṯ tāmûṯ*) occur repeatedly in the legal collections of the Pentateuch condemning criminals to death (Matthews 1996, p. 211). Victor Hamilton notes that all of the *môṯ tāmûṯ* passages in the OT deal with either a punishment for sin or an untimely death as the result of punishment so that in the story of the fall, the expression clearly conveys the announcement of a death sentence by divine or royal decree (Hamilton 1990, pp. 173–74). In the NT, the forensic language is pervasive, especially in Paul's treatment of condemnation and justification in Romans. Recall Dunn's conclusion "that God's righteousness towards the peoples he has created includes wrath and judgment as well as faithfulness and salvation is clearly implicit in the sequences Rom. 1.16–18 and 3.3–6" (Dunn 2008, pp. 64–65). Those who deny that *dikaiosynē* is a forensic term pay insufficient attention to Rom 4.4–5, "where the forensic background is clear in the allusion to the legal impropriety of a judge 'justifying the ungodly'".[29]

3. Conclusions

In sum, it is unbiblical and misguided to try to reduce the entire moral character of God to His love. God's moral perfection is most adequately conceived as His righteousness, which is a complex attribute comprising both His *agape* love and His retributive justice, both of which are plausibly essential to God.

Funding: This research received no external funding.

Conflicts of Interest: The author declares no conflict of interest.

Notes

[1] Laura Garcia reports that most theists would therefore sooner give up omnipotence or omniscience than God's moral perfection, which is taken to be the attribute most essential to God (Garcia 2009, p. 218).

[2] The biblical data are meticulously surveyed by John S. Feinberg, *No One Like Him*, Foundations of Evangelical Theology (Feinberg 2001, chp. 8).

[3] Herman Bavinck, while acknowledging that the Scriptures rarely call God good in this "absolute sense," nevertheless thinks that God's goodness is manifested as these other properties (*Reformed Dogmatics*, 4 vols., trans. John Vriend, ed. John Bolt [Grand Rapids, Mich.: Baker Academic, 2003], 2: 213–14, 223–24), thereby making goodness more fundamental.

Classically, there has been a debate among Protestant theologians whether the expression *dikaiosynē theou* refers to an attribute of God Himself or to the righteousness which He reckons to believers. Lutheran theologians were especially insistent on the latter understanding. This is a righteousness which is given to us, not a property inhering in God Himself. It is clear, I think, that biblically the expression *dikaiosynē theou* is multivalent. "The righteousness of God through faith" (Rom 3.22) clearly refers to reckoned righteousness, since God's attribute is not "through faith", nor is it "for all who believe". God's inherent righteousness, like His power or wisdom, is an essential property of God which He has objectively and independently of whether any human beings at all exist, much less have faith in Him. So the righteousness referred to in v22 is a righteousness from God which believers possess. But then just as clearly, "he himself is righteous" (Rom 3.26) designates a property that God Himself has. Here we do have reference to a property possessed not by believers but by God, akin to His wisdom or power. At least three times in the Pauline corpus, Paul uses *dikaiosynē theou* to refer to God's inherent righteousness (Rom 3.5, 25–26).

Bavinck provides a clear discussion of both of these aspects of divine righteousness (Bavinck 2003–2008, vol. 2, pp. 221–24). While "God's righteousness is most often conceived in a favorable sense and described as the attribute by virtue of which God vindicates the righteous and raises them to a position of honor and well-being," nonetheless "the punishment of the wicked is often ascribed to God's righteousness" (pp. 222–23).

See brief background in (Seifrid 2001, pp. 417–19).

See Carson's incredulity that anyone should think that the *dik-* words have nothing to do with justice or righteousness (Carson 2004, p. 51). Henri Blocher draws attention to the combination of such words in II Thess 1.5-9: "Apart from 2 Timothy 4:8 (recompense awarded by the Righteous Judge), 2 Thessalonians 1: 5-9 is most remarkable: the unfolding of God's 'righteous judgment' (v. 5, *dikaias kriseōs*) implies that it is 'just' (v. 6, *dikaion*) for God to requite (*antapodounai*) persecutors, thereby achieving 'vengeance' or satisfaction of justice (v. 8, *ekdikēsin*) in flaming fire, the punishment (v. 9, *dikēn*) of everlasting ruin" (Blocher 2004, p. 475).

In any case, the reductionistic interpretation of *dikaiosynē theou* as covenant faithfulness has been shown to be lexicographically untenable. Charles Lee Irons' *The Righteousness of God: A Lexical Examination of the Covenant-Faithfulness Interpretation*, (Irons 2015), is the definitive work on this expression and a convincing refutation of the reductionistic interpretation of the new perspective. According to Irons, in the OT. "Righteousness is a *Normbegriff* [normative concept], and the norm is God's own moral law, which is grounded in his unchanging nature as a God of perfect holiness, justice, and truth" (p. 340).

See (Seifrid 2004, p. 44). Or, more accurately, "of God's saving acts of righteousness".

According to Irons both vindication and punishment are expressions of divine righteousness. Proponents of the new perspective have focused solely on the positive role of God's righteousness in vindicating and saving His people, when in fact the flip side of that vindication is the punishment of the wicked who are oppressing God's people and opposing God. Irons counts 41 examples in the Old Testament and 35 in the Dead Sea scrolls where God's righteousness is used in the sense of God's judicial activity that results in the punishment of Israel's enemies, thereby delivering and vindicating His people (Irons 2015, p. 296).

See (Dunn 2008, pp. 63–64). Cf. Seifrid's comment: "Biblical usage of righteousness language is distinct from Greek thought *not* in the lack of the idea of a norm, but in that it does not *define* the norm it presupposes in terms of the *idea* of the good .... The Hebrew Scriptures operate with the simple but profound assumption that 'righteousness' in its various expressions is ultimately bound up with God and his working" (Seifrid 2004, pp. 43–44).

See (Bavinck 2003–2008, vol. 2, pp. 223) for many examples.

(Wessling 2021, p. 148). A sufficient condition of this thesis is said to be that "a complete understanding of God's love, plus a complete description of the relevant circumstances (excluding additional moral premises), would in principle enable one to determine each actual or possible item of behavior (including behaviors of thought and character) that God would judge that He should do, is acceptable to do, or should not do".

For an extended discussion see my *Atonement and the Death of Christ: An Exegetical, Historical, and Philosophical Exploration* (Waco, Tex.: Baylor University Press, 2020), chap.4 (Craig 2020). In Rom 1.18–3.20 Paul describes the human predicament as a result of the universality of sin and our consequent condemnation before a just God. Not one of us, as lawbreakers, will be acquitted before the bar of God's justice; the verdict of "guilty" is pronounced over every human being. Jew and Gentile alike are said to stand under the wrath of God. Any adequate interpretation of the succeeding passage Rom 3.21–26 must find therein Paul's solution to the problem of man's condemnation before a just Judge and the attendant dissolution of divine wrath.

On the Hebrew words and their significance, see *Theological Dictionary of the Old Testament*, (Seybold 1978), sec. II.2.c *In Statements Concerning Divine Judgment; Theological Dictionary of the Old Testament*, ed. G. Johannes Botterweck, Helmer Ringgren, and Heinz-Josef Fabry, vol. X, trans. Douglas W. Scott, *s.v.* "*nāqam*," (Lipiński 1999). When used by the prophets in connection with certain verbs like *šālam* (to repay), *gemûl* has the sense of "payment, reward, recompense, or revenge". According to Seybold, Psalms of individual lament like Ps 28.4; Lam 3.64, in "complete harmony" with the prophetic oracles like Is 59.18, offer prayers for *gemûl* as "a judicial and retributive intervention of Yahweh". The verbal root *nqm* expresses the notion of revenge, in Yahweh's case in accord with retributive justice, the *lex talionis*. Similarly, "We speak today of 'getting one's just reward,' meaning that one is getting due punishment" (Jack R. Lundbom 2004, p. 439). The Greek words are not only abundantly used in the LXX to translate the relevant Hebrew terms but are used in the NT to indicate, among other things, divine retribution and vengeance

(*New International Dictionary of New Testament Theology and Exegesis*, 2d ed., ed. Moisés Silva, vol. I: *A–Δ, s.v. "didōmi (avtapodidōmi avtapodoma, avtapodosis)"* and *"dikē (ekdikeō, ekdikēsis)"* (Silva 2014).

16   Kinghorn generally tends to conflate divine wrath and justice. He is correct in thinking that comparing God's love and God's wrath "is … in a sense like comparing apples to oranges" (Kinghorn and Travis 2019, p. 35). But the relevant comparison is not between God's love and God's wrath but between God's love and God's justice, both of which are comprised by His righteousness.

17   See, e.g., (White 2011; Tonry 2011). Ironically, some theologians, unaware of this sea change in theories of justice, denounce in the strongest terms a God of retributive justice (Stephen Finlan 2007, pp. 97–98), not realizing that their objection to the justice of penal substitutionary atonement depends on a view of divine justice as retributive, lest God punish the innocent on consequentialist grounds.

18   (Kinghorn and Travis 2019, p. 73). A problem here is that, as Garcia notes, flourishing or well-being is a type of non-moral good, and it seems wrong to treat moral value as simply a function of non-moral value (Garcia 2009, pp. 221, 229). She explains, by contrast, that on Jorge Garcia's virtue theory the whole set of moral virtues can be reduced to one over-arching virtue, viz., genuine concern for the good of persons, so that the love of persons is both the root and key component of all the virtues (p. 229). Thus, divine moral perfection consists in "exemplifying perfect love" (p. 230). Perhaps Kinghorn means to endorse such a virtue theory, since he is thinking of persons' good in terms of their relationship to God. Unfortunately, such a theory still neglects divine justice.

19   (Kinghorn and Travis 2019, pp. 75–78). Cf. Arthur Holmes (2007, p. 52), *Ethics: Approaching Moral Decisions*. In addition to Holmes' concerns, one of the main criticisms of consequentialist theories of justice is the fact that on such theories it may be just to punish the innocent in view of the good consequences. On the horrendous impact of consequentialism on the American penal system, see the moving account of Kathleen Dean Moore, *Pardons: Justice, Mercy, and the Public Interest* (Moore 1989, chp. 5).

20   See (Kinghorn and Travis 2019, pp. 1–21). Biblical expressions of God's wrath, he explains, are meant to convey both God's anger at injustice in our world and His actions to set things straight, to settle accounts, to visit punishment upon evildoers. What Kinghorn seems to fail to appreciate is that the reason that God's anger is not an "uncontrolled outburst" is because it is righteous anger, that is to say, guided by justice. Therefore in His role as Supreme Judge, God is, *pace* Kinghorn, most definitely like "a judge in a courthouse, suspending his personal feelings in order to act objectively" (p. 5). In denying that God's acts of wrath are motivated by righteous anger, Kinghorn forgets that it is *righteous* anger, i.e., anger that is guided by divine justice that is at issue.

21   (Kinghorn and Travis, p. 80). God's wrath "is intended by God to lead us in some way toward reconciliation with him. That is, divine wrath is a prodding of some sort, designed to lead us to repentance and eventual reconciliation" (pp. 88–89).

22   The Christian consequentialist could say that punishment in hell does have a consequentialist justification, namely, the sequestration of the wicked from the community of the redeemed, just as hardened criminals are removed from society. But since God could achieve this end by simply annihilating the damned, the consequentialist will need to find some non-retributive reason for God's preserving them in existence.

23   See (Mullins 2021). Mullins errs, however, in thinking that "You cannot have an ultimate defeat of evil if you have a bunch of damned people in hell continuing to engage in a sinful rebellion against God". *Au contraire*, in the biblical view of things God's defeat of evil consists precisely in His punishing the wicked.

24   (Kinghorn and Travis 2019, p. 144). Cf. his explanation:

"Divine wrath is an intentional pattern of action from God, directed toward some individual or group of individuals, and intended for the purpose of some divine goal. … this goal will be a benevolent one, intended to further people's long-term flourishing. … I arrive at the following definition of divine wrath. Our experience of God's wrath toward us is *God pressing on us the truth about ourselves*". (pp. 91–92)

Wessling calls such a view *"divine communicative punishment"* (Wessling 2021, p. 152). Kinghorn differs from Wessling in that Kinghorn recognizes that there comes a point of no return at which, presumably, God as an omniscient being knows that further communication is pointless.

25   (Kinghorn and Travis 2019, p. 145; cf. pp. 139, 142). Kinghorn inconsistently says, "They have become the kind of people who experience all of God's actions as acts of wrath instead of as acts of love and care and faithful prompting" (p. 145). For on his view, God has ceased all such loving actions toward the damned, since He has ceased to press upon them the truth about themselves.

26   (Wessling 2021, p. 152). Kinghorn fails to take due cognizance of the passage he himself cites, "He who believes in the Son has eternal life; he who does not obey the Son shall not see life, but the wrath of God rests (*menei*) upon him" (Jn 3.36).

27   (Kinghorn and Travis 2019, p. 147). I find incredible the fatuous claim by some like C. S. Lewis that God's allowing the damned to persist in their misery is actually an expression of divine benevolence.

28   See Jay Sklar (2005, pp. 11–12) who shows, against those who think of death as merely the natural consequence of sin, that God's response to sin is punitive judgment. See more broadly the classic treatment in Jonathan Edwards (1998, pp. 146–233).

29   (Dunn 2008, p. 64). See also Rom 5. 12–14, where the distinction between death as a consequence of sin and death as a penalty for sin becomes crucial in Paul's thinking. Death from Adam to Moses was a consequence of sin, but after the giving of the law it became as well a penalty for sin.

References

Bavinck, Herman. 2003–2008. *Reformed Dogmatics*. Edited by John Bolt. Translated by John Vriend. 4 vols. Grand Rapids: Baker Academic.
Blocher, Henri. 2004. Justification of the Ungodly (*Sola Fide*): Theological Reflections. In *Justification and Variegated Nomism: A Fresh Appraisal of Paul and Second Temple Judaism*. Edited by Donald A. Carson, Peter T. O'Brien and Mark A. Seifrid. WUNT 2/181. Vol. 2: The Paradoxes of Paul. Tübingen: Mohr Siebeck, pp. 465–500.
Carson, D. A. 2004. The Vindication of Imputation: On Fields of Discourse and Semantic Fields. In *Justification: What's at Stake in the Current Debates*. Edited by Mark Husbands and Daniel J. Treier. Downers Grove: InterVarsity Press, pp. 46–79.
Craig, William Lane. 2020. *Atonement and the Death of Christ: An Exegetical, Historical, and Philosophical Exploration*. Waco: Baylor University Press.
Dunn, James D. G. 2008. The New Perspective: Whence, What and Whither? In *The New Perspective on Paul*, rev. ed. Grand Rapids: Eerdmans, pp. 1–97.
Edwards, Jonathan. 1998. *The Works of Jonathan Edwards, Vol. 1: The Great Christian Doctrine of Original Sin Defended (1834)*. Peabody: Hendrickson.
Feinberg, John S. 2001. *No One Like Him: The Doctrine of God*. Foundations of Evangelical Theology. Wheaton: Crossway.
Finlan, Stephen. 2007. *Options on Atonement in Christian Thought*. Collegeville: Liturgical Press.
Garcia, Laura. 2009. Moral Perfection. In *The Oxford Handbook of Philosophical Theology*. Edited by Thomas P. Flint and Michael C. Rea. Oxford: Oxford University Press, pp. 217–38.
Geach, Peter. 1977. *Providence and Evil*. Cambridge: Cambridge University Press.
Grotius, Hugo. 1889. *A Defence of the Catholic Faith Concerning the Satisfaction of Christ, against Faustus Socinus*. Translated by Frank Hugh Foster. Andover: Warren F. Draper.
Hamilton, Victor P. 1990. *The Book of Genesis: Chapters 1–17*. The New International Commentary on the Old Testament. Grand Rapids: William B. Eerdmans.
Holmes, Arthur. 2007. *Ethics: Approaching Moral Decisions*. Downers Grove: IVP Academic.
Irons, Charles Lee. 2015. *The Righteousness of God: A Lexical Examination of the Covenant-Faithfulness Interpretation*. WUNT 2/386. Tübingen: Mohr Siebeck.
Kant, Immanuel. 1999. *Metaphysical Elements of Justice*, 2nd ed. Translated by John Ladd. Indianapolis: Hackett.
Kinghorn, Kevin, and Stephen Travis. 2019. *But What about God's Wrath? The Compelling Love Story of Divine Anger*. Downers Grove: IVP Academic.
Lipiński, Edward. 1999. *Theological Dictionary of the Old Testament*. Edited by G. Johannes Botterweck, Helmer Ringgren and Heinz-Josef Fabry. Translated by Douglas W. Scott. s.v. "nāqam". Grand Rapids: William B. Eerdmans, vol. X.
Lundbom, Jack R. 2004. *Jeremiah 37–52*. Anchor Bible 21C. New York: Doubleday.
Matthews, Kenneth A. 1996. *Genesis 1–11:26*. The New American Commentary 1A. Nashville: B&H Publishing Group.
Moore, Kathleen Dean. 1989. *Pardons: Justice, Mercy, and the Public Interest*. Oxford: Oxford University Press.
Morris, Leon. 1983. *The Atonement: Its Meaning and Significance*. Downers Grove: InterVarsity Press.
Mullins, R. T. 2021. Response to Love Divine by Jordan Wessling. Paper presented at the meeting of the American Academy of Religion, San Antonio, TX, USA, November 19.
Seifrid, Mark A. 2001. Righteousness Language in the Hebrew Scriptures and Early Judaism. In *Justification and Variegated Nomism: A Fresh Appraisal of Paul and Second Temple Judaism*. Edited by D. A. Carson, Peter T. O'Brien and Mark A. Seifrid. Vol. 1: The Complexities of Second Temple Judaism. WUNT 2/140. Tübingen: Mohr Siebeck, pp. 415–42.
Seifrid, Mark A. 2004. Paul's Use of Righteousness Language against Its Hellenistic Background. In *Justification and Variegated Nomism: A Fresh Appraisal of Paul and Second Temple Judaism*. Edited by D. A. Carson, Peter T. O'Brien and Mark A. Seifrid. Vol. 2: The Paradoxes of Paul. WUNT 2/181. Tübingen: Mohr Siebeck, pp. 39–74.
Seybold, Klaus. 1978. *Theological Dictionary of the Old Testament*. Edited by G. Johannes Botterweck and Helmer Ringgren. Translated by John T. Willis, and Geoffrey Bromiley. s.v. "gāmal". Grand Rapids: William B. Eerdmans, vol. III.
Silva, Moisés. 2014. *New International Dictionary of New Testament Theology and Exegesis*, 2nd ed. Vol. I: A-Δ, s.v. "didōmi (avtapodidōmi, avtapodoma, avtapodosis)" and "dikē (ekdikeō, ekdikēsis)". Grand Rapids: Zondervan.
Sklar, Jay. 2005. *Sin, Impurity, Sacrifice, Atonement: The Priestly Conceptions*. Hebrew Bible Monographs 2. Sheffield: Sheffield Phoenix Press.
Tonry, Michael, ed. 2011. *Retributivism Has a Past; Has It a Future? Studies in Penal Theory and Philosophy*. Oxford: Oxford University Press.
Wessling, Jordan. 2021. Divine Goodness and Love. In *T&T Clark Handbook of Analytic Theology*. Edited by James M. Arcadi and James T. Turner. London: T. & T. Clark, pp. 141–54.
White, Mark D., ed. 2011. *Retributivism: Essays on Theory and Policy*. Oxford: Oxford University Press.

Comment

God's Moral Perfection as His Beneficent Love. Comment on Craig (2023). Is God's Moral Perfection Reducible to His Love? *Religions* 14: 140

Kevin Kinghorn

Asbury Theological Seminary, Wilmore, KY 40390, USA; kevin.kinghorn@asburyseminary.edu

Abstract: William Lane Craig insists that I am wrong in reducing God's moral goodness to his beneficent aim of drawing all people to himself. For Craig, God's moral goodness, best conceived in terms of righteousness, must also include God's retributive justice toward the wicked, who deserve the punishment they receive. My response is that Craig's argument rests on two assumptions about value, neither of which, I argue, Christian theists have good reason to affirm.

Keywords: retributive justice; desert; divine goodness; righteousness; divine love; final value

Citation: Kinghorn, Kevin. 2023. God's Moral Perfection as His Beneficent Love. Comment on Craig (2023). Is God's Moral Perfection Reducible to His Love? *Religions* 14: 140. *Religions* 14: 1205. https://doi.org/10.3390/rel14091205

Academic Editor: Klaus Baumann

Received: 30 March 2023
Revised: 6 September 2023
Accepted: 15 September 2023
Published: 20 September 2023

1. Introduction

In a recent article (Craig 2023), William Lane Craig criticizes my claim that all God's actions toward us are motivated by God's beneficent love for us. Craig focuses on my book, *But What About God's Wrath?* (Kinghorn 2019), in which I looked at various biblical passages that describe God as acting in wrath toward people. I argued that the biblical depictions of God's wrath are best understood as God "pressing upon people difficult truths about themselves". These divine acts can be extremely painful to us, and they are acts of last resort. But they remain one means God has for prompting repentance so that individuals can be reconciled to God and to one another. Thus, the actions of God described in the Bible as wrathful would be intended as ultimately restorative, consistent with the beneficent concern that, I claim, motivates all God's actions toward us.

Craig objects that such a single motivation cannot adequately account for the biblical picture of God's *righteousness*. In response to immorality, this righteousness manifests itself in punishment of the wicked. It is the wicked who have opposed God and have oppressed God's people. And God's vindication of his people needs to involve giving the wicked the punishment they deserve. If God were to fail to uphold the demands of retributive justice, then he would be less than morally perfect.

In what follows, I highlight how Craig's line of argument relies on two big assumptions about the nature of value. One of these assumptions is more central to his core argument than the other. But I want to contest both of them. Focusing on the more central assumption Craig makes, I go on to suggest why Christian theists have good reason to reject it.

2. Craig's First Assumption about Value

The less central, but still noteworthy, assumption Craig makes has to do with the property of moral *goodness*. He cites John Feinberg's survey of biblical passages that reference God's goodness, offering his own summation: "When the biblical authors speak of God's goodness, what they typically have in mind is not God's moral goodness but God's beneficence or generosity" (Craig 2023, p. 1). It is yet unclear here what "moral goodness" amounts to. But whatever it is, we are to distinguish it from God's beneficence. Regarding God's beneficence, Feinberg himself notes that the biblical descriptions of God's goodness do emphasize the idea that "God is concerned about the well-being of his creatures and does things to promote it". Additionally, though, "God is interested in doing what is morally good and right". And the biblical writers "capture that idea by referring to his *righteousness* and *holiness*" (Feinberg 2006, p. 366).

Craig shares with Feinberg this working assumption that, when God does something that is "morally good", God is not necessarily acting out of beneficence to further anyone's well-being. But this working assumption is controversial among moral philosophers. A plausible (and, in my view, convincing) line of argument can be offered that all instances of what is *good* are ultimately instances of what is *good for* someone.[1]

Certainly philosophers and theologians writing downstream of Plato have commonly taken *goodness* to be an irreducible, normative, stance-independent property. But a look at how we humans came to appreciate the concept *good* points to a metaphysically less extravagant story. In brief, the story starts with its functional use in Greek society. Alasdair MacIntyre notes that "the word ἀγαθός, ancestor of our *good*, is originally a predicate specifically attached to the role of a Homeric nobleman" (MacIntyre 2003, p. 6). The term was both descriptive and evaluative.

Over time, the conceptual link was lost between the term and the specific description of a Homeric ideal. Changes in societal roles and expectations have naturally led to differing views about which characteristics are ideal or commendable. Accordingly, differing views have emerged as to the conditions under which it is appropriate to offer the positive evaluation that something is "good". And so we arrive at W. D. Ross's conclusion that the best way to understand the historic use of the term is to see it as one of "indefinite commendation" (Ross 2002, p. 66).

Why would we commend anything as "good"? One answer, in the tradition of Plato, is that we recognize it as possessing an irreducible, normative property of *goodness*. Another (and, in my view, more plausible) answer is that we recognize it as benefiting some subject— that is, as being *good for* some subject. Philippa Foot is one who did much this past century to revitalize this more Aristotelian framework that we cannot separate the idea of goodness from the idea of an organism flourishing in its particular form of life (see Foot 2001).

A semantic analysis of the term "good" lends support to the idea that we identify things as good because we see them as good for someone. On Paul Ziff's careful analysis, our use of the term "good" is our indication that something "answers to the interests" of some real or imagined subject (Ziff 1960). Stephen Finlay reaches a similar conclusion by focusing on the structure of our English sentences and the varied ways in which "good" is used in them: *S* is good; *S* is a good *X*; *S* is good for *X*; *S* is good with *X*; *S* is good at *X*-ing; *S* is good for *X*-ing; and so on. Finlay concludes that there *is* a unified logical form to all our uses of the term "good". In keeping with Ziff's analysis, Finlay argues (convincingly, in my view) that our references to things being "good" ultimately make sense only as references to them being "good for" some subject (Finlay 2014).

A semantic analysis of "good" certainly does not establish any firm conclusions about the *nature* of goodness. But it does at least suggest that the property of goodness might be no more than the property of what is good for subjects. I have offered fuller arguments elsewhere for this conclusion about the nature of goodness.[2] In this section, my very brief look at what *goodness* amounts to is not intended to settle long-standing debates. I am only noting that there are controversies to navigate in claiming that God's concern for "morally good" outcomes is not reducible to his concern for subjects' well-being (i.e., for what is good for subjects).

Here is how this point affects Craig's larger line of argument. His discussion of God's righteousness begins by noting that it encompasses two broad and distinguishable concerns: to further the well-being of creatures and to do "what is morally good and right". He goes on to contend that one particular morally good outcome to which a righteous God is sensitive is the outcome of the wicked receiving the punishment they deserve. (I look at this further claim in the next section.) My main point in this section is that Craig's argument—that God's righteousness includes his concern to do what is morally good *in addition to* his beneficent concern for the well-being of creatures—cannot get off the ground if moral goodness simply *is* a matter of what is good for subjects. For there would be no morally good states to which God could be sensitive beyond those states involving subjects' positive well-being.

3. Craig's Second Assumption about Value

The majority of Craig's article is spent on a more particular claim about a specific, non-welfarist value (i.e., a kind of "moral good" not linked to well-being). The value in question is associated with the "punishment of the guilty", which Craig identifies as an "intrinsic good" (Craig 2023, p. 4). This point is my main point of contention with Craig. Actually, the key point of contention is that I reject the idea that divine punishment or discipline has *non-instrumental* value (sometimes called *final* value). And non-instrumental value is, strictly speaking, not quite the same as intrinsic value.[3] But for our purposes this distinction need not concern us.

Could the punishment of guilty persons have non-instrumental value? Craig discusses this question in connection with rival theories of justice. "Retributive theories" affirm that "punishment is justified because the guilty deserve to be punished". In contrast, "consequentialist theories" maintain that "punishment is justified because of the extrinsic goods that may be realized thereby, such as deterrence of crime, sequestration of dangerous persons, and reformation of wrongdoers" (Craig 2023, p. 3).

Now, I am a little uncomfortable with the way Craig frames things here. To speak of "punishment" being "justified" raises a worry in my mind about question begging. "Punishment" can be viewed as, by definition, an exclusively retributive measure—in contrast to the more restorative idea of discipline. I would not want us to assume at the outset that, when God works against the immediate well-being of a wicked person, God is issuing "punishment" in contrast to "discipline". That has to be argued for, not stipulated through terminology. (Craig does not attempt any question begging in this way. I am simply noting that instead of "punishment" I would be more comfortable using a broader term like "hard treatment"—or at least clarifying that "punishment" could be either retributive or restorative.)[4] Also, I would prefer to ask about God's *desired goal* when acting, as opposed to asking about what would "justify" a divine act of punishment. So-called moral justification seems to me a nebulous idea. I think it is much clearer just to ask about the ultimate goals or purposes God is seeking to achieve when acting toward wicked people.

One final quibble before moving on: I would prefer not to equate "prospective" accounts of justice with "consequentialist" accounts of justice, as Craig does. *Consequentialism* as a normative ethical theory is often understood to involve several commitments that I for one would not want to make. The biblical account of justice is, in my view, restorative and not retributive, but I would not want to say that this account commits me to anything like an unvarnished consequentialist theory of ethics.[5] I do think Craig's categories of "prospective" and "retrospective" accounts of justice are helpful, and I am happy to follow that terminology.

These are minor quibbles. Craig is certainly right on the larger, central point that "retrospective" accounts of justice are to be contrasted with "prospective" accounts. My own understanding of God's restorative justice would, as he notes, be prospective. God's (current) punishment or discipline of the wicked would be a means to the (prospective) further end of their repentance and restoration to healthy relationships with God and with others.[6] In contrast, Craig's understanding of God's retributive justice is retrospective.

On to Craig's view. When God exercises (retributive) justice in restoring a "correct moral order in the world" (Craig 2023, p. 2), he looks back at the wicked actions people perform. If God were to explain his motivation in justly punishing the wicked, he would not point to future good outcomes for people. He would point only to people's past wicked actions. Of course, whenever God performs acts directed to the wicked he may *also* be looking forward to future, good outcomes (such as people's restoration). But as regards the motivation to establish *justice* in a right, moral ordering of the world, God would simply be addressing people's past wicked actions (or perhaps their wicked character as displayed in those actions).

So why exactly is God's punishment of the wicked needed as part of God's estab-lishment of a right, moral order in the world? Craig makes the standard move among defenders of retributive justice by insisting that this punishment is *deserved*. God's response to sin must be to impose "justly deserved punishments" (Craig 2023, p. 6). For there is "something of value, something good" in the wicked receiving their deserved punishment (Craig 2023, p. 6). And a morally perfect God is sensitive to this value and acts to realize it.

But *why* is it good, or valuable, that a wicked person receive painful treatment? This is the question that ultimately needs answering. We could of course list various *prospective* reasons: It may cause the person to rethink her self-reliance; it may prompt the person to turn to God; and so on. But such prospective matters, relevant to questions of the possible *instrumental* value of painful treatment, are not at issue. I am asking about the reasons why there may be *non-instrumental* value in a wicked person receiving painful treatment.

We come now to the big assumption that lies behind Craig's central claims about desert and the value of retributive treatment. This assumption is hardly unique to Craig. There is a long history in Western moral philosophy of assuming that there is value in *proportionality itself* obtaining between a person's virtuous/vicious character and the positive/negative treatment she receives.

Sometimes philosophers have been explicit about this value. Kant, e.g., asserted that the "highest good" is happiness "in exact proportion with the morality of the rational beings who are thereby rendered worthy of it" (Kant 1899, p. 456). This past century, W. D. Ross identified "the allocation of pleasure to the virtuous" as one of four "intrinsic goods" (the others being virtue, pleasure, and knowledge) (Ross 2002, p. 140). Ross was at the tail end of what Thomas Hurka calls "a golden age for moral theory", the period in British moral philosophy that began with Sidgwick and included Hastings, Rashdall, Prichard, Broad, and Ewing. Hurka observes that, during this time of rich moral theorizing, "two commonly accepted objective values were virtue and desert", with desert understood, as Ross put it, as "the proportionment of happiness to virtue" (Hurka 2001, p. 6; Ross 2002, p. 27).

Ross recognized that there is no real argument available in support of this (purported) value of proportionality between virtue/viciousness and positive/negative well-being. It is a value, Ross insisted, that we "must recognize" intuitively (Ross 2002, p. 136). And he claimed that we do, in fact, all have a "decided conviction" that it is good when a virtuous person receives happiness in line with his character (Ross 2002, p. 138).

Ross's view represents the received wisdom on desert that has been handed down to us today. Most contemporary philosophers writing on desert affirm that, if a person deserves X, then there is intrinsic value in the person receiving X.[7] Nathan Hanna refers to this view as "the standard view", observing that "many of those who accept it just assume it" (Hanna 2019, pp. 109–10).

Does Craig assume the standard view? He certainly seems to. We might circle back to Craig's claim that God's moral perfection includes two broad concerns: for the "well-being of his creatures" and for "what is morally good and right". It is difficult to think how this concern for "what is morally good and right" *would not* involve a concern for the (purported) final value of proportionality obtaining between people's character and their treatment. After all, surely no one would claim that there is value in the painful experiences *themselves* of creatures. Rather, as Craig emphasizes, the value at stake is derived from the fact that the suffering of wicked creatures is *deserved*. But since there is not intrinsic value in the suffering itself, the only place for value seemingly has to be in the proportionality that obtains between a creature's suffering and his vicious character.[8] This assumption about value is, again, not a novel one. It is "the standard view" (as Hannah put it) of the value associated with desert. If we do assume the standard view, then Craig's broader line of argument does become quite understandable: God is sensitive to the value of proportionality and performs acts of retributive justice to realize it. Accordingly, God's "moral perfection", best conceived in terms of God's "righteousness", has to comprise "both His *agape* love and His retributive justice" (Craig 2023, p. 6).

What should we make of the standard view? Once again, this view affirms that there is intrinsic value in a person receiving happiness/unhappiness in proportion to her virtuous/vicious character. I do agree with Hannah that this view is the standard one among moral philosophers. I also think Hannah is right that, most times, this view is just assumed. I further think that Christian theists should be the first ones challenging this view!

We Christian theists affirm that God is triune and, thus, essentially relational. We affirm that God's purpose for us is that we participate in relationships with God and with others through which we attain ultimate flourishing. Why think that a relational God would be sensitive to the (impersonal) value of "proportionality itself obtaining" between a person's virtue/viciousness and her positive/negative well-being?

In his defense of the "intrinsic good" realized by God's punishment of the wicked, Craig offers a suggestive moral framework that, to my mind, can be filled out most readily with impersonal moral principles. He notes various biblical passages that reference God's corrective actions and concludes that "The God of the Bible is not just a benevolent father figure but, as Hugo Grotius emphasized in his critique of Faustus Socinus, God is the impartial Ruler and Judge of the creation, responsible for maintaining its moral order" (Craig 2023, p. 4). As to how God's "impartiality" in dealing with the wicked is important in maintaining our world's "moral order",[9] I presume the idea would be something like God establishing proportionality between *every* person's character and his or her respective well-being.[10]

Certainly Western philosophers from the early modern period onward, having moved away from Socrates's framing question of what the good life consists in, have sought to identify various moral principles that might help frame our thinking about how we ought to live.[11] It has been claimed that we should think of justice as grounded in the principles of utilitarianism or contractualism or egalitarianism. Theorists from Kant to Rawls have suggested formulas for discovering, through reason or through intuition, various moral principles that are said really to exist and to be awaiting our discovery. What we have been calling the standard view of desert—that there is value in proportionality itself obtaining between a person's character and her treatment—stands in a line of principles offered by philosophers as grounds for how people ought to be treated. One thing it has in common with these other impersonal principles is that it is not derived from the personal goals God is described in the Bible as having for his creation.

I would argue that scripture depicts God as creating humans for the enduring purpose of having loving fellowship with him (I argued for this conclusion more fully in *But What About God's Wrath?* and I offer a summary defense of it in Section 3). Our participation in the life of God also includes participation in loving, interdependent relationships with other humans and with all the rest of the created order. I find no reason in scripture to think that God would give weight to any moral principle that did not somehow help lead us and the rest of the created order toward these relationships for which we were created. I cannot see why God would be sensitive to the value of any purported moral principle, except where such a principle is an instrumentally valuable guideline in helping bring about those states of final value (which, again, are flourishing relationships as God intended). Accordingly, I cannot see why a Christian theist should want to affirm the standard view of the value of deserved punishment, which I think is pretty clearly assumed within Craig's understanding of a good and right moral order.

Perhaps Craig would want to avoid this conclusion by saying that retributive justice enacted toward the wicked is needed as part of the *vindication* of victims so that these victims might flourish as God intends.[12] In one place, Craig objects to those who "have focused solely on the positive role of God's righteousness in vindicating and saving his people, when in fact the flip side of that vindication is the punishment of the wicked who are oppressing God's people and opposing God" (Craig 2023, p. 2, n. 10). But such a move would be unpromising. The oppressed are not vindicated by the punishment of their oppressors. They are vindicated by the *truth* of their cruel treatment being brought to light and publicly acknowledged by all parties within a community. Sometimes, proportional treatment does help bring to light an offender's actions or character. ("Wow, that corporation received a huge fine from the EPA. Their environmental abuses must have been really egregious!") At other times, though, proportional treatment fails to bring a truthful narrative to light. And when it does not, we are unsatisfied that proportional treatment has accomplished what we were hoping it would accomplish: namely, the reestablishment of both the victim's and the perpetrator's standings in a community, where these standings accurately reflect who they are and how they have affected one another (see Kinghorn 2021, §6.4–6.6).

Further, there are various ways (other than meting out proportional treatment to oppressors) for God to demonstrate solidarity with the oppressed, to honor them, and to take up their cause. The Book of Revelation is, as I read it, a great *unmasking* of, among other things, coercive powers that masquerade as real or highest powers (which I think Christian theists should take to be God's loving, creative power). If the nature of sin is indeed self-destruction, then oppressors naturally experience destruction when God removes the contingencies that have heretofore allowed them some measure of flourishing (e.g., benefiting from the fruit of oppressed individuals' labor, utilizing the social capital of others' goodwill, etc.). In short, God can vindicate the oppressed, with oppressors experiencing public downfall, without actively punishing oppressors as an act of retribution.[13]

Now, it is true that, if an *oppressor* is to repent at some point and become part of the healthy community God intends for all people, the oppressor's acknowledgement of his own past actions toward others may need to include such elements as apology and, to the extent possible, recompense.[14] This apology and recompense might be costly. Perhaps also there is some role for victims to have a say in whether, and how, the community should respond punitively to the oppressor in restoring what the community understands the shape of healthy relationships to be. Even so, this is again where Christian theists should be the first ones embracing the value of the oppressor's ultimate flourishing. If Christian maturation includes taking up Christ's willingness to extend forgiveness to the repentant, along with God's broader commitment to the goal that all people experience fullness of life eternally, then earthly victims now included within the heavenly community of perfected relationships will surely want their earthly oppressors to repent and find a way into that heavenly community.

So the "vindication of God's people" is an unpromising reason why Christian theists should think it good for oppressors to meet with proportional, negative treatment. Proportional treatment is but one way to bring oppressors' actions to light and to affirm God's perspective on their true histories and on their true standing before him. If the suffering of oppressors is not necessary (or even, at times, sufficient) to vindicate victims, then surely this is not the preferred way for God to finally vindicate all victims (or for victims who have been thoroughly conformed to Christ's likeness to want to be vindicated). From previous discussions, also unpromising (as a reason to think it good for oppressors to suffer) is the assumption behind "the standard view" of desert: that there is intrinsic value in proportionality itself obtaining between a person's virtue/viciousness and her positive/negative well-being. So I conclude that Christian theists have no good reason to affirm—and much reason to reject—any final value in wicked people meeting with proportional suffering.

4. Reading the Biblical Witness

Craig is certainly right that many passages in scripture do describe God as responding to persistent human wickedness with actions that both (1) are intended to rectify this sinful warping of God's intentions for humankind and (2) involve painful experiences for those who have acted wickedly. Sometimes, the ultimate motivation behind God's response is clearly described as restorative. ("In vain I punished your people; they did not respond to correction" (Jeremiah 2:30).) Sometimes, there is no mention of any restorative goal. ("But by your hard and impenitent heart you are storing up wrath for yourself on the day of wrath, when God's righteous judgment will be revealed" (Romans 2:5).)[15] The question is whether God's painful treatment of people is always for some restorative purpose, whether explicitly stated in some particular passage or not.

In *But What About God's Wrath*, I offered both philosophical and biblical reasons for concluding that, when God acts correctively, his ultimate motivation should be viewed as always restorative.[16] Craig, of course, rejects this conclusion, insisting that God sometimes acts retributively and not merely restoratively. In my reply here, I have thus far appealed largely to considerations in value theory in claiming that there is no final value associated with retributive justice to which God might be sensitive. I offer a few comments now on the biblical witness.

I will not attempt examinations of particular passages.[17] Rather, I very briefly just raise some broader, methodological points. First, as J. S. Mill pointed out, matters of "expediency" within a community can readily take on a "character of absoluteness"—and rightly so. Expediency here includes such good ends as the education of children, consensus building within a community about the harm of certain behaviors, and deterrence of those behaviors. To accomplish such expedient aims, our discourse with one another understandably becomes absolutist, deontic, and juridical in nature. Those actions judged especially bad are not merely discouraged but are declared "not to be done, period!" (on threat of punishment). Even if the ultimate motivations for punishment are ones of expediency, a community's language—"If you do this, we will do to you in kind!"—hardly reflects this fact.

Craig is again right in noting that many biblical passages do describe God's response to wickedness with terms that lie within the conceptual category of absolutism and not of expediency. Yet, that point itself surely does not settle the question whether God's ultimate motivation in allowing or causing hard treatment of the wicked is an expedient one (e.g., the expedient end of their repentance and restoration). How do we settle it? Difficult questions of methodology abound. We, of course, need to consider the larger biblical picture of what God has revealed as his plans for humankind and, therefore, what he does and does not value. Perhaps we need to draw from reflections on value theory to help shape our expectations of what God might be valuing in a particular biblical narrative. Perhaps we need to engage thoughtfully with how others in the Christian tradition have interpreted the shape of justice in the Bible.

On this last matter, Craig does identify one trend. Commenting on Jordan Wessling's claim that God's moral attributes are all fundamentally a matter of love, Craig states that this thesis seems to him to be "the lingering vestige of classical liberal theology, which eschewed the justice and wrath of God in favor of love" (Craig 2023, p. 3). He then notes a more recent development: "In contrast to classical liberal theology, neo-liberal theology, if we may coin a term, affirms God's wrath but sees it wholly as a manifestation of His love aimed at the reformation of sinners" (Craig 2023, p. 3).

I, of course, would want to make this last affirmation. But I would not see classical liberal theologians as my natural allies on topics such as God's wrath or God's justice. Instead, I would want to note a different trend in looking for allies. I would want to look at the growth of global Christianity over the past few decades. The center of the tradition has moved southward and eastward. And those of us in North America and Europe have been introduced to an array of theologians and biblical scholars from cultures that do not conceive of justice apart from reconciliation and do not comprehend the human problem to be one of guilt from objective wrongdoing. As a missiology colleague from India recently said to me, these cultures "are relational in how they think about everything!"[18] Understandably, then, many biblical scholars from the global Church just do not find a God in the pages of scripture whose justice is retributive or who, more broadly, bears much resemblance to Grotius's image of an impartial judge.

Another trend I welcome is the theological retrieval movement of the past few decades in which both Roman Catholic and Protestant theologians have focused anew on early Church fathers, especially in the Eastern tradition. Irenaeus, Origen, Athanasius, Gregory Nazianzen, and Gregory of Nyssa are among those early writers who either have no place for retributive justice or view it as much less central than restorative justice to the kind of moral order God is pursuing (see Reardon 2015). Certainly one can remain tethered to Christian orthodoxy and reject the idea that God is committed to retributive justice as a final, valuable end. I, of course, acknowledge that Craig can make his opposing claims about retributive justice, also well within the boundaries of orthodoxy. But in this debate about retributive justice, I do think a great deal is at stake in terms of how we view the character and commitments of God. In this article, I have drawn from considerations in value theory in order to defend the view that God unceasingly pursues benevolent ends toward us—saints and sinners alike—whenever he acts in pursuit of the outcomes he desires for his creation.

Conflicts of Interest: The author declares no conflict of interest.

Notes

1   David Baggett has suggested to me that there is quite a bit of middle ground between Craig's position and the position that *goodness* is reducible to what is *good for* subjects. One might challenge Craig's views by claiming, more modestly, that whatever is good has as part of its meaning or nature the goodness of someone or other. That proposal would indeed be a challenge to Craig's view, as it would not allow him simply to divorce matters of goodness from matters of goodness for. I pursue here, though, the stronger claim that the property of being *good* is reducible to the property of being *good for* someone.

2   See (Kinghorn 2016, chp. 1 & 2).

3   See (Korsgaard 1983) for the distinction.

4   Regarding the narrower sense of punishment as retribution, there may be a number of conditions required for genuine *punishment* to occur: guilt of the transgressor; the transgressor's recognition that the hard treatment he is receiving is on account of this guilt; the intention of the punisher to give the hard treatment on account of this guilt; the position of the punisher as an appropriate administrator of punishment; and so on (see Kyle 2013 for a discussion of the conditions for punishment). For present purposes, I ignore this list of conditions and simply assume, with Craig, that there is a sense of "punishment" narrower than "hard treatment" and linked to the (purported) value of retributive justice.

5   Craig notes in passing an objection sometime leveled at "consequentialist theories of justice", namely that "on such theories it may be just to punish the innocent in view of the good consequences" (Craig 2023, p. 5, n. 19). Craig comments that we need "a view of divine justice as retributive, lest God punish the innocent on consequentialist grounds" (Craig 2023, p. 4, n. 17). This has always seemed to me a strange objection—at least if it is used against Christian theists offering restorative theories of justice. If "punishment" simply means hard or painful treatment, then almost all Christian theists actually *do* allow that God, presumably for prospective reasons, does sometimes allow or even cause both the guilty and the innocent to suffer short-term pain, consistent with his longer-term plans to draw them and others into eternal, perfected relationships through which they find their ultimate flourishing. Job is a reminder here. On the other hand, if "punishment" is conceptually tied to "declaring guilty", then in punishing the innocent God would be declaring an untruth. Aside from the dubious idea that God's essential nature is consistent with declaring untruths, surely Christians reject the notion that the God-centered community of perfected relationships—to which God is drawing all people—could be built on untruths about who the people in that community were and are. In short, there seem no prospective reasons why the God of Christian theism would declare the guilty innocent. Thus, I do not see how restorative theories of justice put forth by Christian theists would be at all vulnerable to the kind of objection Craig notes against unnuanced forms of consequentialism.

6   I should note that some of these others may themselves find further restoration in various ways. For example, in correcting an oppressor so that his actions are publicly exposed, God may thereby provide a way for the oppressor's victims to find deeper, healthier relationships with family and friends who now understand them more fully and can stand more fully with them in solidarity. In short, when God disciplines an oppressor, God's aims of restoration need not be limited to the *oppressor's* restoration. Due to limits of space, though, I continue to discuss only the restoration of the wicked as God's goal when he disciplines them.

7   See (Sher 1987, chp. 8 & 11; Pojman 1997, p. 566; Miller 1999, pp. 135–6; Hurka 2001, pp. 7–8; Schmidtz 2006, pp. 85–6; Kristjánsson 2006, chp. 2; McMahan 2009, pp. 8–9; Kershnar 2010, chp. 1 & 6; Kagan 2012, p. 17; Berman 2013, p. 89; Zaibert 2017, pp. 14–16).

8   I suppose one might suggest that it is not *proportionality* here that has value but, rather, *deserved suffering* that has value. Following G. E. Moore's account of "organic wholes", one might claim that the suffering of people with vicious character is an organic whole with positive value—even while the parts that make up that whole (suffering, people with vicious character) each have negative value (see Zaibert 2018, chp. 2). But Moore's intuitive appeal to the supposed goodness of vicious people's suffering only gains traction if one finds a kind of order or appropriateness in this organic whole. And the kind of order in question is surely just proportionality obtaining between vicious character and negative well-being. So we seem back at our question of whether we have reason to think that there is value in proportionality itself obtaining between a person's character and her well-being.

As opposed to, e.g., God's "impartiality" in calling both Jew and Gentile to participate in the New Creation, which, incidentally, seems to me to be the clear focus of Paul's emphasis on God's impartiality in Romans—despite Craig's frequent attempts to draw affirmations of God's retributive justice from this Pauline letter.

I do not mean to suggest that Craig has no room to say that God, in seeking a right, moral order, desires that the wicked repent and embrace his offer of forgiveness and eternal life in fellowship with him. Craig indeed has room to say that God values and desires the well-being of the wicked. There is even room for Craig to say that God values the restoration of the wicked much *more* than he values the just punishment of the wicked. I am only focused on Craig's commitment to the supposed value of just punishment, wherever it ranks within the list of final values to which God is sensitive. It might also be worth noting that, when God *does* restore the repentant sinner then, on Craig's view, there would seem to be a *trade-off* of valuable states of affairs. Yes, Craig could say that there is enormous—perhaps infinite—value in a sinner's restoration to eternal, abundant life with God. Still, there has been *something* of value lost along the way (recall Craig's statement that there is "something of value, something good" in the wicked receiving their deserved punishment). I myself would much prefer to say that it is *altogether* (intrinsically) bad that sin exists, that suffering exists, and that sinful people persist in suffering—and *altogether* good when these states no longer obtain.

See (Darwall 1995). Tellingly, Grotius (whom Craig cited above) is the one whose work, *The Law of War and Peace*, Darwall identifies as "the founding work of modern natural law" (Darwall 1995, p. 5). This modern natural law tradition is to be contrasted with, and was largely a reaction to, the kind of natural law tradition formulated by Aquinas. In this earlier tradition, God's eternal laws "applied and made accessible" to us in the form of natural laws specify "the distinctive perfection or ideal state of every natural thing" (Darwall 1995, p. 5). Framing questions of "what makes for the good life?" and "how ought we to live?" then come to much the same thing. But a moral framework not centered on questions of how to further subjects' well-being goes searching for non-welfarist moral principles to explain why we ought to do certain things. I would also want to raise this historical point in response to a comment Craig makes about my own continued emphasis on God's beneficent goal of our flourishing. Craig cites Laura Garcia in commenting that my emphasis neglects God's justice, which is an aspect of his moral goodness: "A problem here is that, as Garcia notes, flourishing or well-being is a type of non-moral good, and it seems wrong to treat moral value as simply a function of non-moral value (Craig 2023, p. 5, n. 18; cf. Garcia 2008, pp. 221, 229). If by "moral" we mean the modern (downstream of Grotius) quest for a grounding of "the moral ought" in something other than God's telos for us—which is abundant life in communion with God and others—then I suppose my framework for understanding normative concepts (like "good" and "right") does indeed center on non-moral goods. But I would absolutely reject this modern understanding of the nature of normativity with its subsequent framing of the moral/non-moral distinction.

2 Though I note that this rationale for punishing the wicked is different than Craig's earlier rationale that such punishment is an "intrinsic good". For if we claim that punishment achieves the good purpose of restoring the status of victims, then we are claiming that punishment is *instrumentally* valuable.

3 In our current world of imperfectly loving attitudes and limited imagination, it may be that victims often only understand God's message that he is on their side if they see him as acting *against* those who are *not* on their side. But this is a far cry from affirming that God's preferred way of vindicating the oppressed is by punishing their oppressors or that this retributive punishment is somehow conceptually linked with the vindication of victims.

4 See (Swinburne 1989, pp. 81–87) on the conditions for genuine atonement between oppressor and victim.

5 As a quick sidenote, Craig asks why, if I view God's hard treatment of individuals as always restorative, I would not want to claim that God "simply annihilate(s) the damned and put(s) them out of their misery" (Craig 2023, p. 6). In fact, I *am* inclined toward an annihilationist view of those who have decisively rejected all avenues that God's grace might take toward them. But in my book on wrath, I sought to avoid taking a stance on such eschatological matters as how likely it is that some (or many) people have decisively rejected God; whether postmortem opportunities for repentance may be available; and whether the biblical references to eternal separation from God imply separation from every aspect of the *life* coming from God (i.e., imply death for those truly separated from God). Instead, I sought only to explain the sense in which we can rightly say that those who have decisively rejected God have eternally "placed themselves under God's wrath"—consistent with my overall argument that God's wrath has a restorative purpose.

6 Much more detailed interpretations of the biblical witness as pointing to a restorative view of divine justice, over against a retributive view, include (Hays 1989; Marshall 2001; Travis 2009; Wright 2016).

7 In my book on wrath, I did look at some key passages often interpreted along retributive lines (see also the recent overview of Romans and Isaiah, which very much represents my own position, in (Rutledge 2022, chp. 5)). Beyond what I have said in that book, I think the parable of the Rich Man and Lazarus (Luke 16:19–31) is particularly instructive as to how a passage of scripture that speaks of divine judgment can present us with what looks like a clearly retributive *or* a clearly restorative message—depending on the assumptions we bring to the text as to whether there could be final value in wicked people receiving proportionally negative treatment. I look at this parable in (Kinghorn 2021, pp. 214–15) and, with particular attention to the value of retributive justice, in (Kinghorn forthcoming, §4.5).

8 As was, it is well worth noting, the culture of first-century Palestine and the earlier cultures of the ancient Near East. In sharp contrast to Craig's interpretive framework for understanding various New Testament passages about God's justice, see the more relational and Eastern interpretive lens provided in (W 2019).

References

Berman, Mitchell. 2013. Rehabilitating Retributivism. *Law and Philosophy* 32: 83–108. [CrossRef]

Craig, William Lane. 2023. Is God's Moral Perfection Reducible to His Love? *Religions* 14: 140. [CrossRef]

Darwall, Stephen. 1995. *The British Moralists and the Internal "Ought", 1640–1740*. Cambridge: Cambridge University Press.

Feinberg, John. 2006. *No One like Him: The Doctrine of God*, Rev. ed. Foundations of Evangelical Theology. Wheaton: Crossway Books.

Finlay, Stephen. 2014. *Confusion of Tongues: A Theory of Normative Language*. New York: Oxford University Press.

Foot, Philippa. 2001. *Natural Goodness*. Oxford: Clarendon Press.

Garcia, Laura. 2008. Moral Perfection. In *The Oxford Handbook of Philosophical Theology*. Edited by Thomas P. Flint and Michael C. Rea. Oxford: Oxford University Press.

Hanna, Nathan. 2019. Hitting Retributivism Where It Hurts. *Criminal Law and Philosophy* 13: 109–27. [CrossRef]

Hays, Richard B. 1989. *Echoes of Scripture in the Letters of Paul*. New Haven: Yale University Press.

Hurka, Thomas. 2001. The Common Structure of Virtue and Desert. *Ethics* 112: 6–31. [CrossRef]

Kagan, Shelly. 2012. *The Geometry of Desert*. New York: Oxford University Press.

Kant, Immanuel. 1899. *Critique of Pure Reason*. Translated by J. M. D. Meiklejohn. New York: The Colonial Press.

Kershnar, Stephen. 2010. *Desert and Virtue: A Theory of Intrinsic Value*. Lanham: Lexington Books.

Kinghorn, Kevin. 2016. *A Framework for the Good*. Notre Dame: University of Notre Dame Press.

Kinghorn, Kevin. 2019. *But What about God's Wrath? The Compelling Love Story of Divine Anger*. Westmont: InterVarsity Press.

Kinghorn, Kevin. 2021. *The Nature of Desert Claims: Rethinking What it Means to Get One's Due*. Cambridge: Cambridge University Press.

Kinghorn, Kevin. forthcoming. *God and Value Judgments*. Cambridge: Cambridge University Press.

Korsgaard, Christine. 1983. Two Distinctions in Goodness. *Philosophical Review* 92: 169–95. [CrossRef]

Kristjánsson, Kristján. 2006. *Justice and Desert-Based Emotions*. Aldershot: Ashgate Pub. Limited.

Kyle, Brent. 2013. Punishing and Atoning: A New Critique of Penal Substitution. *International Journal for Philosophy of Religion* 74: 201–18. [CrossRef]

MacIntyre, Alasdair. 2003. *A Short History of Ethics: A History of Moral Philosophy from the Homeric Age to the Twentieth Century*. London: Routledge.

Marshall, Christopher. 2001. *Beyond Retribution: A New Testament Vision for Justice, Crime and Punishment*. Grand Rapids: Wm. B. Eerdmans.

McMahan, Jeff. 2009. *Killing in War*. Oxford: Oxford University Press.

Miller, David. 1999. *Principles of Social Justice*. Cambridge: Harvard University Press.

Pojman, Louis. 1997. Equality and Desert. *Philosophy* 72: 549–70. [CrossRef]

Reardon, Patrick Henry. 2015. *Reclaiming the Atonement: An Orthodox Theology of Redemption*. Chesterton: Ancient Faith Publishing.

Ross, W. D. 2002. *The Good and the Right*. Oxford: Clarendon Press.

Rutledge, Jonathan. 2022. *Forgiveness and Atonement: Christ's Restorative Justice*. Routledge Studies in Analytic and Systematic Theology. New York: Routledge.

Schmidtz, David. 2006. *Elements of Justice*. Cambridge: Cambridge University Press.

Sher, George. 1987. *Desert*. Princeton: Princeton University Press.

Swinburne, Richard. 1989. *Responsibility and Atonement*. Oxford: Clarendon Press.

Travis, Stephen H. 2009. *Christ and the Judgement of God*, 2nd ed. Milton Keynes: Paternoster.

W, Jackson. 2019. *Reading Romans with Eastern Eyes: Honor and Shame in Paul's Message and Mission*. Downers Grove: IVP Academic.

Wright, N. T. 2016. *The Day the Revolution Began: Reconsidering the Meaning of Jesus's Crucifixion*. San Francisco: HarperOne.

Zaibert, Leo. 2017. On the Matter of Suffering: Derek Parfit and the Possibility of Deserved Punishment. *Criminal Law and Philosophy* 11: 1–18. [CrossRef]

Zaibert, Leo. 2018. *Rethinking Punishment*. Cambridge: Cambridge University Press.

Ziff, Paul. 1960. *Semantic Analysis*. Ithaca: Cornell University Press.

 *religions*

Article

A Critical Assessment of Shafer-Landau's Ethical Non-Naturalism

J. P. Moreland

Department of Philosophy, Biola University, 13800 Biola Ave., La Mirada, CA 90639, USA; jp.moreland@biola.edu

Abstract: I focus on the ethical non-naturalism of Russ Shafer-Landau. First, I spend a good bit of time specifying the nature of two versions of naturalism and arguing that one is embraced ubiquitously—more importantly, should be embraced—by contemporary naturalists. I do so because if I am right about this, before we investigate the details of Shafer-Landau's ethical non-naturalism, there will be a significant burden of proof for him to meet. In my view, that burden is strong enough to justify the claim that a critic's epistemic task is merely to provide undercutting defeaters for Shafer-Landau's position, and not to proffer rebutting defeaters, though I will attempt to supply both. After presenting a crucial characterization of contemporary naturalism followed by a critique of naturalist emergent properties, I state and critique Shafer-Landau's ontology followed by the same for his epistemology. Both will be evaluated with a particular focus on their plausibility to support his ethical non-naturalism.

Keywords: emergent properties; ethical non-naturalism; naturalism; faint-hearted; naturalism; staunch; Shafer-Landau; Russ

1. Introduction

David Papineau opines that contemporary naturalism is a consequence of the build-up of scientific evidence during the twentieth century. (Papineau 2001) I agree, but regardless of whether he is correct, one thing is certain: We are now confronted with a large and often disparate menagerie of standpoints that claim to represent naturalism. This is particularly true when it comes to naturalist ethical theory. I think it is fair to say that when it comes to ethical theory, most naturalists adopt either some version of non-cognitivism or ethical naturalism (See Moreland and Horner forthcoming).

However, there is a growing number who embrace ethical non-naturalism and, along with it, the existence and knowability of objective intrinsic value and moral duties. In my view, both in their sophistication and accurate representation of this approach, Erik Wielenberg and Russ Shafer-Landau are regarded as the leading advocates of ethical non-naturalism. I have criticized Wielenberg's position elsewhere (Moreland 2020).

So, in this article I will focus on the views of Shafer-Landau. Accordingly, in what follows, I will spend a good bit of time specifying the nature of two versions of naturalism and arguing that one is embraced ubiquitously—more importantly, should be embraced—by contemporary naturalists. I do so because if I am right about this, before we investigate the details of Shafer-Landau's ethical non-naturalism, there will be a significant burden of proof for him to meet. In my view, that burden is strong enough to justify the claim that a critic's epistemic task is merely to provide undercutting defeaters for Shafer-Landau's position, and not to proffer rebutting defeaters, though I will attempt to supply both. After presenting a crucial characterization of contemporary naturalism followed by a critique of naturalist emergent properties, I will state and critique Shafer-Landau's ontology followed by the same for his epistemology. Both will be evaluated with a particular focus on emergent properties, and I believe those working in metaethics can benefit from the rich distinctions and assess their plausibility to support his ethical non-naturalism.

Citation: Moreland, J. P.. 2023. A Critical Assessment of Shafer-Landau's Ethical Non-Naturalism. *Religions* 14: 546. https://doi.org/10.3390/rel14040546

Academic Editors: David Baggett and Joseph Rivera

Received: 7 December 2022
Revised: 1 March 2023
Accepted: 14 April 2023
Published: 18 April 2023

Before I provide a characterization of worldview naturalism, structural supervenient properties, and emergent properties, a few preliminary comments are in order. First, philosophers of science and mind have led the way in studying supervenient detailed analyses of these notions. Accordingly, I will turn to philosophy of science and mind in the upcoming section. This and the points to follow are important for the contribution I hope to make about Shafer-Landau's ethical non-naturalism. In an earlier draft of this article, a very astute anonymous referee raised a number of criticisms of that draft. I have incorporated several of them in this article, but I believe that a cluster of objections were largely due to a misunderstanding of my approach. That misunderstanding was my fault. I was not making my precise approach clear enough. In this and the following preliminary comments, along with their application to specific challenges that arise from the literature in the metaethics of Shafer-Landau's moral realism, I hope to provide a needed context for how my approach attempts to solve these issues.

Second, while supervenience strictly speaking is merely a doctrine of property (or world) co-variance, it is now ubiquitously understood to include a ontological grounding condition construed as ontological dependency between supervenient properties that are constituted by subvenient entities and *sui generis* emergent properties whose conditions for their initial exemplification and continued sustaining are grounded in their associated subvenient base.

Third, in philosophy of science during the first half of the twentieth century, emergent properties were defined epistemologically:[1] Property P is an emergent property of some particular x at level ln just in the case when P is a property of x at ln, and no amount of knowledge of (or descriptive statements about) entities at subvenient levels below ln would justify a prediction of (or logically entail a descriptive statement about) P at ln. In this sense an emergent property (or a statement about it) is surprising and unexpected relative to knowledge of (or statements about) lower levels.

Since the 1960s, emergent properties have been understood in a straightforward ontological way (see below) with the result that Nagelian and property reduction came to replace linguistic and semantic reduction.

Philosophy of mind followed the same path. From the 1920s through the late 1950s. linguistic reduction (e.g., as in Analytic Behaviorism) or semantic reduction were replaced by the two ontological reductions mentioned above. For example, in the 1960s, Type Identity Physicalism employed non-synonymous, co-referring expressions to flank the identity symbol in contingent identity statements (e.g., painfulness = being a C-fiber firing). Thus, the issue of whether properties of consciousness were emergent or reducible was taken to be an *a posteriori* issue; except for rare exceptions, gone was the importance of analytic/synthetic physicalism or naturalism.

To be sure, conceptual analysis continued to be used as one tool among others, but the resulting conceptual equivalencies or lack thereof were examples of use and not mention—they were means to get at the relevant features of the mind-independent world. Consequently, a failure to achieve a conceptual analysis that establishes synonymity between two concepts or terms is not taken to show non-identity of the associated referents. The important issue in any purported reductive claim regarding properties and their instances was whether one is faced with a genuine emergent property or with a case where the property turns out to be identical to one employed in the hard sciences.

This shift away from the analytic/synthetic focus was facilitated even more with the publication of Saul Kripke's *Naming and Necessity*.[2] Beginning with the early modern empiricists, those with an empirical bent (with apologies to Kant and his *synthetic a priori* propositions) held to two types of propositions each of which was characterized by three clustered kinds: (1) Analytic, necessary, *a priori*; (2) Synthetic, contingent, *a posteriori*. Type (1) propositions were analytic truths, and thus, they were *a priori* and necessary. Type (2) propositions were synthetic truths and, thus, were *a posteriori* and contingent. Kripke famously showed that there were contingent *a posteriori* and necessary *a priori* truths. The synthetic/analytic distinction became less important, and the debate about property reduction vs. emergence became more directly focused on the ontology involved. Properties, not property-talk, or entities in the world, not semantics, now constitute the primary focus, even if conceptual analysis is a tool among others to get at that ontology. Some still focus on synthetic/analytic physicalism, but this is often associated with debates about *a priori/a posteriori* physicalism.

To summarize, I take this statement from leading physicalist Andrew Melnyk to be canonical:

The claim that a particular mental property is identical with a particular physical or functional property is not advanced as any kind of a priori claim, e.g., as a conceptual or analytic truth. It must be supported by empirical evidence. For example, it is argued that the identification of mental property M with physical property P would provide the best explanation of an observed correlation between instances of M and instances of P. Physicalism is claimed to be analogous to such a posteriori scientific hypotheses as that genes are segments of DNA or that chemical elements are systems of physical particles (Melnyk 2019).

It is time to apply these insights to a set of issues that must be addressed before I can proceed with my approach to Shafer-Landau.

(i) Do issues about emergent properties generalize to other areas of philosophy, especially those in metaethics? For two reasons, the answer is yes. First, discussions of emergence began in the philosophy of science, and debates about property emergence vs. Nagelian or property reduction surfaced in a wide range of topics, e.g., biology, systems theory, chemistry, and philosophy of mind. Second, Frank Jackson's defense of staunch naturalism (see below) addressed alleged emergent properties in four areas of philosophy: indexical properties associated with the first-person point of view, properties of consciousness, secondary qualities, and normative, e.g., moral properties (Jackson 1998; Sturgeon 1986).

(ii) Some claim that Shafer-Landau seldom, if ever, talks about emergent properties in developing his ontology for moral realism. Thus, critiques of emergent properties (see below) are beside the point. I acknowledge his lack of explicit reference to emergent properties. However, I think that is because his discussion fails to appropriate insights from philosophy of science and mind that are relevant to his views. Discussions about ethical non-naturalism within metaethics seldom bring issues about emergent properties into their discussions.

More importantly, emergent properties are implicit in his ontology. I take his approach to be a specific version of what Bernard Linsky and Edward N. Zath call Platonized Naturalism (Linsky and Zath 1995). This is a view according to which (a) when viewed from the perspective of abstract objects (e.g., properties construed as abstract universals), various concrete objects or events exemplify abstract objects. (b) When viewed from within the Standard Mereological Hierarchy and the perspective of the associated objects or events, when the right physical conditions obtain, the coming-to-be and continued ontological grounding of the exemplified property are understood as emergent properties ontologically dependent on the right subvenient bases.

Shafer-Landau explicitly states that moral principles and specific moral properties are exemplified to form moral facts construed as instances of the principles and properties. He cites specific cases of the right kind in which non-moral facts regularly exemplify these properties (Shafer-Landau 2004). It is clear that the coming-to-be-exemplified and the continued ontological sustaining of these properties are grounded in specific kinds of non-moral facts. If this is correct, then moral properties and their fact-instances meet the conditions for being emergent prope rties.

There is an additional consideration that supports Shafer-Landau's employment of emergent properties, viz., his constitutive non-naturalism according to which the rightness or goodness of anything will be brought about by the descriptive facts that constitute it in a particular instance.[3] It is the particular arrangement of descriptive features that causes something to have moral status. How does this happen? While a conjunction of moral principle/property and non-evaluative, descriptive facts explain the moral status of a moral fact, only the latter are causal. Moral properties are epiphenomenal. But moral properties supervene and are not type identical to their subvenient purely descriptive properties and property-instances. Thus, moral properties are irreducibly emergent epiphenomenal properties that emergently supervene on the appropriate factual subvenient bases. This is exactly what those in philosophy of science and mind mean by emergent properties.

In an important article, Nicholas L. Sturgeon defends a view quite similar to Shafer-Landau's with an important difference. Sturgeon's main goal is to provide defeaters to two claims made by Gilbert Harman: Alleged moral facts are irrelevant to explaining our moral beliefs and observations because (a) moral explanations are of a kind that does not make it possible to test moral claims empirically in ways scientific claims can be tested; (b) moral claims can be tested empirically if we have in hand a natural reduction for moral claims.

Among his responses, Sturgeon tweaks one of Harman's thought experiments and uses it against him. Harman invites us to consider the following: Albert is beating a cat who should have known better than to stray into his yard. Jane sees him and believes that what he is doing is wrong. Now, says Harman, it may initially seem plausible to hold that part of the reason Jane has this belief is due to the moral fact that Albert's action is wrong. But this would be mistaken because there is nothing about the occurrence of Jane's belief that requires anyone else to believe in the postulated moral fact. Thus, the moral explanation provides no useful test of whether Albert's action is wrong. Irreducible moral facts (if such there be) are epiphenomenal and explanatorily useless.

Among his responses, Sturgeon presents an altered version of the thought experiment. Everything is kept as it was except now another person—Mary—is introduced into the picture. Mary has never thought that there is anything wrong with beating animals. However, based on observational evidence, Mary has come to believe that Jane's moral judgments are quite good and correct in most cases. She also holds that Jane is a good person with a deep moral life and her moral sensitivity is reliable. Based on this observational evidence, Mary comes to believe what Jane believes about Albert's actions. Mary did not accept this as true to begin with. Observational evidence changed her mind. Mary did not have a reductive analysis in hand, and her moral beliefs were caused to change by empirical evidence just as scientific beliefs are. Thus, Harman's two theses are false.

Harman replies that irreducible moral properties/facts are epiphenomenal and, thus, can never be the cause of one's moral beliefs. Perhaps descriptive wrong-making features of certain acts can explain what we observe, but the wrongness of those acts is explanatorily irrelevant.

Sturgeon digs his heels in and argues that epiphenomenalism in these cases is wrong. The supervenience of moral facts upon non-moral facts does not render the former epiphenomenal. Rather, the supervenience of moral facts is like the supervenience of biological facts upon chemical and physical ones, and this is a kind of "causal constitution of the supervening facts out of the more basic ones, which allows them a causal efficacy inherited from that of the acts out of which they are constituted."

There are two crucial mistakes in Sturgeon's final argument that informs Shafer-Landau's project. First, as noted above, philosophers of mind have written volumes on constitution-supervenience which are exactly like Sturgeon's characterization of them. Supervenient properties are constituted by their subvenient base entities and a new structural arrangement. Above, I called this structural supervenience. Unfortunately, if all supervenient properties are structural ones, then one's ontology will be that of the hard sciences and bereft of emergent properties, including moral ones. In this case, *sans* emergent moral properties/facts, ethical non-naturalism reduces ontologically to ethical naturalism irrespective of the absence or presence of linguistic or semantic reduction.

Second, absent causal overdetermination, if there is either an irreducible mental or value description or a genuinely mental or value property that is an aspect of an object/event that also has a physical description or ontological aspect, then the mental component is causally epiphenomenal and does no work in explaining one's action. For example, if a state of feeling thirsty emerges on a brain state of certain neurons firing, and one is thereby caused to get a drink, it was the neurons firing that caused the action. The feeling of thirst was epiphenomenal. Or so most naturalists would argue. If this is so, then Sturgeon's employment of his views of supervenience, etc., is hard to harmonize with his claim that epiphenomenalism is false.

(iii) Objection: Employment of an emergence theory for moral properties would be a form of naturalism. Since Shafer-Landau in an ethical non-naturalist, this is something he simply would not do. We have already seen reasons for thinking that Shafer-Landau does, in fact, quantify over emergent moral properties, and I will not rehearse those. But what should we make of this objection?

I think a simple distinction is sufficient to defeat this claim. We need to distinguish ethical non-naturalism from worldview naturalism as it applies to genuinely emergent properties in many areas of philosophy. Ethical non-naturalism amounts to the rejection of ethical naturalism and its claim that the ontology of the hard sciences is all there is: alleged emergent entities must be reduced to that ontology or eliminated. As we will see below, ethical non-naturalism is an expression of staunch naturalism applied to moral entities.

By contrast, ethical non-naturalism embraces the ontology of the hard sciences but goes on to adopt a richer ontology that includes, among other things, properties of consciousness and intentional action, along with moral/value properties and principles. The mistake made by the objection under consideration is to think that adopting ethical non-naturalism amounts to an abandonment of worldview naturalism, but this is simply a mistake. As we will see, Faint-Hearted Naturalism is a widely accepted version of worldview naturalism according to which the ontology of the physical sciences provides an inventory of all the fundamental entities in reality, but genuinely emergent properties (e.g., being painful, being good) also exist and are ontologically dependent on or grounded in physical reality. Thus, Shafer-Landau's ethical non-naturalism is a version of Faint-Hearted Naturalism and in no way an abandonment of naturalism *tout court*.

A consideration of the following statement by Shafer-Landau in light of the next section on worldview naturalism makes this point, at least as far as I can see.

In effect, what the moral skeptic is giving us is a universe exclusively regulated by scientific laws, containing only the things that are ratified by science. Ethical objectivists give us a fuller, more expansive ontology. This includes all that science does, but adds an additional layer—moral principles and facts.

2. The Nature of Naturalism as a Worldview: Preliminary Remarks

2.1. Staunch vs. Faint-Hearted Naturalism

In this section, I will take both versions of naturalism to be robust, ontological doctrines. I have already explained above why most philosophers of science and mind are not particularly interested in analytic or synthetic naturalism, though a small minority remain. My purpose here is to take insights from philosophy of science and mind about the nature of naturalism, emergence, and property reduction, and use them to assess Shafer-Landau's ethical non-naturalism.

Staunch naturalism is the view that the cosmos and all entities within it—e.g., particulars, properties, relations, events, processes—are and only are physical. Strong physicalism adopts the same ontology concerning consciousness, the human person, and other entities studied in the philosophy of mind. While he does not use the term, Galen Strawson's understanding of standard physicalism and his claim that it is the ubiquitously adopted view is consistent with my claims about staunch naturalism: "I take [standard] physicalism to be the view that every real, concrete [i.e., spatio-temporally located] phenomenon in the universe is ... physical" (brackets mine).[4] According to Strawson, standard physicalism entails (NE): "Physical stuff is, in itself, in its fundamental nature, something wholly and utterly non-experiential." (Ibid., p. 11.)

Staunch naturalists/strong physicalists eschew *sui generis*, irreducible, ineliminable emergent properties.[5] Faint-hearted naturalism and weak physicalism differ only in that they embrace emergent entities, usually properties, but in a few cases, systems and even substances.

Strictly speaking, neither version of naturalism makes any reference to the existence or non-existence of abstract entities. However, with supplementation, we get Platonized Faint-hearted Naturalism = $_{def.}$ a version of Platonized naturalism according to which certain abstract entities—relevant properties, laws/standards, and relations—are exemplified, and when exemplified, are understood as emergent properties—more plausibly, emergent property-instances—located in the spatio-temporal, physical, causal realm. Such properties, laws/standards, and relations can be known by human cognizers.

2.2. Emergent vs. Structurally Supervenient Properties

There is an important distinction between emergent and structural properties/supervenience. Emergent properties (EPs) are completely unique, new kinds of properties different from those that characterize their subvenient bases. Moreover, EPs are simple, novel properties different from and not composed of subvenient entities. Being painful is an example. Keep in mind that in the first half of the twentieth century, emergent properties were defined epistemologically:[6] Property P is an emergent property of some particular x at level l_n just in the case where P is a property of x at l_n, and no amount of knowledge of (or descriptive statements about) entities at subvenient levels below l_n would justify a prediction of (or logically entails a descriptive statement about) P at l_n. In this sense an emergent property is surprising, unexpected, and utterly brute. Thus, the prior probability of emergent properties, given complete knowledge of lower levels, would be zero.

By contrast, a structural property (SP) is constituted by a new configurational pattern of subvenient parts, properties, relations, and events. It is not a new kind of property; it is merely a new pattern of subvenient entities. In what follows, I will set aside global supervenience and employ only strong property supervenience with a modality of (*de re*) metaphysical necessity.[7]

3. Why Contemporary Naturalists Ought to Be Staunch Naturalists (and Most Are)

Space considerations forbid me from developing the points in this section. Fortunately, I have done that elsewhere (Rickabaugh and Moreland 2023), so here I will provide a precis that I trust has enough details for the reader to get the important ideas and their relations to each other. Among other things, what follows makes explicit and provides justification for why J. L. Mackie advanced his argument from queerness against non-natural moral properties and facts (Mackie 1977). The ontological component of his argument entails the rejection of the exemplification of moral properties and the obtaining of moral facts due to their being utterly different from any other properties and facts (ibid.). This conviction led him to affirm that "Moral properties constitute so odd a cluster of properties and relations that they are most unlikely to have arisen in the ordinary course of events without an all-powerful god to create them" (ibid.).

3.1. The Inner Logic of Scientific/Philosophical Naturalism

Intellectually responsible naturalists cannot merely deny God's existence. Additionally, they must provide an account of what ideas naturalists ought to hold regarding epistemological commitments, a broad creation story (the Grand Story) about how all entities have come-to-be, and a resulting ontology such that all entities can be located in the Grand Story as certified by naturalist epistemological commitments.

Just exactly what are the central features of contemporary naturalism? (Rosenberg 1996) Though versions vary, there is a specific form that is rightly enjoying widespread hegemony. Further, by clarifying the relationship between a naturalist ontology, epistemology, and creation account, a picture will emerge regarding what ought to constitute that ontology. This picture places a substantial burden of proof for alternative naturalist ontologies bloated beyond what is justifiable within the constraints that follow from a naturalist epistemology and creation account.

Fundamentally, naturalism is the view that the spatio-temporal universe of entities postulated by our best current (or ideal) theories in the physical sciences, particularly physics, is all there is. Scientific naturalism includes: (1) different aspects of a naturalist epistemic attitude; (2) an etiological, microphysical, combinatorial account of how all entities have come-to-be, constituted by a bottom-up, event-causal story (especially the atomic theory of matter and evolutionary biology); and (3) a general ontology with and only with entities bearing a relevant similarity to those in a completed form of physics. Whether this ontology should be expanded to include *sui generis* emergent properties or abstract objects, will occupy our attention shortly.

The ordering of these three ingredients is crucial. The naturalist epistemology justifies the etiology which together justifies and places constraints on ontological commitments. Moreover, naturalism requires coherence among these three areas of the naturalistic turn.

Thus, in setting up his naturalist project, David Papineau sets philosophy within science—philosophical investigation should be conducted within the framework of our best empirical theories. It follows, says Papineau, that " ... the task of the philosophers is to bring coherence and order to the set of assumptions we use to explain the empirical world" (Papineau 1993).

Hence, there should be a coherence among third-person scientific ways of knowing; a physical, evolutionary account of how our sensory and cognitive processes came-to-be; and an ontological analysis of those processes. Any entities that are taken to exist should bear a relevant similarity to entities that characterize our best (or ideal) physical theories, their coming-to-be should be intelligible in light of the Grand Story, and they should be knowable by scientific means.

3.2. The Naturalist Epistemic Attitude

First and foremost, naturalism expresses an epistemic posture, specifically, scientism. Wilfrid Sellars expressed this posture when he said that "in the dimension of describing and explaining the world, science is the measure of all things, of what is that it is, and of what is not that it is not" (Sellars 1963). Steven Wagner and Richard Warner claim that naturalism is "the view that only natural science deserves full and unqualified credence" (Wagner and Warner 1993).

Most contemporary naturalists embrace either weak or strong scientism (Moreland 2018). According to the former, nonscientific fields offer some intellectual results, but they are vastly inferior to science in their epistemic standing. According to the latter, unqualified cognitive value resides in science alone. Either way, naturalists are extremely skeptical of any reality-claims that are not justified by scientific methodology in the hard sciences. That methodology is a third-person one, and the entities justified by it are capable of exhaustive description from a third-person perspective. Entities that require the first-person perspective as their basic mode of epistemic access are met with skepticism.

Naturalists believe this posture is justified by the success of science relative to other fields of inquiry. In addition, some naturalists justify this standpoint by appealing to the unity of science. As John Searle notes, since for these naturalists, science exhausts what we can know, then belief in the unity of science entails a belief in the unity of all knowledge because it is scientific knowledge:

> Every fact in the universe is in principle knowable and understandable by human investigators. Because reality is physical, and because science concerns the investigation of physical reality, and because there are no limits on what we can know of physical reality, it follows that all facts are knowable and understandable by us. (Searle 1992)

For such naturalists, the exhaustive or elevated nature of scientific knowledge entails that either the only explanations that count or the ones with superior, unqualified acceptance are those employed in the hard sciences.

Second, scientific theories that are paradigm cases of epistemic/explanatory success (e.g., the atomic theory of matter, evolutionary biology) employ combinatorial modes of explanation. Thus, any process that constitutes the Grand Story and any entity in the naturalist ontology should exhibit an ontological structure analyzable in terms that are isomorphic with such modes of explanation. Colin McGinn has defended this idea along with what he takes it to entail, viz., the inability of naturalism to explain EPs:

> Can we gain any deeper insight into what makes the problem of consciousness run against the grain of our thinking? Are our modes of theorizing about the world of the wrong shape to extend to the nature of mind? I think we can discern a characteristic structure possessed by successful scientific theories, a structure that is unsuitable for explaining consciousness . . . Is there a "grammar" to science that fits the physical world but becomes shaky when applied to the mental world? Perhaps the most basic aspect of thought is the operation of *combination*. This is the way in which we think of complex entities as resulting from the arrangement of simpler parts. There are three aspects to this basic idea: the atoms we start with, the laws we use to combine them, and the resulting complexes . . . I think it is clear that this mode of understanding is central to what we think of as scientific theory; our scientific faculty involves representing the world in this combinatorial style. (McGinn 1999)

We have seen that many philosophers express different aspects of the naturalist epistemic attitude. Let us turn to an overview of the Grand Story.

3.3. The Naturalist Grand Story

I use "the Grand Story" for the naturalist account of how all things came-to-be.[8] Speaking generally, all of reality—space, time, and matter—came from the original "creation" event, and the various stars, galaxies, and other heavenly bodies developed combinatorially as the expanding universe went through various stages. On at least one of those heavenly bodies—earth—some sort of pre-biotic soup scenario explains how living things came into being from non-living chemicals. The combinatorial processes of evolution gave rise to all life forms, including human beings. Thus, all organisms and their parts exist and are what they are because they contributed to (or at least did not hinder) the struggle for reproductive advantage.

Note three important things about the Grand Story. First, at its core are two theories that exhibit combinatorial explanation: the atomic theory of matter and evolutionary theory.

Second, it expresses a scientific version of philosophical monism with two features: (1) An acceptable explanation must come from the hard sciences, and must show why something, e.g., a state of affairs, had to happen, given certain conditions. For example, $PV = nRT$ is a lawlike description of an ideal gas (P, V, T and n are pressure, volume, temperature and the number of moles of gas, respectively; R is a constant.). But it is not a scientific explanation. For that we must employ ideal gas theory that, in turn, explains why the pressure of a gas must increase with an increase in temperature at constant volume. (2) No non-physical entities exist, including EPs.

When naturalists embrace EPs, however, they must depict them as being rooted in, emergent from, dependent upon, and necessitated by their subvenient physical states constituting the Grand Story. Further, their origin and continued existence are brute facts for which, in principle, there are no explanations. Later, we examine whether EPs should be allowed in a naturalist ontology.

Third, the Grand Story is constituted by bottom-up, event causality, eschewing irreducible teleology and agent causation in which the first relatum of the causal relation is a substance and not an event. Further, the Grand Story is deterministic in two senses: diachronically such that the state of the universe at any time t, coupled with the laws of nature, determine or fix the chances of the state of the universe at subsequent times; and synchronically such that the features of and changes regarding macro-wholes are dependent on and determined by micro-phenomena.

3.4. The Naturalist Ontology

(a)   Faint-Hearted vs. Staunch Naturalism One More Time

Characterizing a naturalist ontology requires distinguishing staunch (SN) and faint-hearted naturalism (FN). I describe that distinction above, but since it is so important for what follows, I provide a precis here to get this distinction before the reader. Staunch naturalists (e.g., David Papineau) accept a strict/strong version of physicalism (all individuals, events, states of affairs, properties, relations, and laws are entirely physical) for the natural world, while faint-hearted naturalists (e.g., John Searle) embrace various EPs.

(b)   The Location Problem

Let's focus on criteria for naturalist ontological commitments. The canonical place to start is with what Frank Jackson calls "the location problem" (Jackson 1998). According to Jackson, given scientism, naturalists are committed to a widely accepted physical story about how things came-to-be (the Grand Story) and what they are. This generates the location problem: the task of locating some entity in that story.

For Jackson, the naturalist must either locate a problematic entity in the basic story or eliminate it. Roughly, an entity is located in the basic story just in case it is entailed by that story. Entailment is accomplished by some sort of reduction. Jackson provides examples of location. First, just as density is a different property from mass and volume, it is not an additional feature of reality over and above mass and volume because an account of things in terms of mass and volume implicitly contains, i.e., entails, the account in terms of density.

More importantly, Jackson focuses on the location of macro-solidity. He acknowledges that prior to modern science there was a widely accepted commonsense notion of macro-solidity, viz., being everywhere dense. However, due to modern science, this notion has been replaced with being impenetrable. So understood, macro-solidity may be located in the basic micro-story: given a description of two macro-objects in terms of their atomic parts, lattice structures, and sub-atomic forces of repulsion, this description entails that one macro-object is impenetrable with respect to the other. Here, SE and EP are reduced to weak supervenience and structural properties, respectively. This move relieves the naturalist from embarrassing—inexplicable—brute entities and preserves the correct ontology developed within the naturalist epistemology and Grand Story. In turn, this (allegedly) retains the naturalist claim to explanatory and epistemic superiority.

Jackson says that the naturalist must locate (reduce) or eliminate four troublesome entities: mental properties/events, first-person indexical facts, secondary qualities, and moral properties.

3.5. The Logic of the Standard Mereological Hierarchy

What has come to be known as the Standard Mereological Hierarchy has become the ubiquitously accepted world picture allegedly bequeathed to us by the hard sciences. Speaking of the hierarchy, Jaegwon Kim asserts what he takes to be obvious and without need of defense:

> Today, any proposed general ontology of the world … is defined by its relation to materialism, the position that the world consists exclusively of bits of matter and structures made up of bits of matter, all behaving in accordance with physical law. Everything is an arrangement of matter and living organisms and minded creatures are no exceptions. (Kim 2018)

To elaborate, the Standard Mereological Hierarchy is the picture within which philosophers must work. Construed ontologically, it is an ascending, hierarchically arranged taxonomy of individuals, properties, and relations. The fundamental level is microphysical entities.

Call this level n. Focusing on living organisms, in the category of individual, the hierarchy ascends through level n+1, n+2, etc.—atoms, molecules, cells, living organs/systems, living organisms, psychologically endowed living organisms, ecosystems. The relation between a level and the one above it is the standard part/whole relation of extensionalist mereology. Moreover, level n is fundamental and not ontologically dependent on any lower level since there is none. Each level above n lists individuals that are dependent on the level below it in two ways (Inman 2019):

Essentially$_1$ Grounded: (IG) x is essentially$_1$ grounded in $y =$ def. There is a two-place predicate "F" such that it is part of the identity of x that x is related by F to y.

Rigid Existentially Grounded: (RG) x is rigidly grounded in $y =$ def. @ (E$x \rightarrow$Ey). (NB. The @ should be replaced with the box).

To clarify (IG), let x be some aggregate of parts, y be one of y's parts, and F be the part-whole relation or, perhaps, its converse. In (RG), "E" is "exists" and the arrow is strict entailment. (RG) means that y's existence is necessary for x's existence. Each principle in its own way implies mereological essentialism for individual wholes at level n+1 relative to n as they are depicted in the hierarchy.

In the category of property, all properties above level n are structural properties composed of the parts at the lower level standing in a new structural arrangement constituted by numerous instances of external relations between and among those parts (e.g., being H_2O, being a *homo sapiens*). In the category of relation, all relations are external.

It is important to keep in mind that IG and RG are expressions of ontological grounding or (non-causal) metaphysical priority or dependency. For example, RG captures the idea that it sometimes happens that one thing (x) may depend on another specific entity (y) for its existence. It is metaphysically impossible for x to exist without that very entity y existing. The word "rigid" is meant to capture the idea that x cannot exist without that specific y such that if there is a replacement of or variation within y, x ceases to exist. The classic example of RG is mereological essentialism applied to mereological aggregates.

Jackson grasps the connection between accepting the epistemic superiority of naturalism and deciding between SN and FN and the importance of working within the limits set by the Standard Mereological Hierarchy. For Jackson, epistemic superiority entails SN.

This inner logic of naturalism implies at least three ontological constraints:

1. Entities should conform to the naturalist epistemology.
2. Entities should conform to the naturalist Grand Story.
3. Entities should bear a relevant similarity to those found in chemistry and physics *or* be capable of one-to-one or one-to-many correlation with entities in chemistry/physics or depend necessarily on entities in chemistry/physics. This is an expression of microphysical priority.

Regarding the naturalist epistemology, all entities should be subject to combinatorial modes of explanation, be entirely publicly accessible, be knowable entirely by third-person scientific means, and be knowable by faculties formed by the evolutionary struggle for reproductive advantage. Regarding the Grand Story, one should be able to show how any entity had to appear, given combinatorial, microphysical, event-causal processes. At higher levels above the fundamental one (if there is such), mereological aggregates and structural properties fit nicely into the Grand Story and satisfy the epistemological criterion of simplicity compared to substantial selves (or homeodynamic systems) and EPs. Thus, the first disjunct of (3) follows nicely from (1) and (2), but the second and third disjuncts do not.

Unfortunately, when construed in terms of EPs, the second disjunct of (3) "solves" the so-called hard problem of consciousness or the emergence of moral properties by simply naming the problem (they are "emergent") or by employing weak supervenience and dismissing the need for further explanatory work. Further, the second disjunct fails to satisfy criteria (1) and (2). The third disjunct of (3) suffers from this latter problem and from difficulties with justifying the claim that emergent entities are "necessitated" by their subvenient microphysical bases.

4. Problems with Naturalistic Emergent Properties

4.1. The View

For those who accept the existence of genuine, irreducible, non-physical conscious states and, at the same time, affirm naturalism, the most popular current strategy is to adopt faint-hearted naturalism and weak (usually, nonreductive) physicalism, and appeal to some sort on natural emergence. According to the staunch-naturalist account, matter at the most basic level—the microphysical level—is or will be completely describable within an ideal physics. Staunch naturalist David Papineau's view on this matter is canonical. While acknowledging that progress towards an ideal science may require categorial supplementation of some sort, he maintains the following: "What I do not believe is that they [the current categories of physics plus future supplementation] will need supplementation by psychological categories" (Papineau 1993, 2002) (brackets mine).

That ideal description will be able to capture the complete nature of basic matter, and it will entail that basic matter is bereft of any mental entities, including mental potentialities. So far, a faint-hearted naturalist would agree. However, they go on to affirm that when matter reaches a certain, "appropriate" level of complexity, a completely new range of *sui generis* emergent properties, especially conscious and moral properties, appears from a subvenient base wholly bereft of, say, consciousness/intrinsic rightness/goodness or potentialities for them.

4.2. Seven Criticisms of the View

For one thing, an appeal to emergent properties has always seemed suspect to us if it is offered as an explanation: "emergence" is not a solution but a name for the problem to be solved. It is a label and that is all. This is especially problematic in the current setting in which scientists and philosophers of science are increasingly elevating the importance of seeking mechanisms that explain how and why emergent properties appear under a specific set of base conditions (Tabaczek 2019).

In a closely analogous context, Jaegwon Kim has convincingly made the same charge against the widely employed, but illicit, inclusion of dependency in strong property supervenience (Kim 1998). He notes that such supervenience is merely a principle of property covariance and, as such, it is consistent with a number of disparate views on the mind/body problem, including some forms of property or substance dualism. According to Kim, supervenience is a name that provides no explanation of the problem to be solved, viz., the dependency and determination of the mental on or by the physical.

Kim's solution to this problem is to adopt a version of physicalist functional realizationism, which entails that mental properties supervene on physical properties because physical properties realize mental properties. The point here is not to evaluate Kim's solution; rather, it is to acknowledge his charge that slapping the label "supervenience" on the problem of mental dependency on the physical is no solution at all. Some further theoretical work is needed to satisfy that problem-solving need.

I am making the same claim about the naturalist employment of "emergence." I recognize that supervenience *tout court* is not precisely analogous to genuine emergence, but I think that Kim's treatment of strong property supervenience *is* appropriately analogous to our claim about "emergence." In fact, employment of "emergence" is more egregious than using "supervenience" in the Kim discussion. Why? As Kim shows, at least the "supervenience" case allows room for the development of an explanatory theory that grounds and explains why supervenient dependency is true.

But this is not possible for emergent properties. Recall that until the middle of the twentieth century, emergent properties were characterized epistemically, e.g., as being unpredictable from exhaustive knowledge of base entities. Genuine emergence is the Platonic Form of being a brute fact, and as such, there is in principle no deeper explanation of emergent properties on offer. Consequently, the charge that emergence is just a name for the problem and not a solution seems justified.

In the present context, while I do not agree with his overall position, it is instructive to notice an important aspect of Colin McGinn's Mysterian Naturalism (McGinn 1999).[9] According to McGinn, given that there is no knowable, current naturalistic solution to the origin of consciousness or its regular correlation with matter, due to our cognitive limitations, he sets out two conditions for any solution to these issues: (i) It must be a naturalistic solution. (ii) It must depict the emergence of consciousness and its regular correlation with matter as necessary and not contingent facts.

More specifically, there must be three kinds of unknowable natural properties that solve the problem. First, there must be some general properties of matter that enter into the production of consciousness when assembled into a brain. Thus, all matter has the potentiality to underlie consciousness. Second, there must be some natural property of the brain he calls C* that unleashes these general properties under the right conditions. Third, just as the brain must have a hidden unknowable structure that allows consciousness to emerge from it, so consciousness must have a hidden unknowable essence that allows it to be embedded in the brain.

The important point about McGinn's project is this: He recognized that a naturalist employment of "emergence" to solve the problems of the origin of consciousness and its regular correlation with matter is no explanation at all. It is what needs to be explained, and on this basis, McGinn offers a solution for the label. The simple fact that he does this demonstrates his recognition of the explanatory vacuity of the label "emergence".

Second, as a label, it leaves open other empirically equivalent views, viz., that the new kind of property may reside in a new substance (see below) or be due to God's regular intention that the property appear under the same set of circumstances. As Timothy O'Connor has noted, if the lawlike link between occurrent subvenient properties and their associated occurrent emergent properties is contingent, then the only adequate explanation for the link and the appearance of an emergent property is God's direct activity and stable intention that things be so (O'Connor 2000). Now it seems to many, perhaps most, philosophers who do not start with a prior commitment to strong physicalism, that the link is indeed contingent, as seen in several well-known thought experiments.

Third, emergence seems to be a case of getting something from nothing, a case of magic without a Magician. If matter is relevantly similar to what current physics and chemistry tell us, and it is bereft of any sort of mental entities, then matter does not have mental potentialities. Given this, it is hard to see how the mere spatial rearrangement of, say, atomic simples to form a more complicated spatial structure would be an adequate cause for bringing into existence *ex nihilo* a completely new sort of entity.

Fourth, this "*ex nihilo*" problem generates another difficulty with emergent properties. To see this, consider the following tensed definition of coming-to-be (Chisholm 1989):

B_t "X comes into existence" = Df. There is a property P which is such that x has P, and there is no property Q which is such that x had Q.

Stated without tense, we have:

B_{nt} "X comes into existence at t" = Df. There is some property P which is such that Px at t, and for all times t' prior to t there is no property Q such that Qx at t'.

Now, consider two contrasting views of the composition of time:

Instantism: Temporal intervals are derived and not fundamental entities. Intervals are wholly grounded in dimensionless instants.

Intervalism: There are extended temporal intervals that are fundamental in that they are not wholly grounded in the existence of other entities.

B_t and B_{nt} are meant to capture the idea that coming-to-be takes place at an instant of time and is not an extended temporal process or interval. For example, it is not a case of alteration or elanguescence (when something gradually transitions from existence to non-existence.) Further, these definitions, while consistent with Instantism, do not entail it. If, as seems likely, intervals have unextended boundaries at their beginning, then coming-to-be would occur at that boundary.

The important point about B_t and B_{nt} is the fact that coming into existence is not a process that could be governed by something, e.g., a (Non-Humean) law of nature. Thus, there is no naturalistic or scientific explanation whatsoever as to why one entity comes into existence at t as opposed to any other entity. Under the view being considered, emergence is a case of coming-to-be and, as such, it leaves as a bizarre brute fact that whenever matter is at such and such configuration, the same emergent property—e.g., being painful—always emerges. Besides the fact that the naturalist ontology is now chock full of emergent brute facts—an embarrassing state of affairs, given the naturalist's favorite trump card of ontological parsimony—there is also the improbable coincidence, bordering on a miracle, that the same emergent property always seems to show up when the same physical conditions obtain, and in principle there is no explanation for this.

Galen Strawson has given considerable reflection to our last two points (Strawson 2006). He notes that when it comes to liquidity or heat (the objective physical phenomena and not our experience of them), we have a good story to tell as to how and why these (structural) properties regularly appear under certain circumstances. But when it comes to genuinely emergent properties—he focuses on experiential phenomenal qualia—due to the nature of emergence, there is in principle no story to tell.[10] He argues that if it is actually the case that Y is emergent from X, then in the relevant sense, it must be the case that Y is wholly dependent on and only on X such that all the features of Y can be metaphysically intelligibly traced, in principle, back to X. If this is not true, then Y did not emerge solely from X.

Based on this, Strawson rightly asserts that emergence cannot be brute since, given the nature of brute emergence, there is absolutely nothing about the intrinsic or relational nature of X in virtue of which Y emerges. That is simply what it means for emergence to be brute. Brutality rules out nothing. Thus, Strawson concludes, emergence is a genuine miracle, not only because it is the appearance of something from nothing in virtue of which it appears, but given that whenever the "appropriate" physical conditions obtain, there is also the bizarre fact that the very same emergent property appears.

However, this is utterly ridiculous and, indeed, incoherent. In principle, there is no reason why, says Strawson, a negative number could not emerge from the addition of certain positive numbers. I could not agree more with his summary warning: "If someone says he chooses to use the word "emergence" in such a way that the notion of brute emergence is not incoherent, I will know that he is a member of the Humpty Dumpty army and be very careful with him" (Strawson 2006).

Since emergence provides no explanation for why either emergence obtains or there is a regular covariance between a physical base property and an emergent property, this leads to troublesome metaethical implications. Surely it is strongly conceivable that there are physical duplicate worlds of the actual world that resemble zombie worlds in philosophy of mind in that they have no moral norms or value properties. Moral/axiological inverted worlds seem similarly conceivable, worlds like ours in all physical respects but in which torturing children is right and caring for the poor is wrong. Further, there could be worlds in which moral properties, etc., emerge in a random, fluctuating basis such that kindness and cruelty alternate between being right or wrong. Surely, any metaethical theory that entails such possible worlds is deeply flawed.[11]

Fifth, sorites problems are lurking in the neighborhood. Could this emergent property, say being painful or moral rightness, be instantiated with one less atomic part in the subvenient base when that base is the "right" level of complexity? Surely the answer is yes. How about two fewer atomic parts? And so on. *Sans* ontological vagueness, at some point, the emergentist must say that the subtraction of one small atomic part has a huge, disproportionate metaphysical effect on the disappearance of the emergent property or properties, e.g., all the irreducibly mental properties constituting consciousness. Grant that humans are physical objects of some sort that exemplify intrinsic goodness. Given the sorites problem, at some point the removal of one tiny atom out of myriads causes that intrinsic goodness to cease being exemplified. Surely, such a dramatic ontological effect cannot result from such a tiny, seemingly insignificant cause. Keep in mind that the sorites problem here is ontological and not epistemological or conceptual.

But how can such a significant metaphysical effect be due to such an insignificant cause? And why was the "right" level of complexity one atomic part greater than the actual level? And the very notion of "the right level of complexity" is completely vacuous. Why? What is the right level? Answer: Whatever the level is when the emergent property appears. When does the emergent property appear? When the right level of complexity is reached. There are no independent criteria for identifying the "right level of complexity" besides the appearance of the so-called emergent property.

Sixth, David Chalmers has raised an additional difficulty with SE, given some form of panpsychism or (we add) strict Microphysicalism—the Quality Combination Problem (viz., plausibly explaining how microqualities combine to yield macroqualities, e.g., phenomenal and moral ones?) of which one especially difficult version is the Palette Problem (viz., given the highly likely fact that there is a limited number of microqualities but a large number of macroqualities, how do so many get yielded from so few resources?) (Chalmers 2017).

Chalmers considers unfavorably two attempts to resolve the Palette Problem: small-palette solutions (viz., somehow, all macroqualities can be generated from just a few microqualities, if we find the right ones with sufficient flexibility and generality) and large-palette solutions (viz., the full range of macroqualities are included among the micro-qualities). Against the former, Chalmers argues that it is pure speculation and still faces the Quality Combination Problem (viz., how do microqualities combine to yield simple macroqualities?).

Against the latter, Chalmers argues that there are, in fact, only a small number of causally efficacious microqualities; the rest will be epiphenomenal. To deny this, one would have to deny the simplicity of physics with a small number of properties and laws. Says Chalmers, "Large-palette solutions seem once again to be stuck with a form of epiphenomenalism or radical revision of the fundamental dynamics of the physical world." (Ibid, p. 206.)

Seventh, Ben Page has advanced a Bayesian argument to the effect that the obtaining of the correct conditions for the emergence of consciousness (and, presumably, moral properties) in the actual world is substantially more likely, given theism compared to atheism (Page 2020). Thus, these emergent properties (if there are such) confirm theism over atheism.

The prior probability of conscious (and intrinsically valuable) beings is higher on theism than on atheism. Why think this? Page argues that given theism, God would have several reasons for creating conscious (and intrinsically valuable) beings and bring about whatever conditions that would do the job: It seems likely that God would want to have love relationships with creatures, to share His knowledge and what it is like to experience various things with them; being creative, God desires to create all kinds of beings, those like human persons being one kind, and so on. But on atheistic hypotheses about the actual world, there is no such being who wants to bring about creatures like us. There is no teleological driving force behind the laws of nature that would be directed towards bringing about the conditions required for our coming-to-be.[12] Rather, on atheist worlds with laws like ours, it is extremely unlikely that those conditions would obtain.

5. Ontological Difficulties with Shafer-Landau's Ethical Non-Naturalism

In this section I will present three features of Shafer-Landau's ontology relevant to his ethical theory and provide criticisms of each after they are presented. I will close this section by offering one general problem with his entire approach.

5.1. Three Features of Shafer-Landau's Ontology[13]
5.1.1. Non-Natural Moral Properties and Facts

Schafer-Landau (Shafer-Landau 2003) holds to the existence of non-natural moral and value properties, facts, truths, moral principles/rules/standards that are objective and non-perspectival. Moral standards are general conditionals linking moral facts with moral evaluations (e.g., taking someone's possessions without their permission is wrong.). A particular moral fact obtains as a result of the conjunction of moral standards and specific non-moral facts (e.g., Jane's action last night of taking Bill's property without his permission was wrong). Worlds without agents have no moral facts but moral standards still exist in those worlds. Additionally, he advocates for non-reductive moral non-naturalism according to which moral properties exist and are not identical to natural scientific properties. Finally, moral properties and facts are epiphenomenal.

There are several problems with this aspect of Shafer-Landau's ontology, but since some appear below, I will postpone my responses to them until later. Here I make one criticism. I agree with Christian Miller who notes that by restricting moral realism to only being a view about the objectivity of moral standards, Shafer-Landau's moral realism is both too broad and too narrow (Miller 2006). It is too narrow because it leaves out views that are versions of moral realism. For example, a moral realist could deny the existence of moral standards and accept the reality of objective moral facts. It is too broad because it includes views that are not versions of moral realism. Shafer-Landau's position would wrongly seem to count versions of ethical expressivism[14] as moral realist positions.

5.1.2. Universal Moral Laws and Absolutism

According to Shafer-Landau (2004), there are universal moral laws (standards, rules) in the sense that they apply to everyone who can understand them whether they do or do not endorse them. These laws exist in all possible worlds, including those without agents. Ethical objectivism entails this view of "universal" and adds that moral laws are claims about what people ought to do. The content of moral rules is fixed independently of our opinions. Ethical objectivism is about the status of moral laws; absolutism is about the stringency of moral laws (there are moral laws that should never be broken). Shafer-Landau accepts ethical objectivism and remains neutral about absolutism.

As I see it, the fundamental problem with this aspect of Shafer-Landau's position is that it is a paradigm case of begging the question against alternative views, especially theistically-grounded metaethical views as well as versions of ethical naturalism. He could respond that his criticism of moral skepticism justifies some version of objectivism and that it is a self-evident Moorean fact that values and moral standards and properties are normative. I will examine this latter claim below when I assess Shafer-Landau's epistemology. For now, I want to address his critique of moral skepticism in defense of objectivism.

The main problem here is that Shafer-Landau seems to know only about moral skepticism as a skeptical-threat argument, and he addresses all of his criticisms to this interpretation. Applied to moral claims, if successful, a skeptical-threat argument demonstrates that there is no such thing as an objectively true moral proposition. An undercutting defeater of such an argument shows that there is no good reason to believe moral skepticism. A rebutting defeater seeks to show that there are sufficient reasons to reject moral skepticism.

But there is a second and, in my view, better interpretation of the point of moral skepticism in this context, especially as employed by theistically grounded metaethical theorists. This is the Inference-to-the-Best-Explanation (IBE) approach according to which one grants the existence of objective moral rules and value properties and goes on to seek among a pool of explanatory options the best explanation for their existence.

I acknowledge that Shafer-Landau criticizes theistic ethics. But for two reasons, I don't think this carries much weight in this discussion. First, as far as I know Shafer-Landau has not provided a serious interaction with what is widely acknowledged as an explosion of sophisticated literature in natural theology defending the existence of God (Craig and Moreland 2009). Thus, if the moral argument for God is the sole focus of critique as it seems to be with Shafer-Landau, that critique may be plausible within that limited scope, but it could still be the case that belief in the existence of God is epistemically justified, all things being considered. If so, then God's existence is still within the pool of options for an IBE regarding the existence of objective moral rules and values. An IBE approach to moral skepticism seeks to argue that moral facts/principles and value properties are much more to be expected based on theism that on naturalism; thus, theism has a better response to moral skepticism. Moreover, some of the arguments for God's existence (e.g., the argument from reason) provide defeaters for Shafer-Landau's critique of theistic ethics. In light of the contemporary situation, it is question-begging for Landau to assert his ethical non-naturalism and the success of his critique of theistic ethics. That assertion is premature.

Second, the lion's share of his defense of ethical objectivism relies on his critique of moral skepticism, and as we have seen, he fails to address the IBE interpretation of this view.

5.1.3. Where Do Moral Standards Come From?

Shafer-Landau breaks this question into two different issues (Shafer-Landau 2004). First, to the simple question of where such standards come from, he holds that no one made them up since not every law requires an author. Second, to the question of whether moral standards are eternal or just popped into existence, he acknowledges that they certainly seem to be eternal and to have existed before humans (agents) came to be. But, he says, this seems implausible.

To address this implausibility, he argues that there are two strategies one can employ. First, one can deny that an authorless morality must be eternal laws. After all, laws governing DNA did not exist before DNA existed in organisms, and we can in principle date the origin of such laws as the time when DNA first existed. The same goes with moral laws. Second, one can deny the absurdity of eternal moral laws by recalling the distinction between moral principles, conditionals such that if certain conditions obtain, then a certain moral verdict follows (e.g., if x kills, then x did something wrong) and moral facts.[15] By contrast, moral facts are the realization of moral principles, the instantiation of goodness/rightness/intrinsic virtue. Moreover, he adopts a Platonist view of principles according to which some are never exemplified. Thus, moral principles are eternal but moral facts are not.

What should we make of these claims? It will come as no surprise that I do not think they are plausible. First, consider the assertion that there are authorless moral laws. Moral laws are prescriptive and, as such, we discover them to have imperatival force and impose duties on us. However, imperatives and duty-impositions come from persons with wills. I suppose one could respond that they are grounded in emergent normative properties. I have already presented several serious problems with natural emergence, so I do not think this is a plausible response for a naturalist. Regarding an objective non-natural moral order, I think evolutionary naturalist Michael Ruse got it right when he noted.

Morality is a biological adaptation no less than are hands and feet and teeth. Considered as a rationally justifiable set of claims about an objective something, ethics is illusory. I appreciate that when somebody says 'Love thy neighbor as thyself,' they think they are referring above and beyond themselves. Nevertheless, such reference is truly without foundation. Morality is just an aid to survival and reproduction . . . and any deeper meaning is illusory (Ruse 1989).

As far as I can tell, our uniform experience of the origin of laws with imperatival force and duty-imposition come from persons, and Shafer-Landau's authorless moral laws run against this uniform experience. To be sure, moral laws differ from laws of government, custom, or other social groups. What they all have in common, however, is imperatival force and duty-imposition. Surely this problem places a significant burden of proof on Shafer-Landau's authorless moral laws. Moral norms exhibit a high degree of incumbency when compared to norms in law or custom; accordingly, they transmit a kind of authority and accountability that is hard to conceive as being generated by impersonal sources.

Second, consider Shafer-Landau's commitment to the existence of intrinsic value properties—especially objectively good virtues—in worlds without agents. Now I have defended a hybrid of Platonism and Aristotelianism about universals elsewhere

(Moreland 2013; Kim 2011). Here I want to call attention to a relevant issue. I grant that there are Platonic properties in that they can exist without being exemplified. Examples would be being a triangle, being such and such color. So far, I agree with Shafer-Landau.

However, there are other properties that are Aristotelian in that they require at least one particular to exemplify them in order to exist. Chief among these are properties that require conscious being to have them. They conform to the old adage that necessarily, thoughts have thinkers. Among these properties are being a thought, desire, sensation, and being loving, kind, just, truthful. Take the virtue of being loving. It is hard to conceive of how such a property could simply exist as an impersonal entity. It is hard to know what that would even mean, but it is not hard to see how being loving could exist if and only if it is exemplified by a subject of consciousness.

Since being loving does not seem to depend for its existence on any or all finite, contingent beings, there would seem to be a transcendent Subject of consciousness who exemplified being loving before humans appeared or in agentless, personless worlds. It seems far more reasonable to take the existence and exemplification of being loving as a property of a person and a mode of personal reality as opposed to being an impersonal stand-alone property whose exemplification is a mode of impersonal reality.

Third, Shafer-Landau is guilty of a fundamental ontological conflation of realization and exemplification. He explicitly identifies the two, but anyone familiar with general ontology knows to keep them distinct. As Jaegwon Kim canonically observed, concepts are realized by items that play a role specified by the concept. By contrast, properties are exemplified by things and characterize their being (Kim 2011). Consider NFL quarterback Patrick Mahommes. He has a number of properties that characterize him and, arguably, are constituents within his being: being a certain height, mass, shape, color, and so on. Does Mahommes also have the property of being a quarterback? No. Being a quarterback is a concept, a functional role he realizes, plays, satisfies. It is not a property he exemplifies. If an ideal observer inventoried Mahommes' properties, being a quarterback would not be included. Shafer-Landau seems unfamiliar with this widely acknowledged distinction, and by equating them, it makes one wonder just how much work he has done in basic ontology.

Finally, consider his assertion that authorless moral laws need not be eternal by citing cases in which a law (e.g., governing DNA in organisms) comes into existence when the item it governs first comes to be. Surely this is another confusion, especially given his Platonic views that some principles (e.g., of geometry) and some properties (e.g., triangularity) could exist without ever being exemplified. It seems obvious that within Shafer-Landau's own ontology, it is more consistent and avoids laws popping into existence from nothing if one holds that in such cases, a law is first exemplified rather than first coming to be. If I am right about this, then the ontological status of such laws (and properties) would seem to be described as abstract entities, entities that are timeless and spaceless. Abstract entities are eternal in that there never was a time when they did not exist.

It is important to keep in mind an important distinction between a traditional realist—e.g., Platonist—construal of properties and property-instances. The former are universals taken as abstract necessary beings in that they exist in all possible worlds. Viewed ontologically, the latter are particulars; viewed diachronically, they are instances of emergent properties. Thus, realist understandings of properties are fully consistent with taking them as emergent properties. While abstract, when the "right" subvenient conditions obtain, the property is instantiated and when viewed from the subvenient/supervenient perspective, the property and its instance are emergent.

5.2. The Problematic Nature of Contingent Brute Facts

In Section 3, I provided a detailed critique of emergent properties given naturalism. Here, I want to revisit that topic and focus on a different difficulty that emergent properties present for Shafer-Landau's ontology, one that targets a fundamental aspect of his view. That aspect involves the problematic nature of brute facts or entities. Alexander Pruss has provided a thorough critique of contingent brute facts which he takes to be true propositions

(Pruss 2009). I have no problem with this but in what follows, I will take a brute fact to be a state of affairs, e.g., Joe's being in pain, Arthur's action being wrong. Shafer-Landau shares this view of moral facts.

Contingent brute facts have two important characteristics: (1) *Qua* brute, there is in principle no explanation for their obtaining. (2) *Qua* contingent, they could have not obtained, and others could have obtained instead. Given (1), the obtaining of a contingent brute fact is utterly inexplicable. Moreover, if such a fact could appear brutely then it becomes inexplicable why just any and every fact does not appear brutely. Finally, the regular obtaining of the same type of brute fact when certain conditions obtain (e.g., people being in pain given that their C-fibers are firing) is so improbable that it seems to be almost incoherent and miraculous.

In this regard, as Timothy O'Connor has noted, if the lawlike link between occurrent subvenient properties and their associated occurrent emergent properties is contingent, then the only adequate explanation for the link and the appearance of an emergent property is God's direct activity and stable intention that things be so (O'Connor 2000). If O'Connor is right, as I think he is, this would be bad news for Shafer-Landau's appropriation of contingent brute facts.

Regarding (2), the obtaining of a contingent fact cries out for an explanation. Indeed, throughout history, the search for an explanation for the obtaining of contingent facts is what has constituted part of the very notion of what it is to search for knowledge and explanations. When someone announces that the contingent fact is brute, that is tantamount to giving up on the explanatory enterprise.

Necessary facts and entities do not need an external explanation for their existence. Indeed, the search for one is a category fallacy. The existence of such entities flows from their nature as being necessary.

By way of application to Shafer-Landau's ontology, let us grant that when certain states of consciousness obtain (e.g., being in pain, intentionally murdering an innocent person), they *de re* metaphysically necessitate the relevant moral/value properties (being right, being wrong, being good, being bad). So far so good. The problem is that the conscious states of personal agents are utterly contingent. As far as I can tell, the obtaining of moral properties (which is a moral fact) for Shafer-Landau amounts to moral properties being second-order ones that are exemplified if and only if a relevant first-order property of consciousness is exemplified. This is why he holds that in agentless worlds there are no moral facts, namely, there are no morally relevant conscious facts in those worlds (e.g., evil intentions).

The fact that the obtaining of the properties of consciousness is contingent is supported by two lines of reasoning. First, Shafer-Landau seems to agree with me that they are emergent properties and, as such, since their obtaining is brute, one cannot simply announce that they are somehow necessitated by subvenient conditions.

This line of reasoning needs supplementation by my second point: The contingency claim is based on the widespread and, in my view, successful employment of a host of thought experiments (e.g., the knowledge argument, the possibility of absent or inverted qualia, zombie worlds, and disembodied existence) that highlight the contingency in question. In regard to the employment of these thought experiments to support the reality and contingency of qualia, Kim observes.

The [property-dualist] case against qualia supervenience therefore is not conclusive, though quite substantial. Are there, then, considerations in favor of qualia supervenience? It would seem that the only positive considerations are broad metaphysical ones that might very well be accused of begging the question (Kim 2011).[16]

I conclude that Shafer-Landau's ontological support of his version of ethical non-naturalism rests on the reality of a relevant range of contingent brute facts or entities. I have argued that this is a serious problem for his overall position.

6. Difficulties with Shafer-Landau's Moral Epistemology

Earlier, I referred to the ontological aspect of J. L. Mackie's argument from queerness. This aspect is widely known and debated. However, the argument also contained a lesser-known epistemological component, viz., knowing such queer entities would require "some special faculty" of moral perception or intuition, utterly different from our ordinary ways of knowing everything else (Mackie 1977). This "special-faculty" problem has caused several philosophers to adopt an externalist, usually causal or reliabilist accounts of modal knowledge and justification. In this last section, I want to expand on this problem and add further considerations about the epistemological difficulties with Shafer-Landau's epistemology. To accomplish this, I will provide a precis of Shafer-Landau's view, followed by an evolutionary argument against his and similar epistemologies. Next, I will consider and provide defeaters for the main ethical non-naturalist rejoinder to evolutionary arguments.

6.1. A Precis of Shafer-Landau's Moral Epistemology

Shafer-Landau adopts a combination of internalist foundationalism (he is tentative about this and limits its range) and reliabilism. Roughly, we can know moral truths because some of them are self-evident, and we can employ moral reliabilism to extend our knowledge to non-self-evident moral truths (Shafer-Landau 2003, 2004). Here is a precis of his position.

Step 1: Provide defeaters for constructivism and non-cognitivism.

Step 2: Moral knowledge begins with non-empirical, non-natural, perhaps, *a priori* access to moral facts and true moral propositions. Thus, we begin by *assuming* there are such self-evident moral facts and truths.

Step 3: Mere intuition fails due to the widespread reality of moral disagreement.

Step 4: Thus, a version of moral reliabilism is the proper way to move from knowledge of self-evident moral facts/truths to those that are not self-evident. This account of reliabilism is based on current empirical theories of moral psychology, and we arrive at an account of moral reliabilism without causation. A moral process is reliable if it triggers more true than false moral beliefs.

Before we proceed, a few words of evaluation are in order. First, in step 1, constructivism and non-cognitivism are far from exhaustive. This leaves several naturalistic alternatives as live options without any criticism of them.

Second, his employment of "self-evident" is ambiguous and confused. He claims that we must assume the reality of moral facts, yet he says that foundational ones are self-evident. He explicitly rejects the view that moral beliefs about act and trait tokens are inferred from self-evidently known moral principles. Along with this, he denies a role for intuition in moral knowledge. However, the ubiquitous way of understanding a self-evident truth p is to claim that p achieves this status as follows: p is justifiably believed or known if either p is adequately grasped and understood or p is appropriately attended to and is clearly and directly known by acquaintance.

Moreover, Shafer-Landau holds that either basis just mentioned is sufficient for justification/knowledge, although these are clearly internalist notions that Shafer-Landau explicitly rejects. Yet he fails to provide an alternative account of the nature and knowability of the self-evident. Finally, though he goes back and forth between *de re* knowledge of moral facts and *de dicto* knowledge of moral truths, it is clear from his rejection of intuition that *de re* knowledge by acquaintance is off the table. However, without such *de re* knowledge, it becomes opaque as to how one is to know the truth of associated *de dicto* propositions or the reliability of the faculties that trigger them. I will say more on faculty reliability below.

6.2. An Evolutionary Argument against Shafer-Landau's Epistemology

An evolutionary argument against naturalist epistemology—including Shafer-Landau's—seeks to undercut the assumption of the cognitive adequacy of the cognitive faculties we have. As we will now see, this assumption is a very problematic one for naturalists who are Darwinists.

As Mark Linville notes, "[T]he naturalist's commitment to a Darwinian explanation of certain salient features of human psychology presents an undercutting defeater for our moral beliefs as a whole" (Linville 2009). According to Michael Ruse and E. O. Wilson, "Ethical premises are the peculiar products of genetic history, and they can be understood solely as mechanisms that are adaptive for the species which possess them . . . .No abstract principles exist outside the particular nature of individual species" (Ruse 1989; Ruse and Wilson 1986).

This statement may be taken as canonical for evolutionary naturalists such as Shafer-Landau, and, in my view, Thomas Nagel has presented the most persuasive case for what follows from it (Nagel 1997). The central problem is that, given Evolutionary Naturalism, the fact that people have certain moral faculties or processes that bring about moral dispositions/beliefs and the reasons they have them are quite independent from whatever would make the dispositions proper and the beliefs true. Our moral dispositions/beliefs and their development are survival conducive, not truth conducive. If Darwinian processes had turned out such that we had evolved with different survival faculties/processes that produced other survival enhancing dispositions, our beliefs would have tracked those.

The fact that those beliefs do or do not correspond to a non-natural, non-causal, non-empirical, objective moral realm has nothing to do with the faculty/process-generated moral beliefs/dispositions we develop. Thus, Evolutionary Naturalism generates an argument for moral skepticism and, lacking any warrant whatsoever for belief in moral facts (values, duties), for agnosticism towards or the denial of irreducible moral facts. Given Evolutionary Naturalism, we have no reason at all to believe the world has anything other than natural facts and subjective reactions to them.

Thus, Evolutionary Naturalism undercuts practical reason, according to Nagel. Our moral dispositions/beliefs are not counterfactually sensitive. We would form our beliefs irrespective of their veridicality. They are mere expressions of contingent moral faculties/processes that bring about a contingent set of dispositions that evolved with no regard to their correspondence to an independently existing moral order; they are not genuine insights into a non-contingent realm of objective value and duty. Wilson chides "ethical philosophers who wish to intuit the standards of good and evil, but who do not realize that their moral sentiments really spring from the hypothalamus and the limbic system, not from veridical intuition into an independently existing, objective moral realm" (Rachels 1990).

Shafer-Landau takes himself to have objectively reliable moral processes and dispositions, and warranted, true moral beliefs that correspond to an objective moral realm. However, those dispositions and beliefs are there only because of their survival value. If there were no objective moral realm, or if the objective moral realm were constituted by different values and duties, the ones Shafer-Landau adopts would all be false and inappropriate. Nevertheless, he would hold them anyway due to their survival value. He would not exhibit counterfactual sensitivity towards the content of the objective moral realm he posits. Thus, even if it is there in the way he adopts, he would have no reason at all to believe it is there or that he has genuine insight into it. That is, indeed, a big problem.

The final defeater involves our apparent ability to know things about exemplification itself and abstract objects. As I have argued elsewhere, we have knowledge of abstract properties that is quite different from our knowledge of concrete property-instances. However, such knowledge seems to be ruled out by naturalism if, for no other reason than it involves the employment of a "spooky" non-sensory intuitive faculty that is impossible to locate in the naturalist ontology.[17]

Moreover, Laurence BonJour noted that it is virtually impossible to accommodate traditional realist properties (especially Platonic ones) with naturalist depictions of human cognizers as physical entities and the physical causal interactions that constitute cognitive processes such as perception (BonJour 1998). For the naturalist, knowledge of some entity e entails a standard physical, causal interaction between e and the knower, but such a causal interaction is impossible when e is a causally effete abstract object.

Shafer-Landau could respond by appealing to some cognitive faculty with the power of rational intuition capable of grasping abstract objects. Once again, this would be a case of helping himself to an entity that just cannot be located in the most reasonable naturalist epistemology, Grand Story, and resulting ontology, bereft of queer, brute, non-natural entities. As Thomas Nagel correctly observed, adopting the existence of the ability to exercise rational intuition or grasping abstract objects is one that is secularly uncomfortable; it should make naturalists nervous, and is suspiciously religious or quasi-religious. Thus, it brings up the "fear of God," precisely because such abilities are much more at home in a theistic than an atheistic worldview (Nagel 1997). A naturalist appropriation of them is borrowed capital on the cheap.

Alternatively, Shafer-Landau could appropriate his moral reliabilism about knowledge of abstract objects. However, this move would face the undercutting defeater provided by the Nagelian evolutionary argument.

6.3. The Main Ethical Non-Naturalist Rejoinder to the Evolutionary Argument

In brief, the main rejoinder to the evolutionary argument goes like this: Our moral intuitions about a host of moral facts are so strong, that they provide defeater defeaters for the less epistemically weighty evolutionary argument. Maybe we just got lucky, but whatever the case, fundamental moral intuitions are self-evident and reliable moral processes clearly exist, and that is all one needs to appropriate to defeat the evolutionary argument.

Unfortunately, this argument is unsuccessful. The objection conflates and confuses two ways of presenting the evolutionary argument: a skeptical threat argument or an Inference to the Best Explanation (IBE). As a skeptical threat argument, evolutionary argument seeks to show that we should be skeptical that we actually have moral knowledge. The objection under consideration is the claim that, yes, the evolutionary argument should make us skeptical except for one thing: We do have moral knowledge and our warrant for knowing this is stronger that than for the evolutionary argument for skepticism. It seems that we just got lucky. This may or may not be a successful response to the skeptical-threat employment of the evolutionary argument, but I, and many theists, employ the IBE use of the argument. Here, one grants that we have moral knowledge and goes on to seek the best explanation for why this is true. The theist will argue that theism is a much better explanation of this fact than is the "we just got lucky" response. As Christian theist Dolores Morris astutely notes:

> Yes! Absolutely! Objective moral values are *clearly* a part of reality … The question of course, is how this all came to be … These atheistic theories tell us that we ought to act morally, but they do so with a conception of the universe that makes it difficult to see why and how we should believe that these shared moral values have anything like true normative objectivity. Objective morality may not be impossible on an atheistic worldview, but it feels like an ad hoc addition. (Morris 2021)

Morris goes on to say that objective morality is very much at home and natural in a theistic worldview.

6.4. Responding to Leibowitz's Defeaters for Evolutionary Debunking Arguments

In an important article, Uri D. Leibowitz seeks to place advocates of evolutionary debunking arguments on the horns of a dilemma, and to provide defeaters for each horn (Leibowitz 2021). I cannot address everything in Leibowitz's article, but fortunately, there is a subset of his article that is particularly relevant to defending my evolutionary argument against the possibility of objectively justified beliefs about true moral realist claims. It is important to note when observing the two arguments that constitute his dilemma's horns, that while they both make reference to an inference to the best explanation, these arguments are skeptical-threat arguments that employ IBE considerations within certain premises to establish the skeptical threat. They are not IBE arguments as depicted above. In what follows, I will present Liebowitz' two arguments followed by my responses to them.

Here is the first argument offered, to which Leibowitz's responses are given as rebutting defeaters for this type evolutionary debunking argument. Let us call this debunking argument EDA #1:

1. Evolution provides the best explanation of moral phenomena.
2. Evolutionary explanations of moral phenomena do not require that our moral judgements are true.
3. If (2), then the chance of any one of our moral judgements being true is slim.
4. If the chance of any one of our moral judgments being true is slim, then even after rational reflection the chance of any one of our moral judgments being true remains slim.
5. If even after rational reflection the chance of any one of our moral judgments being true remains slim, then each one of our moral judgments is unjustified.
6. Therefore, each one of our moral judgments is unjustified.

Here is the second argument, to which Leibowitz's responses are offered as undercutting defeaters for this type of evolutionary debunking argument. Let us call this debunking argument EDA #2:

1. Evolution provides the best explanation of moral phenomena.
2. Evolutionary explanations of moral phenomena do not require that our moral judgments are true.
3. If (2), then we have no reason to believe of any one of our moral judgments that it is true.
4. If we have no reason to believe of any of our moral judgments that it is true, then even after rational reflection we have no reason to believe of any one of our moral judgments that it is true.
5. If even after rational reflection we have no reason to believe of any one of our moral judgments that it is true, then each of our moral judgments is unjustified.
6. Therefore, each one of our moral judgments is unjustified.

What does Leibowitz say in response to these arguments. Regarding EDA #1, his basic rejoinder goes like this. Even if we grant that the argument succeeds in showing that some moral belief targeted by the argument is unlikely to be true, there is still another moral belief in the vicinity that escapes EDA #1. Suppose we judge that A is morally permissible, but considering EDA #1, we would be justified in believing the negation of our initial judgment, i.e., we would judge that it is highly likely that A is not morally permissible. Given a standard, commonsense understanding of moral terms of appraisal, this last judgement would amount to the judgement that it is highly likely that A is wrong. So, while EDA #1 may succeed in showing that some of our moral judgments are unlikely to be true, the argument supports that other related moral judgments are highly likely to be true. Thus, premise (6) is false.

Regarding EDA #2, Leibowitz offers two defeaters. First, he argues that it commits the well-known genetic fallacy. A belief's origin and justification can come apart and evolutionary debunking arguments do not affect theories in moral epistemology that do not aim to show that moral beliefs are justified by tracking their causal origins.

Second, building on his first defeater, Leibowitz claims that even if EDA #2 succeeds in showing that we have no evolutionary grounds for believing our moral judgments to be true, there are other theories in moral epistemology that do show this. So, EDA #2 fails to establish the general claim made in (6).

I offer two general responses to Leibgowitz's critique of these two debunking arguments. First, it may be that the specific people who support these two debunking arguments use them to undercut specific moral judgements and generalize to undercut each and every moral judgment. Call this the bottom-up approach according to which both arguments begin with defeating any particular moral judgment and, by generalization, it concludes by defeating each of our judgments.

Whether or not the bottom-up approach defeats evolutionary debunking arguments such as EDA #1 and EDA #2, I do not think that Leibgowitz's responses defeat what I call top-down debunking arguments such as the one presented above by Nagel and which I advocate. According to the top-down approach, all of our moral judgments and beliefs are produced by unreliable faculties and processes. This is true for two reasons: (i) Our moral faculties/processes are counterfactually insensitive to truth or rationality conditions; thus, the latter are irrelevant to our moral judgments/beliefs. (ii) Evolutionary processes select traits solely because they aided (or did not hinder) the survival-enhancing 4 Fs: feeding, fighting, fleeing, reproducing. Truth and rationality are irrelevant.

Moreover, as Plantinga, Reppert, and many others have argued, the evolutionary accounts of our rational faculties/process—e.g., sensations, "intuitions," reasoning and rational deliberation—are victims of the top-down evolutionary debunking argument just as much as our moral faculties/processes are (Plantinga 1993; Reppert 2009).[18] For the purposes of assessing Leibgowitz's responses, let us assume the point made by Plantinga and others.

Let us apply these general points to some of Liebgowitz's specific arguments. Consider his counterargument to EDA #1 according to which the evolutionary debunking argument may defeat our justification for thinking A is permissible but in so doing, it justifies another belief—that A is wrong. However, if our moral faculties/processes themselves are unreliable, then once we judge that A is wrong, the evolutionary argument now makes it the case that it is highly unlikely that this judgement is true. By inference, it is now highly likely to be true that A is morally permissible. Thus, we have entered a skeptical dialectical loop from which there is no escape, or so it seems to me.

Next, consider the second counterargument to EDA #2 according to which even if some moral judgments are defeated by evolutionary debunking arguments, others which are the result of alternative moral epistemologies and not tracing a moral judgment to its origins would still be justified. The problem here is that if Plantinga et. al. are right, then this counterargument uses reason in formulating and judging to be reasonable some alternative moral epistemologies. However, given that all of our faculties/rational processes are unreliable, then the formulation of justified moral epistemologies falls prey to the general evolutionary debunking argument. Further, a major way of developing a moral epistemology is, at least in part, by employing reflective equilibrium. An important aspect of reflective equilibrium is an attempt to establish coherence among general moral theories, specific moral principles or more specific moral rules, and particular test cases involving an independent, *prima facie* justified moral judgement. This means that moral judgements and the moral faculties/processes that produce them are an uneliminable aspect of developing a moral epistemology. As such, this developmental task will be undercut by the evolutionary debunking argument, though, perhaps, in a different way than moral epistemologies that focus on tracing a moral judgment back to its origin are undercut.

The final counterargument against EDA #2 is the charge that it commits the genetic fallacy. This is, indeed, a fallacy. However, there are clear cases in which discounting the justification for some claim based on its origin is a proper way of reasoning and not a genetic fallacy. One place this happens is when the origin of a claim directly impacts it credibility. Consider this example. Suppose you are riding a train from London to Wales. While you are looking out the window, you see etched into the hillside an indented set of shapes: WALES IN 10 KM. Now suppose you knew that trains in the UK sometimes used signs and sometimes used digging out letters in hillsides to inform riders of the next place the train stops and how far away it is. In this case, you would be justified in believing that Wales was 10 km ahead.

But suppose that you found out from highly reliable sources that the upcoming sign about Wales had been randomly shaped by erosion and flooding. It could still be the case that Wales is in 10 km, but given the causal story about the origin of the hillside scratchings, you would no longer be justified in judging Wales to be coming up in 10 km. In a court case, if you learn that a witness has a conflict of interest regarding his testimony or that due to childhood abuse, he was a chronic liar, then his testimony might be true but given your information about the causal origins of the witness's reliability, you would no longer be justified in believing his testimony.

I think that the top-down evolutionary threat argument is just like these. If a solid causal story about the processes that lead up to the formation of our rational and moral faculties/processes provides a significant defeater for the reliability of the beliefs or judgments they produce, then this counts against the justification of those judgments or beliefs. Arguing this is not to commit a genetic fallacy.

There is a final point I want to make that seems to me to be the most important one. Liebgowitz is arguing against evolutionary debunking arguments construed as skeptical threat arguments. His appeal to best explanation claims occurs with premises of the two arguments he seeks to defeat, but those claims are used to justify the idea that an evolutionary account of our moral judgments and beliefs is the best one we have and, thus, this account raises a skeptical treat against those judgments and beliefs which he seeks to rebut or undercut. For these two EDA arguments to count as examples of IBE, their structure needs to be different. An IBE would grant that our moral and rational faculties/processes are reliable and, thus, our moral judgments are generally true and justified. These are taken as givens. The issue becomes this: From within a pool of the most important positions that attempt to explain these givens, an inference is made to the best explanation for them. The two key members of that pool are naturalism—staunch and faint-hearted, sometimes supplemented with Platonism—and theism. I cannot undertake an assessment of those like me who claim that theism is the best explanation for these givens, but I offer three brief reasons for the theistic inference.

First, a number of facts must be true: people have consciousness and intentionality, rational powers, including the ability to be directly aware through rational intuition of important moral properties (e.g., rightness, goodness), they must have libertarian freedom to perform genuinely intentional actions and be responsible moral judgers and agents, and they must exemplify immanent teleology since reasoning—moral or otherwise—involves a deliberative process for the sake of obtaining true or justified beliefs.

Staunch naturalists deny all of these, and faint-hearted naturalists can accept them only by appealing to the contingent, brute fact of their emergence. However, such facts are in principle incapable of having reasons offered for their emergence since that is what it means for them to be brute. Their contingency cries out for an explanation for why they obtain rather than alternative states of affairs. For natural emergence advocates, since natural entities are characterized by the ontology of the (especially) hard sciences, the physical subvenient base from which these properties emerge are examples of coming-to-be *ex nihilo*. Moreover, their regular obtaining when the "right" physical conditions obtain is nothing short of a miracle. The theist is in no such pickle. The theist's fundamental being is not strings, particles, mere stuff and the like, but the theistic God who exemplifies all of the features that constitute the relevant facts listed above that inform an IBE. Thus, in a theistic universe, it is easy to explain the existence of these facts, but naturalists cannot offer an explanation. They must simply point to a range of brute facts.

A Platonic naturalist may have an explanation for the existence of value properties as abstract objects. However, since the time of Plato, non-theistic Platonists have acknowledged that they have no explanation, e.g., no efficient cause, to explain why these abstract objects were ever exemplified. Plato saw this and appealed to the demiurge to solve the problem, a minimal theistic solution. Further, Platonic moral realism cannot explain these features of the facts mentioned above: libertarian freedom and responsible intentional action, immanent teleology. There is no explanation for what grounds equal human rights or why our various faculties are reliable.

Third, as noted earlier in this article, Ben Page has argued (successfully in my opinion) that on theism, the prior probability of the universe containing conscious—and I would add, moral—persons is much, much higher than on naturalism. I will not repeat his argument here.

In any case, when I provided a critique of Shafer-Landau's moral epistemology, I explicitly claimed that I was using an IBE and not a skeptical-threat argument. Whether successful or not, this fact means that Liebgowitz's article is irrelevant to my IBE argument.

I have provided a rational context for assessing Shafer-Landau's ethical non-naturalism by presenting the inner logic of contemporary naturalism and highlighting the distinction between staunch and faint-hearted naturalism, arguing that the former is substantially preferable to the latter. Since Shafer-Landau is a faint-hearted naturalist, before we examine the specifics of his views, he faces a severe burden of proof, or so I argued. I sought to raise that burden of proof by providing a critique of emergent properties, given naturalism. Next, I presented Shafer-Landau's ontology and epistemology and argued that neither is adequate in supporting his ethical non-naturalism. The reader may not be convinced by my case, but I hope it is powerful enough to give readers something to think about when assessing Shafer-Landau's ethical non-naturalism.

Funding: This research received no external funding.

Data Availability Statement: Not applicable.

Conflicts of Interest: The author declares no conflict of interest.

Notes

[1] For a classic comparison of the epistemic and ontological characterizations, see Nagel (1979), pp. 366–80. For what I take to be the most authoritative recent treatment of emergence and reduction construed in a straightforward ontological way, see Tabaczek (2019), pp. 41–97.

[2] Kripke (1972). Interestingly, in the article entitled "Moral Realism" in the online *Stanford Encyclopedia of Philosophy*, the author is preoccupied with the ontology of moral realism and the truth conditions of moral claims so interpreted. Other subareas of the article are discussed in relation to the ontological issues. A short section covers semantic issues, but the discussion is preoccupied with minimalism (a version of redundancy theory for truth) and its problems. Synthetic/analytic issues are not significantly present in the artricle. See Sayre-McCord (2021).

[3] Shafer-Landau (2003), pp. 98–114. Interestingly, Shafer-Landau explicitly claims that causal closure issues and irreducible properties of consciousness are structurally paralled with irreducible moral properties.

[4] Strawson (2006), pp. 3–31. The quote is from page 3. Strawson's idiosyncratic use of "physicalism" includes irreducible experiential states as a kind of physical state, and he distinguishes his view from "physicSalism", the faith commitment that the nature or essence of all concrete reality can in principle be captured in the terms of physics. The definition of "physicalism" in the quote is not his own panpsychist one, but is more akin to physicSalism and what we mean by staunch naturalism.

[5] For my purposes, I set aside the distinction between Global Naturalists (who deny the existence of abstract objects) and Local Naturalists (who accept abstract objects, usually with the proviso that the only abstract objects that are exemplified must be physical properties or relations.) For a good treatment of this distinction put in different terms and including a case that naturalists ought to be Global, see Grossmann (1992), pp. 1–46; Rickabaugh and Moreland (2023), chp. two.

[6] For a classic comparison of the epistemic and ontological characterizations of emergent properties, see Nagel (1979), pp. 366–80.

[7] Kim (1998), pp. 1–27. Kim employs nomological necessity in his understanding of the sort of modality implied by "strong."

[8] The best precis of the Grand Story is found in McGinn (1999), pp. 12–18.

[9] McGinn (1999), especially pp. 46–54, 66–76, 95–101. I have subjected McGinn's view to a careful analysis and critique. See Moreland (2008), chp. five.

[10] When John Searle developed his biological naturalism, he dismissed the problem of (genuinely) emergent properties such as those constituting consciousness by making a tight analogy between them and structurally supervenient properties, e.g., solidity, liquidity. This allowed him to find emergent mental properties to be ordinary physical, structural ones and their appearance to be unsurprising. See Searle (1992), pp. xii, 13–19, 25–28, 32, 56–57, 85–93, 95, 118–24. For a response to Searle, See Moreland (2008), chp. three.

[11] I am indebted to an anonymous referee for these suggestions.

[12] Thomas Nagel sees the problem here and advances a non-theistic teleological view of our universe to overcome it. See Nagel (2012). For a critique, see Moreland (2012), pp. 415–24.

[13] Important sources for Shafer-Landau's ontology are (Shafer-Landau 2003, 2004).

[14] Roughly, the view that holds two theses: psychological non-cognitivism (ethical claims express mental states with a world-to-mind direction of fit, e.g., desires, pro-attitudes) and semantic ideationalism (the semantic contents of an ethical claim are

objectively given their associated mental states such that an expression of some ethical claim p expresses confidence or agreement with p that just is the meaning of "p is true."

[15] I think Shafer-Landau needs "murders" rather than "kills" doing the latter. In cases of a car accident, self-defense, war, or capital punishment, the wrongness of killing is controversial to say the least.

[16] Brackets mine.

[17] For examples of the spookiness charge, see Murphy (2018), pp. 317–27.

[18] Plantinga (1993), chps. 11 and 12; Reppert (2009), pp. 345–90. Nagel seeks to block the inference from the defeat of our moral faculties/processes to our rational faculties/processes, but his arguments are confused and ineffective. For more on this, Moreland (2009), pp. 165–80.

References

BonJour, Laurence. 1998. *In Defense of Pure Reason*. Cambridge: Cambridge University Press.

Chalmers, David J. 2017. The Combination Problem for Panpsychism. In *Panpsychism: Contemporary Perspectives*. Edited by Godehard Brüntrup and Ludwig Jaskolla. Oxford: Oxford University Press, pp. 204–6.

Chisholm, Roderick. 1989. *On Metaphysics*. Minneapolis: University of Minnesota Press.

Craig, William Lane, and J. P. Moreland. 2009. *The Blackwell Companion to Natural Theology*. Malden: Wiley Blackwell.

Grossmann, Reinhardt. 1992. *The Existence of the World*. London: Routledge.

Inman, Ross. 2019. *Substance and the Fundamentality of the Familiar*. New York: Routledge.

Jackson, Frank. 1998. *From Metaphysics to Ethics*. Oxford: Clarendon Press.

Kim, Jaegwon. 1998. *Mind in a Physical World*. Cambridge: MIT Press.

Kim, Jaegwon. 2011. *Philosophy of Mind*, 3rd ed. Boulder: Westview Press.

Kim, Jaegwon. 2018. Against Cartesian Dualism. In *The Blackwell Companion to Substance. Dualism*. Edited by Jonathan J. Loose, Angus J. L. Menuge and J. P. Moreland. Oxford: Wiley Blackwell, pp. 152–67.

Kripke, Saul. 1972. *Naming and Necessity*. Cambridge: Harvard University Press.

Leibowitz, Uri D. 2021. A dilemma for evolutionary debunking arguments. *Philosophical Studies* 178: 45–69. [CrossRef]

Linsky, Bernard, and Edward N. Zath. 1995. Naturalized Platonism versus Platonized Naturalism. *The Journal of Philosophy* 92: 525–55. [CrossRef]

Linville, Mark D. 2009. The Moral Argument. In *The Blackwell Companion to Natural Theology*. Edited by William Lane Craig and J. P. Moreland. Oxford: Wiley-Blackwell, pp. 391–448.

Mackie, John L. 1977. *Ethics: Inventing Right and Wrong*. London: Penguin Books.

McGinn, Colin. 1999. *The Mysterious Flame*. New York: Basic Books.

Melnyk, Andrew. 2019. *Physicalism—Routledge Encyclopedia of Philosophy*. Oxfordshire: Taylor and Francis. Available online: https://www.rep.routledge.com/articles/thematic/physicalism/v-1 (accessed on 13 April 2023).

Miller, Christian. 2006. Review Essay: Russ Shafer-Landau's Moral Realism: A Defense. *Social Theory and Practice* 32: 311–31. [CrossRef]

Moreland, J. P. 2008. *Consciousness and the Existence of God*. London: Routledge.

Moreland, J. P. 2009. *The Recalcitrant Imago Dei: Human Persons and the Failure of Naturalism*. London: S. C. M. Press, pp. 165–80.

Moreland, J. P. 2012. A Reluctant Traveler's Guide for Slouching Towards Theism: A Philosophical Note on Nagel's *Mind and Cosmos*. *Philosophia Christi* 14: 415–24. [CrossRef]

Moreland, J. P. 2013. Exemplification and Constituent Realism: A Clarification and Modest Defense. *Axiomathes* 23: 247–59. [CrossRef]

Moreland, J. P. 2018. *Scientism and Secularism: Learning to Respond to a Dangerous Ideology*. Wheaton: Crossway.

Moreland, J. P. 2020. Wielenberg and Emergence: Borrowed Capital on the Cheap. In *God and Morality: What Is the Best Account of Objective Moral Values and Duties?* Edited by Adam Lloyd Johnson. New York: Routledge, pp. 93–114.

Moreland, J. P., and David Horner. forthcoming. *Metaethics and Worldview*. Nashville: Broadman & Hollman.

Morris, Dolores G. 2021. *Believing Philosophy*. Grand Rapids: Zondervan.

Murphy, Nancey. 2018. For Nonreductive Physicalism. In *The Blackwell Companion to Substance Dualism*. Edited by Jonathan Loose, Angus Menuge and J. P. Moreland. Oxford: Blackwell, pp. 317–27.

Nagel, Ernest. 1979. *The Structure of Science*. Indianapolis: Hackett.

Nagel, Thomas. 1997. *The Last Word*. New York: Oxford University Press.

Nagel, Thomas. 2012. *Mind and Cosmos*. Oxford: Oxford University Press.

O'Connor, Timothy. 2000. *Persons & Causes*. Oxford: Oxford University Press.

Page, Ben. 2020. Arguing to Theism from Consciousness. *Faith & Philosophy* 37: 336–62.

Papineau, David. 1993. *Philosophical Naturalism*. Oxford: Blackwell.

Papineau, David. 2001. The Rise of Physicalism. In *Physicalism and Its Discontents*. Edited by Carl Gillett and Barry Loewer. Cambridge: Cambridge University Press, pp. 3–36.

Papineau, David. 2002. *Thinking about Consciousness*. Oxford: Clarendon Press.

Plantinga, Avin. 1993. *Warrant and Proper Function*. New York: Oxford University Press.

Pruss, Alexander. 2009. The Leibnizian Cosmological Argument. In *The Blackwell Companion to Natural Theology*. Edited by William Lane Craig and J. P. Moreland. Malden: Wiley Blackwell, pp. 24–100.

Rachels, James. 1990. *Created from Animals*. Oxford: Oxford University Press.

Reppert, Victor. 2009. The Argument from Reason. In *The Blackwell Companion to Natural Theology*. Edited by William Lane Craig and J. P. Moreland. Malden: Wiley-Blackwell, pp. 345–90.

Rickabaugh, Brandon, and J. P. Moreland. 2023. *The Substance of Consciousness: A Comprehensive Defense of Contemporary Substance Dualism*. Oxford: Wiley Blackwell, chp. two.

Rosenberg, Alex. 1996. A Field Guide to Recent Species of Naturalism. *British Journal for the Philosophy of Science* 47: 1–29. [CrossRef]

Ruse, Michael, and E. O. Wilson. 1986. Moral Philosophy as Applied Science. *Philosophy* 61: 173–92. [CrossRef]

Ruse, Michael. 1989. Evolutionary Theory and Christian Ethics. In *The Darwinian Paradigm*. London: Routledge.

Sayre-McCord, Geoff. 2021. Moral Realism. In *The Stanford Encyclopedia of Philosophy*. Edited by Edward N. Zalta. Available online: https://plato.stanford.edu/archives/sum2021/entries/moral-realism/ (accessed on 13 April 2023).

Searle, John. 1992. *The Rediscovery of the Mind*. Cambridge: MIT Press.

Sellars, Wilfrid. 1963. *Science, Perception, and Reality*. London: Routledge & Kegan Paul.

Shafer-Landau, Russ. 2003. *Moral Realism: A Defence*. Oxford: Clarendon Press.

Shafer-Landau, Russ. 2004. *Whatever Happened to Good and Evil*. New York: Oxford University Press.

Strawson, Galen. 2006. Realistic Monism: Why Physicalism Entails Panpsychism. In *Consciousness and Its Place in Nature*. Edited by Anthony Freeman. Exeter: Imprint Academic, pp. 3–31.

Sturgeon, Nicholas L. 1986. Harman on Moral Explanations ofNatural Facts. *The Southern Journal of Philosophy* 24: 69–78. [CrossRef]

Tabaczek, Mariusz. 2019. *Emergence*. Notre Dame: University Press.

Wagner, Steven J., and Richard Warner. 1993. *Naturalism: A Critical Appraisal*. Notre Dame: University of Notre Dame Press.

Article

Is It Morally Permissible for Some People to Rape and Murder? Responding to Erik Wielenberg's Argument That Divine Command Theory Fails to Explain How Psychopaths Have Moral Obligations

Adam Lloyd Johnson

Center for the Foundations of Ethics, Houston, TX 77074, USA; adam@convincingproof.org

Abstract: Atheist moral philosopher Erik Wielenberg recently argued that Divine Command Theory is implausible as an explanation of objective morality because it fails to explain how psychopaths have moral obligations. In this paper I explain that everyone agrees the consciences of psychopaths don't work as they should, but there's disagreement among experts as to whether: A. The consciences of psychopaths *don't* inform them of what's right and wrong and that they should do what's right or B. The consciences of psychopaths *do* inform them of these things but merely don't generate the appropriate moral emotions. I argue that, based on the psychological research, a strong case can be made for B and thus under DCT psychopaths do have moral obligations because their consciences inform them of what's right from wrong and that they should do what's right. I also argue that even if A is true, God can, and does, make psychopaths aware of what's right and wrong and that they should do what's right through other means such as rationality, society, parents, culture, direct verbal commands, etc. Therefore, even if A is true, then psychopaths still have moral obligations under DCT because they do know what's right from wrong and that they should do what's right. Lastly, I turn the tables on Wielenberg and point out that his theory is even worse than DCT when it comes to providing an explanation for the moral rights and obligations of psychopaths

Keywords: Divine Command Theory; Erik Wielenberg; David Baggett; psychopath; moral realism; Divine Love Theory; metaethics; obligations; duties; morality; ethics; Robert Adams; William Lane Craig

Citation: Johnson, Adam Lloyd. 2023. Is It Morally Permissible for Some People to Rape and Murder? Responding to Erik Wielenberg's Argument That Divine Command Theory Fails to Explain How Psychopaths Have Moral Obligations. *Religions* 14: 507. https://doi.org/10.3390/rel14040507

Academic Editor: David Baggett

Received: 16 February 2023
Revised: 23 March 2023
Accepted: 3 April 2023
Published: 6 April 2023

1. Introduction

Erik Wielenberg has recently argued that Divine Command Theory is implausible as an explanation of objective morality because it fails to explain how psychopaths have moral obligations (Wielenberg 2020). His reasoning is as follows: in an attempt to explain how and why everyone has certain moral obligations, some Divine Command Theorists have proposed that God has issued commands to people, and therefore they have moral obligations if they recognize moral requirements as extremely authoritative and as having imperative force. However, because psychopaths do not recognize these things, they would not have moral obligations under Divine Command Theory. If they do not have moral obligations, then everything they do is morally permissible and nothing they do is objectively wrong. Thus, according to Divine Command Theory, it is not objectively wrong for some people, i.e., psychopaths, to rape and murder. Since it is implausible for actions such as rape and murder to be morally permissible (not objectively wrong) for some people, Divine Command Theory is an implausible explanation for objective morality.[1]

In this paper, I will defend Divine Command Theory by affirming and strengthening David Baggett's case that the evidence is not strong enough to conclude that the consciences of psychopaths do not recognize moral requirements as extremely authoritative and as having imperative force. In addition, I will argue that even if Baggett is wrong and the consciences of psychopaths do not inform them of these things, then God can and does make such individuals aware of these things via other means besides their consciences. Thus, I will argue that since psychopaths do somehow recognize these things, at least to some degree, they do, in fact, have moral obligations according to Divine Command Theory. Lastly, I will point out that Wielenberg's own atheistic metaethical theory faces even worse problems in terms of providing an explanation for the moral obligations and rights of psychopaths.

2. Understanding Wielenberg's Objection

It is important to understand how Divine Command Theory would lose plausibility points *if* Wielenberg's psychopath objection is successful. Remember that those who believe there are objectively real moral truths (moral realists) propose metaethical theories, Divine Command Theory being one such theory, in which they attempt to explain how and why some actions are morally good while others are morally bad as well as how and why everyone has certain moral obligations; for example, to refrain from rape and murder. That people have such objective moral obligations is a key belief of moral realists. They often try to make their case that morality is objectively real by pointing out that if there were no objective moral obligations, then, for example, the atrocities committed by Hitler were not objectively wrong. Such moral realists argue it is implausible to conclude Hitler did nothing objectively wrong and therefore we have strong reason to believe people do have objective moral obligations.

Now suppose that a moral realist proposed a moral theory, call it the Purple Theory, which concludes that only half of the population have moral obligations to refrain from rape and murder but it is morally permissible for the other half to commit these actions. Such a theory would obviously fail in one of its primary goals; that is, to explain how and why everyone has certain objective moral obligations. Moral realists would dismiss this Purple Theory as implausible for the same type of reason they find it implausible to claim there are no objective moral obligations at all. For them, it is *just as implausible* to conclude half the population would do nothing objectively wrong if they raped and murdered as it is to conclude Hitler did nothing objectively wrong. A moral realist wants to explain why *everyone* has a moral obligation to refrain from such hideous deeds, not just some people. Thus, a metaethical theory like the Purple Theory would lose so many plausibility points that it would be deemed implausible by moral realists. However, how many plausibility points would a theory lose if it concluded that 25% of the population had no such objective moral obligations? What if it concluded 10% had no such moral obligations? What if it concluded 1% had no such moral obligations?

Ideally, a moral theory should explain how and why it is objectively wrong for *everyone* to rape and murder; thus, the more people that do not have these objective moral obligations in a theory, the more implausible that theory becomes. It would be similar to a situation where someone, after years of research confirming that all bees have stingers, proposed a theory to explain *why* this is the case.[2] If, however, her theory concludes that only 75% of bees have stingers and cannot explain why the other 25% of bees have stingers, then her theory as it stands has failed and should be considered implausible. Similarly, moral realists have a strong conviction that everyone has a moral obligation to refrain from rape and murder, but Wielenberg argues that Divine Command Theory should be considered implausible because it cannot explain why this obligation applies to a significant amount of people (i.e., psychopaths).

After quoting several experts on psychopathy, Wielenberg summarized his case as follows:

> "We see, then, that despite the various disagreements about psychopathy, it seems quite plausible that psychopaths cannot grasp morality's authority and force. Suppose that is true . . . . [S]ince psychopaths cannot grasp morality's authority and force, God has not issued any commands to them, and so DCT [Divine Command Theory] implies that they have no moral obligations . . . . [O]n

DCT psychopaths do nothing wrong. DCT therefore implies that there walk among us human beings capable of freely and intentionally doing awful, evil things whom God has exempted . . . from the ordinary requirements of morality. If DCT is true, then for psychopaths, everything is permitted." (Wielenberg 2020, p. 549)

If Wielenberg is correct, and if, according to psychologists, "about four percent of human beings are psychopaths" (Wielenberg 2008, p. 81), then under Divine Command Theory, it is not objectively wrong for over thirteen million people in America to rape and murder—an implausible conclusion indeed, at least for moral realists.

Most divine command theorists have not grasped the weight of Wielenberg's psychopath objection because they mistakenly think it has to do with moral accountability, whereas it actually has to do with moral permissibility. For example, in response to Wielenberg's objection, William Lane Craig wrote that "if psychopaths literally do not know the difference between right and wrong, then I'd say that on any plausible moral theory they are not culpable for their evil acts" (Craig and Wielenberg 2020). In a footnote, he further explained that "[i]n our justice system, guilt is typically a combination of an evil act (actus reus) and a blameworthy mental state (mens rea). A person who has done an evil act but is mentally deranged has no mens rea and so will be found 'not guilty' by reason of insanity." (Craig and Wielenberg 2020, p. 63).

It is clear Craig thought this objection had to do with moral accountability because he argued that Divine Command Theory does not face difficulty with psychopaths since they simply would not be held accountable if they did not know right from wrong. It is reasonable to surmise that, if Divine Command Theory is true, God would not hold someone morally responsible if she does not know the difference between right and wrong. I have noted previously that Paul seems to imply this condition in Romans 2:14–16 but then explains that everyone does know the difference between right and wrong (Johnson 2023, p. 78). Regardless, that is not the issue here—the problem is *not* that under Divine Command Theory psychopaths cannot be held morally accountable. The problem is that, according to Wielenberg, under Divine Command Theory, psychopaths cannot do anything wrong in the first place.

It becomes more clear that Craig missed the thrust of Wielenberg's objection when he wrote that "[i]n virtue of God's general commands to mankind, murder is morally wrong, but someone who lacks a blameworthy mental state is not held morally responsible for committing that wrongful act. So when a mentally deranged person like James Holmes is found not guilty by reason of insanity for his hideous deeds, one does not deny that he has done a wrongful act . . . but that his mental state is blameworthy." (Craig and Wielenberg 2020, p. 74). From this quote we can see that Craig thinks that under Divine Command Theory the psychopath can commit wrong actions but just is not held morally accountable for those actions. But Wielenberg's argument is that Divine Command Theory actually *does deny* that a psychopath has done a wrongful act when he does such a hideous deed. Because he mistakenly thought the issue was moral accountability instead of moral permissibility, Craig did not explain how psychopaths could have moral obligations in the first place if they do not know right from wrong. In other words, if Divine Command Theory requires someone to know right from wrong in order to have moral obligations, and if psychopaths do not know right from wrong, then they have no moral obligations—nothing they do can be considered wrong and we would be incorrect if we told them there are things they should not do.

3. Responding to Wielenberg's Objection

Wielenberg's argument can be summarized as follows:

1. Under Divine Command Theory, someone does not have moral obligations if he does not recognize moral requirements as extremely authoritative and as having imperative force.

2. Psychopaths do not recognize moral requirements as extremely authoritative and as having imperative force.
3. Therefore, under Divine Command Theory, psychopaths do not have moral obligations.

He focuses mostly on defending premise two; for example, he wrote that "[p]sychological research shows that, whether or not psychopaths know the difference between right and wrong, they are incapable of grasping the *authority* of morality" (Craig and Wielenberg 2020, pp. 70–71). He even claimed that "the evidence from psychology that at least some psychopaths cannot grasp morality's authority and force is overwhelming." (Wielenberg 2020, p. 551). He summed up his argument when he explained that "[s]ince psychopaths are incapable of grasping the authority of moral demands, it seems that God has not given them moral obligations, which means that, on Craig's view [Divine Command Theory], they have no obligations at all." (Craig and Wielenberg 2020, p. 59).

Like many divine command theorists, I have argued elsewhere that in order for someone to have moral obligations, God must make that person aware of two things: 1. what is right and wrong; and 2. that he should do what is right, morally speaking (Johnson 2023, pp. 75–80). Wielenberg words it a bit differently in that he says someone must recognize moral requirements as extremely authoritative and as having imperative force—language he takes from Robert Adams (Adams 1999). However, when I say that God must make someone aware 'that he should do what is right', I am including in this awareness a recognition that moral requirements are extremely authoritative and have imperative force. Thus, throughout this paper, I will often use my description but the reader should keep in mind that it entails Wielenberg's.

Wielenberg has argued that "[p]sychopaths are incapable of empathy, love, or guilt and cannot grasp the authority of moral demands" (Craig and Wielenberg 2020, p. 59). In order to defend his position, he quoted several experts who have spent many years researching psychopaths. For example, psychologist Robert Hare explained that psychopaths lack "the shackles of a nagging conscience" (Hare 1993). Marijana Vujosevic wrote that "[s]ince their dysfunctional conscience does not stimulate moral feelings, psychopaths do not become aware of the constraints required to understand that they have obligations. Their conscience does not make them responsive to the constraining power of morality" (Vujosevic 2014). Eric Matthews maintained that psychopaths "do not merely behave contrary to moral standards . . . but seem in some sense not even to understand the notion of a moral standard in any 'serious' sense, that is, as meaning anything more than a conventionally accepted rule" (Matthews 2014, p. 78).

An initial concern with Wielenberg's argument here is that he seems to conflate mortal motivation with moral knowledge when he implies imperative force means 'to be strongly motivated.' But certainly, our obligations do not disappear just because our motivations are lacking. We all struggle with motivation to do the right thing from time to time, but this does not negate our obligation to do what is right. As a reminder, Wielenberg took this phrase 'imperative force' from Adams (Adams 1999, p. 268), but I suggest that the correct way to understand Adams here is that he intended this phrase to mean 'knowing you should do something,' not 'being motivated to do something'.

Even more concerning is Wielenberg's giant leap from the agreed-upon fact that psychopaths have an absent or significantly diminished capacity for moral emotions to the conclusion that they are incapable of grasping the authority and force of moral demands. Interestingly, this leap implies that the root problem with psychopaths is primarily emotive, not rational, which, as we have seen, is what the experts affirm. It also should be noted that considering his overall approach to morality is rationalistic, it is odd for Wielenberg to suggest an emotivist approach to moral knowledge. However, the major concern here is whether he is justified in making this leap from a deficiency in moral emotions to an incapability for moral knowledge.

Elsewhere, Wielenberg qualified himself a bit when he wrote "I do not mean to suggest that there is widespread agreement on the part of philosophers or even psychologists on the exact nature of psychopathy. On the contrary, psychopathy is the subject of various psychological and philosophical disagreements. However, as far as I can tell, there is widespread agreement on the claim that is crucial for my argument here, which is that psychopaths are incapable of grasping morality's authority and force." (Wielenberg 2020, p. 548). While we can agree that the "mainstream view of psychopaths in contemporary psychology and philosophy has it that they have significant neurological deficits that leave them with an absent or significantly diminished capacity for love, compassion, and guilt," (Wielenberg 2020, p. 546) it certainly is not clear that the experts have concluded from this, as Wielenberg has, that they are, therefore, incapable of grasping the authority and force of moral demands. It would do well at this point to note that according Robert Hare, the leading expert on psychopathy,

> "for psychopaths ... the social experiences that normally build a conscience never take hold. Such people don't have an inner voice to guide them; they *know* the rules but follow only those they choose to follow, no matter what the repercussions for others. They have little resistance to temptation, and their transgressions elicit no guilt. Without the shackles of a nagging conscience, they feel free to satisfy their needs and wants and do whatever they think they can get away with. Any antisocial act, from petty theft to bloody murder, becomes possible. We don't know why the conscience of the psychopath—if it exists at all— is so weak. However, we can make some reasonable guesses: Psychopaths have little aptitude for experiencing the emotional responses—fear and anxiety—that are the mainsprings of conscience." (Hare 1993, pp. 75–76)

Hare here seems to affirm that psychopaths lack the proper emotions that often are associated with morality but still know what the moral rules are.

Wielenberg's 'incapability' proposal is suggesting something that goes way beyond any empirical evidence from those who have researched psychopaths. It is one thing to affirm someone does not know certain truths, but quite another to affirm they are incapable of knowing them. How could Wielenberg, or anyone else, know that psychopaths do not merely lack such knowledge but are absolutely incapable of it? Yes, there is agreement that the problem with psychopaths has to do with their internal consciences, but there is disagreement among experts as to whether:

A. The consciences of psychopaths *do not* inform them of what is right and wrong and that they should do what is right, OR

B. The consciences of psychopaths *do* inform them of these things but merely do not generate the appropriate moral emotions.

Wielenberg jumps too quickly from the agreed-upon fact that the consciences of psychopaths do not generate the appropriate moral emotions to the conclusion that their consciences do not inform them of what is right and wrong and that they should do what is right. Based on the evidence we currently have, a reasonable case can be made for B; that is, the only problem with psychopaths is that their consciences do not generate appropriate moral emotions.

For example, consider David Baggett's case in his response to Wielenberg's psychopath objection. Baggett noted several experts, some of whom Wielenberg also quoted, which take the position that the consciences of psychopaths do inform them of what is right and wrong and that they should do what is right but merely do not generate the appropriate moral emotions. Baggett explained that

> "There is an intellectualist interpretation according to which the psychopath can know that such reasons [reasons to comply with the edicts of morality] are invariably strong ones, while also remaining largely or entirely indifferent to them. On this interpretation, it's possible for psychopaths to apprehend moral authority, much as it's possible for an agent to know of the 'prudentially authoritative' reasons that might demand that he, say, go on a diet, without his being in the least inclined to do so". (Baggett 2020, p. 136)

To support this position, Baggett noted that in a review of Hare's work (the well-known expert on psychopaths that Wielenberg often quotes), Christian Perring wrote: "Can or can't we say about the psychopath, 'he doesn't know any better'?". The answer seems to be both yes and no. Yes, in that the psychopath does not *emotionally* understand the rules of morality, even while he *does intellectually* understand them" (Perring 1999). In response to Perring's summary, Baggett encouraged his readers to "[n]otice once more that the vexed question of how best to understand what it means to grasp moral authority—whether affective/motivational or intellectualist—rears its head. It's not that Hare can be faulted for not settling this dispute, but Wielenberg moves too quickly when acting as though it were a settled matter . . . ." (Baggett 2020, p. 140).

From this discussion, we can see that it is important to make a distinction between the cognitive understanding of right from wrong and that a person should do what is right versus the emotions that are often associated with these experiences. It may very well be the case that the consciences of psychopaths merely fail to generate these emotions but still do inform them of what is right and wrong and that they should do what is right. Baggett summarized this position as follows:

> "A psychopath is a person who doesn't feel appropriately about his actions, but reason still leads to moral law. So psychopaths are not incapable of recognizing the moral law, they just lack the right emotional responses to it. Thus they are disadvantaged, but not in a way that precludes knowledge of the moral law . . . . Wielenberg, therefore, may be treating conscience in an overly narrow sense. Perhaps he thinks of conscience as morally appropriate feelings that guide us to right action, but why not include among the faculties of conscience the deliverances of reason?" (Baggett 2022)

If this position is correct and psychopaths merely lack the appropriate moral feelings, then they are not completely without a conscience but simply lack most, if not all, of the emotions that a healthy conscience normally generates.

Baggett has also made an additional point that raises doubts about Wielenberg's claim that the consciences of psychopaths do not at all inform them of what is right and wrong and that they should do what is right. Namely, he noted that psychopathy is measured in degrees, and very few, if any, are diagnosed at the highest level of psychopathy, which seems to imply that while the consciences of psychopaths may not inform them of what is right and wrong and that they should do what is right *as well as* normal consciences do, they still do so at least to some degree. In other words, their conscience still works in that it informs them of these moral truths, but it just does not work as well as it should, which is vastly different than Wielenberg's claim that they are incapable of knowing these things. Baggett elaborated on this point as follows:

> "In at least the vast range of cases, psychopathy manifests along a continuum; it's less a binary matter than one of degree. Even among those who clinically qualify as psychopaths there's a range of scores on Hare's diagnostic, and very few who score as high psychopaths. What this suggests is that among many if not most diagnosable psychopaths there may well be some measure of capacity for guilt, conscience, and remorse. Rather than a complete absence of such faculties, they're compromised to one degree or other. This again reminds us of the misleading nature of treating limiting cases as paradigm cases. If a given psychopath has some measure of capacity for guilt or conscience, then such a person may, to at least some real degree, be able after all to apprehend a modicum of moral authority . . . . It's an open question how big the class is of the limiting case psychopaths; it may well be very small indeed, or perhaps ultimately even empty." (Baggett 2020, p. 142)

Baggett also pointed out that "[h]igh psychopaths are roughly those who score 34 or above on the PCL-R. Unfortunately, almost no studies of moral judgment in psychopaths have participants who score above 34 . . . ." (Baggett 2020, p. 138). He noted that "[i]nterviewees during a PCL-R evaluation can receive the highest score for lack of empathy and for lack of remorse even if they show some signs of limited empathy or remorse (Baggett 2020, p. 142).

Thus, it seems a good case can be made that psychopaths do know, even if it is in a greatly diminished capacity, what is right from wrong and that they should do what is right. Under Divine Command Theory, a moral conscience does not have to be perfectly correct all the time in order to instigate moral obligations; after all, everyone struggles to know what is right from wrong in certain situations. Similarly, even a faint conscience, as long as it informs a person to some extent of what is right and wrong and that he should do what is right, still instigates moral obligations.

So which position is correct, A or B? Since, as we have seen above, experts who study psychopaths seem to vacillate on this question, we should be hesitant to reject a metaethical theory based solely on this issue. There is just a lot we still do not understand about psychopathy and it is for this reason that Baggett believes Wielenberg is overstating his case here in claiming A is true. Baggett provided the following caution in this regard:

> "The work of Robert Hare to which Wielenberg primarily points, groundbreaking as it is, tends not to be as bold as Wielenberg's conclusions. . . . Among what Hare does effectively is broach the question of whether psychopaths are bad or mad. When it comes to the crunch, however, Hare actually remains fairly noncommittal. This may in fact be the right stance to take, in light of the genuinely difficult nature of the question involved, but Wielenberg doesn't emulate Hare's reticence at this point." (Baggett 2020, pp. 138–39)

There is just a lot we do not know about the inner experiences of psychopaths.

One of the factors that makes it difficult for us to know what is going on inside the minds of psychopaths is that the only information we have, and could ever have, about the inner workings of psychopaths is what they themselves tell us. I trust you see the irony of this situation—psychopaths, by definition, are not a very trustworthy source of honest information! For this reason, among others, Baggett is concerned that Wielenberg's

> "appealing to the existence of psychopaths invites a number of difficult philo-sophical questions that the psychological evidence alone underdetermines. We don't look to the psychological literature, as fascinating as it may be, to settle meta-ethical questions . . . . [T]here's a distinct danger of borrowing too freely, presuming too much, and being strategically selective in adducing evidence . . . . The psychological evidence on numerous scores underdetermines answers to central philosophical questions. Many psychologists themselves attest to the challenging and vexed nature of the moral questions that psychopathy raises. Philosophical theorists simply drawing on the empirical findings they find most suitable for their purposes does not a solid interdisciplinary discussion make. . . . A non-exhaustive list of examples includes character, personality, emotion, cogni-tion, rationality, empathy, and moral knowledge. Much still needs exploration, and there remains a great deal of disagreement about explanations of and the relevant concepts germane to psychopathy. . . . The best way forward, however, is not to treat the issue as more definitively settled than it is. Wielenberg's am-bitious and premature use of the category of psychopathy is arguably guilty of overreach." (Baggett 2020, pp. 136–37)

Even if someone concludes that we do not know yet whether A or B is true, I argue that in either case, psychopaths do have moral obligations under Divine Command Theory. If B is true—if the consciences of psychopaths do inform them of what is right and wrong and that they should do what is right but merely do not generate the normal emotions that usually accompany these experiences, as Baggett has argued—then they have moral obligations. This result follows because, according to Divine Command Theory, all that is required for moral obligations is for someone to know what is right and wrong and that they should do what is right. Moral obligations are based on moral knowledge, not emotions and feelings.

However, if Baggett is wrong and A is true—namely, that the consciences of psychopaths actually do not inform them of what is right and wrong and that they should do what is right—then God can, and does, make them aware of these truths via other means, namely, through direct verbal commands from God, rationality, family, friends, culture, etc. It is important to keep in mind that, according to Divine Command Theory, God can make His moral requirements for us known in many ways. In fact, most divine command theorists use the term 'command' broadly in this context to include not only direct verbal instructions from God but also the many other ways God makes His moral requirements known to us, including the ways I enumerated above (Adams 1999, pp. 264–65). While some experts on psychopaths do describe their problem as a failure of their consciences to inform them of these things, in no way do they claim that psychopaths are incapable of knowing these things via other means. Wielenberg's 'incapability' proposal goes way beyond the evidence from empirical research concerning psychopaths. Therefore, regardless of whether A or B is true, psychopaths do know what is right and wrong and that they should do what is right, and thus, according to Divine Command Theory, they do have moral obligations.

4. How Psychopaths Fare under Wielenberg's Moral Theory

As we have seen above, Wielenberg has argued that Divine Command Theory is implausible because he claims it results in psychopaths having no moral obligations. However, let us turn the tables and see if his moral theory does a better or worse job in this regard. In other words, what does Wielenberg's moral theory conclude, either explicitly or implicitly, about the moral obligations of psychopaths?

One of the noteworthy features of Wielenberg's theory is his proposed making relationship in which natural, non-moral properties are responsible for instantiating moral properties. Wielenberg summarized this making relationship well when he responded to this question: what is the source of human moral rights and obligations?

"I propose the following answer: any being that can reason, suffer, experience happiness, tell the difference between right and wrong, choose between right and wrong, and set goals for itself has certain rights, including the rights to life, liberty, and the pursuit of happiness, and certain obligations, including the duty to refrain from rape (in typical circumstances). Having such cognitive capacities *makes* one have such rights and duties." (Wielenberg 2014, p. 56)

Thus, Wielenberg's proposal is that certain natural properties robustly cause, or make, moral properties to become instantiated." As I have explained elsewhere, Wielenberg's critics have pointed out several concerns with his idea that moral properties are instantiated by our cognitive faculties (Johnson 2023, pp. 137–42). The primary concern is that different human beings have different levels of cognitive abilities. Wielenberg's model would seem to indicate then that we should attribute fewer moral rights and duties to those who have lesser cognitive faculties, such as infants or those with mental handicaps. In other words, Wielenberg's model seems to imply that if a particular human being does not have sufficient cognitive faculties, then they have fewer moral rights and duties, or none at all. This is a very precarious path that could be used to justify all sorts of horrendous practices such as eugenics, forced sterilizations, and involuntary euthanasia. Surely Wielenberg himself does not believe that infants and people suffering from dementia have fewer moral rights, but the fact that his model seems to minimize, if not eradicate, such rights is an indication that his model is dangerously wrong.

This concern can be extended to psychopaths as well. As I noted above, Wielenberg's theory maintains that "any being that can reason, suffer, experience happiness, *tell the difference between right and wrong*, choose between right and wrong, and set goals for itself has certain rights, including the rights to life, liberty, and the pursuit of happiness, has certain obligations, including the duty to refrain from rape (in typical circumstances). Having such cognitive capacities *makes* one have such rights and duties."[3] Thus, it seems that Wielenberg's attempted attack against Divine Command Theory boomerangs back and strikes an even worse blow to his own theory. This follows because, according to Wielenberg's psychopath objection, psychopaths are incapable of knowing the difference between right and wrong and that they should do what is right and, according to Wielenberg's proposed making relationship, such persons do not have any moral obligations. But things are even worse than that because, according to Wielenberg's proposed making relationship, such individuals, such as psychopaths if Wielenberg is correct, do not even have any moral rights.

To summarize, according to Wielenberg's psychopath objection, Divine Command Theory is implausible because it concludes that psychopaths do not have any moral obligations. However, this objection of his, when applied back to his own moral theory, concludes not only that psychopaths do not have any moral obligations but that they do not even have any moral rights, which is an even more implausible conclusion.

5. Conclusions

I appreciate Wielenberg's work in moral theory because it causes all of us to think deeply about important issues. His psychopath objection claims that Divine Command Theory is implausible because it results in psychopaths—since they do not know right from wrong and that they should do what is right—having no moral obligations. While this objection is interesting and thought-provoking, it ultimately falls short in showing that Divine Command Theory is implausible.

I argued in this article that unless we develop strong evidence to the contrary, it is reasonable, based on the psychological evidence we currently have, to assume that psychopaths do know right from wrong generally, though not perfectly, and they do know they should do what is right, even if they do not have the normal emotions that a healthy conscience normally generates. However, even if I am wrong and the consciences of psychopaths do not inform them of what is right and wrong and that they should do what is right, God can and does make them aware of these things through other means, and this, according to Divine Command Theory, is all that is required for someone to have moral obligations. Thus, in either case, psychopaths do have moral obligations under Divine Command Theory.

Funding: This research received no external funding.

Institutional Review Board Statement: Not applicable.

Informed Consent Statement: Not applicable.

Data Availability Statement: Not applicable.

Conflicts of Interest: The author declares no conflict of interest.

Notes

[1] I call my own moral theory a Divine Love Theory instead of a Divine Command Theory because God's triune nature plays the central role in my theory, not His commands. However, my Divine Love theory affirms what most Divine Command Theories do, namely, that God's commands generate our moral obligations. Therefore, this objection of Wielenberg's also applies towards my Divine Love Theory. (Johnson 2023). In this book I also defend the overall cogency of Divine Command Theory and cotrast it with other theistic moral theories such as Natural Law.

[2] I have no idea if all bees have stingers, but assume they do for the sake of this illustration.

[3] (Wielenberg 2014, p. 56). Emphasis added.

References

Adams, Robert Merrihew. 1999. *Finite and Infinite Goods: A Framework for Ethics.* New York: Oxford University Press, repr., 2002.

Baggett, David. 2020. Psychopathy and Supererogation. In *God and Morality: What Is the Best Account of Objective Moral Values and Duties?* New York: Routledge.

Baggett, David. 2022. On Psychopathy and Moral Apologetics. *Moral Apologetics.* May 25. Available online: https://www.moralapologetics.com/wordpress/on-psychopathy-and-moral-apologetics?rq=psychopathy (accessed on 17 February 2023).

Craig, William Lane, and Erik J. Wielenberg. 2020. *God and Morality: What Is the Best Account of Objective Moral Values and Duties?* Edited by Adam Lloyd Johnson. New York: Routledge.

Hare, Robert D. 1993. *Without Conscience: The Disturbing World of the Psychopaths among Us*. New York: Guilford Press.

Johnson, Adam Lloyd. 2023. *Divine Love Theory: How the Trinity Is the Source and Foundation of Morality*. Grand Rapids: Kregel Academic.

Matthews, Eric. 2014. Psychopathy and Moral Rationality. In *Being Amoral: Psychopathy and Moral Incapacity*. Edited by Thomas Schramme. Cambridge: MIT Press.

Perring, Christian. 1999. Review—Without Conscience. *Metapsychology*. Available online: https://metapsychology.net/index.php/book-review/without-conscience/ (accessed on 2 February 2023).

Vujosevic, Marijana. 2014. Conscience as the Rational Deficit of Psychopaths. *Philosophical Psychology* 28: 1230.

Wielenberg, Erik J. 2014. *Robust Ethics: The Metaphysics and Epistemology of Godless Normative Realism*. New York: Oxford University Press.

Wielenberg, Erik. 2008. *God and the Reach of Reason: C.S. Lewis, David Hume, and Bertrand Russell*. New York: Cambridge University Press.

Wielenberg, Erik. 2020. Divine Command Theory and Psychopathy. *Religious Studies* 56: 542–57. [CrossRef]

 *religions*

Article
Divine Command Theory, Robust Normative Realism, and the Argument from Psychopathy: A Reply to Erik Wielenberg

Christopher R. Pruett

Philosophy Department, Indiana University East, Richmond, IN 47374, USA; crpruett@ius.edu

Abstract: Erik Wielenberg has offered a fascinating argument from moral psychology against a sophisticated theistic account of moral obligations: Divine Command Theory (DCT). This argument focuses on the pathology known as psychopathy—a perennial interest for those concerned with abnormal and moral psychology. The argument can be labeled *the argument from psychopathy* for convenience. The strength of the argument is that it forces the DCT-ist to maintain that there are some human beings who have no moral obligations yet still do evil actions. This, he argues, is an implausible thesis. Therefore, DCT is false. In this paper, I defend DCT and argue that there is good reason to be neutral or skeptical that psychopaths have moral obligations and, to the degree that they do, they are able to grasp morality in a way consistent with DCT. Furthermore, if the argument does present a serious problem for DCT, then it does so for Wielenberg's own view, Robust Normative Realism (RNR), just as much as DCT.

Keywords: God; religion; philosophy; ethics; metaethics; normativity; psychopathy; divine command theory

Citation: Pruett, Christopher R. 2023. Divine Command Theory, Robust Normative Realism, and the Argument from Psychopathy: A Reply to Erik Wielenberg. *Religions* 14: 107. https://doi.org/10.3390/rel14010107

Academic Editor: David Baggett

Received: 20 November 2022
Revised: 31 December 2022
Accepted: 10 January 2023
Published: 12 January 2023

1. Psychopaths and DCT

Wielenberg sums up his argument in the following way:

1. There are some psychopaths who are incapable of grasping the authority and force of moral demands.
2. God commands person S to do act A only if S is capable of recognizing the requirement to do A as being extremely authoritative and as having imperative force. (R)
3. Therefore, there are some psychopaths to whom God has issued no divine commands.
4. But there are no psychopaths who have no moral obligations.
5. Therefore, DCT is false (Wielenberg 2018).

Immediately, and rightly so, one could grapple with the validity of the argument and deny that 2 is a necessary condition for DCT to be true, thus rendering the argument not as one against DCT—a robust theory of moral obligations—but rather against some particular account of the divine promulgation of moral obligations.[1] But I am willing to grant that it is a necessary condition of DCT and that the implicit premise that (4.5) if DCT is true, then 3 is true. This is not the position of all DCT-ist, however, since this form of divine promulgation seems to assume that there is something internal to the agent that determines whether God issues commands to them. This is the essence of what we could call an *internalist* form of DCT, rather than a moral *externalist* position where there is nothing within the agent that makes a difference as to whether God issues divine commands to them, although it does make a difference, for the externalist, as to whether one is exempt from fulfilling one's moral duties or being morally responsible for not being able to uphold the moral law. Notice further that the "is capable of" clause echoes Kant's ought–implies–can principle, which is important, to varying degrees, to the internalist and externalists. We come back to this discussion later, but it is worth mentioning that an externalist might well reject (R) above.

The nature of divine commands and their communication is a wellspring within DCT-ist literature. Divine commands are the properly communicated will and requirements of God (Evans 2013). This gives us three requirements for one to have moral obligations: (1) there must be a command issued, (2) the command must be issued by a competent authority, and (3) the command must be properly communicated.[2] How then are they "properly communicated"? This is performed in the following way, taken from Robert Adams: (I) a divine command will always involve a *sign* ... that is intentionally caused by God. (II) In causing the sign, God must intend to issue a command, and *what* is commanded is what God intends to command thereby. (III) The sign must be such that the intended audience could understand it as conveying the intended command. This is what counts as a divine command and what is necessary for its proper promulgation (Adams 1999).

From (III), God only issues commands to persons that *could* understand the signs that are involved in commands as conveying the intended command. There is no use in yelling at a deaf person or waving one's hands frantically at a blind person. The ability to grasp a sign might be through intuition or rational principles. For example, when one comes upon the scene of a few teenagers burning a dog (rather than a cat) alive, one can just *see* that it is wrong. There is no moral deliberation about it. It is experienced as a moral abomination. However, there are less clear cases in which moral deliberation is necessary. Perhaps I should volunteer at a soup kitchen rather than keep my promise to attend Tyler's birthday. A combination of moral deliberation and moral experience is also common in complex issues such as abortion or the justification of war. The point is that, for many of us, moral experience is indispensable in many of the moral choices and beliefs that we have. To lack a robust experience of morality—a lack of the sense of authority and imperative force—is to be morally deficient to the extreme. As such, from Adams and Wielenberg, we have a principle from (III), namely (R) above.

As an internalist understanding of promulgation of moral obligations, where the presence of moral requirements upon an individual is based upon something internal to individuals, such as cognitive ability for example, it is not surprising that, as an internalist and DCT-ist myself, I do not find the first two premises problematic.[3] The first premise can be granted regardless of whether one is an internalist or an externalist. The disagreement arises in the importance and relevance of the truth of premise one to moral obligation. The second premise, (R), is just the DCT-ist's version of the moral accessibility principle, which says that in order for one to be a genuine moral agent, one must have sufficient access to the moral realm through things such as moral rationality, moral knowledge, moral development, etc. I should mention, however, that the DCT-ist need not accept premise 1 or 2, even if Adams does. Evans, as an externalist, would not accept 2. Per Evans, "I follow Shafer-Landau on this question and reject internalism. So, for me it is enough that someone knows that some act is morally obligatory or is forbidden to have an obligation ... One would not say that the person has no obligations, just that the person has an excuse for not fulfilling the obligation" (Evans, Personal Correspondence). It is one thing to disagree with Evans' position on moral internalism or externalism. It is another to present the argument as an argument against DCT itself like Wielenberg does, especially given the externalist and internalist construals of divine command promulgation. This argument hinges on what kind of DCT-ist one is, but (again) I am willing to grant 1–3 for the sake of argument. Thus, the sticking point comes with 4. I will argue that there is little reason to accept 4 as true, rather than unknown or simply false. The reasons for this will begin with how a DCT-ist understands moral obligations.

For the DCT-ist, moral obligations have certain features. Moral obligations are decisive, law-like, deontic concepts that apply to every person of a certain level of cognitive or noetic development. To say that I have an obligation to perform X is to say that I am required, or called to, perform X by an authority over and above myself. Obligations are authoritative concepts, or *commands*, that require of me certain actions and forbid other actions. Actions that are not obligatory for me are morally neutral, supererogatory, or non-culpable. This would mean that I do not have a moral obligation to do or not do said action, even if *other people* have an obligation to keep me from performing that action.[4] In addition, and although not all DCT-ists agree with my view here, I take it that moral obligations are also the kinds of things that one is responsible, culpable, blameworthy, or liable for violating.[5] It would make little sense to say, after having failed a supposed moral duty to perform X, that I am still required to perform X even though I lack necessary access to rational and moral faculties to perform X, a fact that is both beyond my control and characteristic of psychopaths. Thus, I take it that there are no moral obligations that one has that one is not culpable for violating.

To further tease out a proper understanding of moral obligations, and as Matthew Flannagan has noted as well, there is a difference between material moral obligations—also called external or objective moral obligations—and formal moral obligations—also called internal or subjective moral obligations. Material moral obligatoriness is the deontic status that applies to an action in virtue of the circumstances that one finds oneself in and the consequences that follow from that action. Formal moral obligatoriness is the deontic status that applies to an action in virtue of one's beliefs about the morally relevant circumstances and consequences (Flannagan 2021). In my view, this distinction is helpful, even if partially delineated. I say "partially delineated" because formal moral obligations seem to be a proper subset of material obligations in that one's beliefs about morally relevant circumstances is a proper part of one's morally relevant circumstances. As such, one's formal moral obligations are not properly called moral obligations since one who has a formal moral obligation to do X might have a conflicting and overriding material obligation to do Y or not-X. To take Flannagan's illustration, David Cerven committed various armed robberies in Auckland before turning himself in and notifying police that he would be waiting at a local park. When the police arrived, he pretended he had a gun and was promptly shot and killed. Flannagan notes that the police had a material (i.e., objective) obligation not to shoot unarmed people, which included Cerven, but were also formally (i.e., subjectively) permitted to shoot Cerven given their morally relevant beliefs about the matter (Flannagan 2021). In my view, the police were morally permitted to do what they did in both circumstances, material and formal, sense their beliefs about the matter are relevant to whether they were materially permitted to shoot Cerven.

When speaking of moral obligations, i.e., material moral obligations, I also take it that one cannot non-culpably fail to do X if X is a moral obligation. There are no moral laws that one, at some level or another, is not responsible for violating. To say that one state of affairs ought to have been otherwise is not to say that one has a moral obligation to bring about that state of affairs given that, for example, one *cannot* bring about that state of affairs. There are certain standards of moral behavior, such that to culpably fail to meet such standards is to say that one had a moral obligation to meet such standards. To non-culpably fail to meet such standards just means to fail concerning them due to various constraints that are not up to the individual, internal or external.

Wielenberg argues that all psychopaths have at least some moral obligations. They are culpable for failing to live up to the moral standard, which would mean that they have at least some moral obligations. He has three reasons for this thesis (premise 4). The first is an appeal to intuition, which is a perfectly valid way to argue. However, I also appeal to the opposite intuition: it seems to me that there are some psychopaths that do not have any moral obligations at all, and if they do, such obligations are compatible with DCT in both their internalist and externalist construals.[6] He attempts to motivate the intuition by saying that it is implausible that psychopaths do nothing wrong, which is implied on DCT for at least some psychopaths if premises 1–3 are to be believed. But what does "wrong" here mean? Does it just refer to moral standards of behavior? If so, then of course such a thing is implausible, but it is also irrelevant since DCT-ists can grant this as well. If not, if something being wrong refers to something else, then why take the view that some psychopaths not being able to do wrong as implausible? This is because he believes that psychopaths are also *culpable* for their failure to meet the moral demand or standard. As has been mentioned, I also believe that doing something morally wrong implies culpability, but as we will see, some psychopaths are plausibly not culpable for failing to meet moral standards and so cannot do anything morally wrong. This is not to say that we have no obligations ourselves to stop psychopaths from performing certain actions, whether they are culpable or not, since they can, in a genuine sense, violate other persons of intrinsic value.

One can violate other people without being a moral agent. But if one *is* a moral agent, one must satisfy two putative conditions: one epistemic condition and the other a control condition. One must have appropriate epistemic access to moral reality, as well as the appropriate level of control over one's morally relevant actions.[7] The presence of both conditions means that one is morally responsible for what happens in a given circumstance. Moral responsibility itself is a rich and fascinating concept that Wielenberg simply notes in passing as involving a robust philosophical debate and that philosophers disagree on whether psychopathic deficiencies imply a lack of moral responsibility. This is surprising since moral responsibility would seem to be a necessary condition of one having moral obligations and is something that one can have only if one is a moral agent. For any action A, person S, and circumstance C, S has a moral obligation to do A in C only if S would be morally responsible for doing (or not doing) A in C, or given morally relevant circumstances prior to C. If we do not know the responsibility status of S in C (or prior to C), then we also should be skeptical that S has any moral obligations in C. Even worse, if it turns out that in no instance of C is S morally responsible for A, then there is no instance of C in which S has a moral obligation to do (or not do) A. To put it simply, where there is no moral responsibility, there are no moral obligations, even if there are, say, legal obligations or obligations of etiquette. It is for this reason, in addition to moral experience, that I have the exact opposite intuition, i.e., that not all psychopaths have moral obligations.

This is *not* to say that the reverse is true, i.e., that one cannot be morally responsible for actions or consequences that are beyond one's control. This is the point of discussions on moral luck. Many philosophers believe that some persons have moral luck, viz. that some persons are genuinely responsible for actions beyond their control. To take a popular example: Imagine that Ted and Jones attempt to murder their victims. Ted is successful in his task, but Jones' gun jams. Both were equally responsible for their attempted murder, and it was a matter of luckTed succeeded and Jones did not. Do they both have the same degree of moral responsibility? If you said "yes", then you believe in moral luck. This kind of moral luck is typically called *resultant* or *consequential* moral luck, but it has its place beside circumstantial and constitutive moral luck.

At bottom, the debate on moral luck comes down to how strongly one understands the control condition for moral responsibility. Taken as strongly as it can, it is the condition that, necessarily, there are no two or more persons that are the same in all features that are under their control yet whose morally relevant status nonetheless differs (Enoch 2008). Perhaps the control condition is not so sweeping. In that case, one could take the condition to apply, without limit, to obligation, permissibility, and character while only taking the condition to apply partially to outcomes or consequences (Kumar 2018). In either instance, the control condition that I press is deliberately formulated to avoid this debate and leave the status of moral luck an open question since all that is required is an "appropriate" level of control for responsibility and obligations, whatever that comes to.

The second motivation to accept 4 is the claim that psychopaths do evil things with evil intentions. Wielenberg says that "unlike babies and those with severe dementia, the agency of psychopaths is largely intact. Psychopaths can and often do perform evil actions from evil motives, and according to Hare, their evil acts 'result not from a deranged mind but from a cold, calculating rationality'" (Wielenberg 2018, p. 8). This deserves some unpacking. First, he never defines what he means by "evil", or what an evil action requires. This is pivotal to his claim that psychopaths do evil actions. To offer a few operative definitions, first define an action as *bad* if and only if it causes, perhaps unnecessary, suffering to a being of intrinsic value. This includes moral agents and non-moral agents or happenings, such as natural disasters. Let us say that an action is evil if and only if it is bad and performed in conjunction with or as a result of intentions that are formed by considering moral reasons. An action that is morally wrong for an agent to do is one that is evil and contradicts a moral duty to not do said action. An action can be evil, but not wrong in the following way:

James is on a remote island where he has been taught from birth that killing people and eating them during the Shingami festival is a sign of respect. No matter how he reasons, he will come to that conclusion or one like it. What he is doing is evil, but not wrong if doing something wrong requires that one be culpable. If doing wrong does not imply culpability, then doing evil is enough for doing something wrong, and premise 2 is false and not required for DCT. It would just turn out that internalism about moral obligations is false.

Given these terms, it is clear that psychopaths do actions that are bad, yet not evil or wrong for them to do. This is also not a new concept. Actions that are bad or evil, yet not wrong, are also known as *infravetatory actions* (Swinburne 2008, p. 7). That does not mean that such actions are permissible. The psychopath who engages in infravetatory actions does so in a way that they are not morally culpable or, in the least, are not violating moral obligations, yet *we* have a moral duty to stop them. Their actions are impermissible on one level or another. The seeming moral insanity of psychopaths (see Schramme 2014, p. 3), not to mention the theologically charged notion of "evil", is enough, I think, to be skeptical that psychopaths can do anything evil as defined in the aforementioned sense (de Sousa and Heinrichs 2010, p. 299). Evil intent is not something that can be realized in the psychopath since they cannot take a moral stance and do not have the option of developing a specifically evil perspective. If evil does *not* require an evil intention but rather is synonymous with "bad", then hurricanes and tsunamis are evil, though clearly not moral agents. Thus, amoral agents could do things that are evil yet not wrong, and so evil would have no obvious connection to moral agency at all. Psychopaths could therefore be amoral agents—incapable of violating moral obligations or being culpable for their actions—and yet still do evil actions, contrary to what Wielenberg says.

Second, if it is true that psychopaths so often do evil things with evil intentions, would it not be correct to call them evil as a result? That is typically what we call people who do the kind of things that psychopaths often do. Perhaps we could call them *agents of evil* (like natural disasters) if evil actions did not require evil intentions, but that does nothing to show that they are *evil agents* (like immoralists). Notice that Hare above describes them as *cold*, not *evil*. There is a reason for that. That is because, even to Hare, while psychopaths might be agents of evil when they harm other persons, they are not evil persons. It is

> more likely that the behavior of psychopaths—including the few that murder and mutilate—stems from a total indifference to the feelings or welfare of others than from sure evil. Their eyes are those of an emotionless predator, not those of Satan. (Hare 2011, p. 210)

They are not moral free riders, moral nihilists, immoralists, or rational moralists (Jacobs 2014, p. 137). They are *usually* viewed as amoralists (Ibid., 144), though they should be thought of as *rational amoralists* (Benn 2014, p. 170). They give rational explanations for their behavior (sometimes) but very rarely give moral reasons for why they did (or did not do) something. They use language without understanding the meaning beyond that language, which is referred to as *Semantic Dementia* in the literature (Adshead 2014). They are predators who sometimes take account of the suffering of their prey in delight, at other times with total indifference (Maibom 2014, p. 91).[8] The amoralist is a person who is not a moral agent and cannot deal competently in moral matters (Schramme 2014, p. 322).

Before getting into the final argument for 4, I want to mention that Wielenberg's view seems strikingly similar to, or at least supported by, Mathew Talbert's *attributionism*, which says that a sufficient condition for moral responsibility is that one treats another with contempt or ill will (Talbert 2014, p. 282). Psychopaths treat others with ill will by disregarding their explicit and implicit demands to have their rights respected and not be wronged. Therefore, as Talbert and Wielenberg would (or should) argue, all psychopaths have at least some moral responsibility. On this view, one would be morally responsible regardless of whether one has moral knowledge, moral rationality, and their developmental history. Psychopaths can therefore be responsible for violating at least some moral obligations that they have. As I will argue, given the current evidence in the literature on psychopaths, this is very unlikely.

The final argument for 4 is that there is a tension between DCT and God not commanding psychopaths like the rest of us. Part of the reason that God commands us to do, or refrain from doing, certain things is for our good. The goodness and badness of certain actions is one of the reasons that God commands us concerning them. If that is true, then it is inexplicable why God still does not command psychopaths to not do some actions, such as rape, given that rape is bad or evil. If God's commands are partially grounded in the badness or goodness of actions, then why would God still not command the psychopath?

This argument can be understood in a few ways, but I take it that the thrust of the argument is something like this: if DCT were true, then there would be no psychopaths because God would have ample reason to command psychopaths to do certain things.[9] As a paradigmatically rational being, God would act reasonably and issue commands to psychopaths for their own good and ours. While it is true that God considers the goodness and badness of actions when issuing commands, the point of issuing commands is, as Evans says, for our good—making us into virtuous persons who can relate to God as a friend. But if God knew that giving commands to psychopaths would not do any good because they are morally deaf, then what is the point in giving commands at all? Screaming louder at a deaf person will do nothing except prove an exercise in futility. On the other hand, God could cure their moral deafness so that His commands could be heard. If so, then why does he not? I am not aware of a single overarching reason, but there are plenty of available possible and, in my view, probable explanations. It is doubtful that God has only one reason, given that God knows the kind of ripples in time that can happen from the smallest change. A few answers come to mind: salvific planning, the greater good, free will, and soul-making theodicies. All of these combined make a robust case for not issuing commands to some psychopaths, who represent an extremely small percentage of human beings at the present time. This does not mean that God will never command psychopaths or heal them of their ailments, but only for a little while. Regardless of what God's reasons are unless there is good reason to think that God does not have such reasons, I do not think that psychopathy can be used in such a way as evidence against theism or DCT. It is not enough to show that some of the available explanations do not work. That is not an argument against DCT but only against some DCT-ists.

To finalize the point that we should view 4 with strong suspicion, I argue that there is good reason to think that 4 is false with respect to high psychopaths. Psychopaths are not moral agents, even if they are, to some extent, rational agents. To say that they are the same thing would be suspiciously similar to identifying rational oughts with moral ones—or one's access to rational oughts with one's access to moral ones—surely an unacceptable position.

In the next section, I hone in on the nature of psychopaths and the admittedly rare condition and argue that we should take Gilbert Ryle's words to heart that "a person who does not care about the difference between right and wrong has not yet learned the difference" (Ryle 1971, pp. 381–90).

2. The Amorality and Moral Incapacity of Psychopaths

The operative case under discussion is psychopathy—an extremely rare condition that represents the extreme edge of abnormal psychologies. If we are going to consider psychopaths when trying to understand moral agency, responsibility, and theories of obligations, we need a clear picture of what we are dealing with. This is the aim of Section 2, so let us begin.

Among moral psychologists, it is generally accepted that we have two options when it comes to psychopaths: either they are (1) not morally responsible for their actions or (2) their moral responsibility will be severely diminished as a result of various factors (Haji 2010a). To what degree (1) or (2) applies to an individual psychopath will depend upon how high he/she scores on certain diagnostic tools, such as Robert Hare's Psychopathy

Checklist Revised (PCL-R), which is the gold standard checklist for psychopathy. The higher the score, the less likely one is to be morally responsible for one's actions and the more psychopathic one is likely to be. Psychopaths are the worst off among those with Antisocial Personality Disorder (APD). In the US, a minimum score of 30 out of 40 is required for a diagnosis that one is *probably* a psychopath.[10] Once one reaches 34 on the scale, they are deemed "high psychopaths" in that they are qualitatively different than "successful" or "low" psychopaths. The point here is that there is a spectrum to the diagnoses, and since we are focused on the ones with the worst deficiencies relevant to moral agency, I will be talking about high psychopaths.[11]

As Wielenberg argues using the current psychological and psychiatric literature, psychopaths are morally blind, which means that they are severely deficient in terms of both affective and rational capacities. More specifically, psychopaths lack identifying empathy, guilt, remorse, fear, love, shame, and moral capacities such as moral and practical rationality, knowledge, practical wisdom, and moral patiency—namely, the understanding that one has vulnerabilities, is dependent on others, and that morality constitutes useful behavior within a moral community, reason-responsiveness, moral judgment, moral intention formation, self-reflection, and the ability to improve morally. Psychopathy is a developmental disorder in which moral development is stagnated from an early age, resulting in an inability to truly care about morality or other persons qua persons or have meaningful relationships (Schramme 2014, p. 322). They view people as mere objects rather than human beings (Hare 2011, p. 93).

Furthermore, the amorality and moral responsibility of psychopaths are things that are so important to the discussion of whether psychopaths have moral obligations, yet, except for a footnote, Wielenberg does not explore them further. In the footnote, he notes that the consensus among the authors of Mcmillan and Malatesti (2010), according to Thomas Schramme, is that psychopaths lack moral responsibility for their actions. If that is true, and it is also true that where moral responsibility is absent, so are moral obligations, then it also follows that psychopaths have no moral obligations. Even Schramme, as a result of the psychopath's moral blindness, argues, quite rightly, that psychopaths are not moral agents or moral persons. It is not that psychopaths have moral obligations and are not blameworthy for violating them. They do not have moral obligations at all, or if they do, then it is for a host of reasons that are compatible with DCT. For example, if the psychopath comes to have sufficient moral knowledge that is required for moral responsibility, then God's commands can indeed be heard, though perhaps to a muffled degree.

As for the amorality of psychopaths, it is "now accepted", according to Gwen Adshead, that emotional experience and reflection are *essential* for moral reasoning (Adshead 2014, p. 119). Without moral reasoning, including self-reflection, one of the primary things that separate us from mere animals, we cannot be moral agents. We could be clever, but not moral reasoners. It is the presence of both rational and emotional/affective capacities that make one a moral person (Schramme 2014, p. 240). We should be very suspicious of the idea that serious deficits of the will concerning morality can happen without other volitional or rational structures being likewise impaired (Jacobs 2014, pp. 148–49; Schramme 2014, p. 323). This is one of the reasons that philosophers are so interested in psychopaths: they seem to be prime cases of amorality. In fact, one of the first clinicians, Philippe Pinel, to write about psychopaths referred to psychopaths as "morally neutral" (Hare 2011, p. 25). The idea of the amoralist is still prevalent among philosophers and psychologists (Haji 2010b, p. 263).[12] Terms such as "morally insane", "amoralist", exhibiting "profound amoralism", and "mentally deranged" are applied to psychopaths often (Kennett 2010, p. 243; Gillett 2010, p. 286).

Such a dismal description of such persons, in addition to the inability of psychopaths to genuinely distinguish between moral rules and rules of convention, is what leads Neil Levy and Jeanette Kennett to conclude that psychopaths are worse off in moral matters than autistic 5-year-old children. The age can be lowered to 3 since even at that age, children can distinguish, in a morally relevant way, between moral and conventional rules (Kennett 2010, p. 263; Levy 2010; Levy 2014). Presumably, Wielenberg would be fine with saying that children that young do not have moral obligations, and even more so those that are worse off in moral reasoning. Being a rational or normative agent is thus not sufficient for being a moral agent. Persons that are not moral agents cannot do anything wrong, in the sense of culpably violating moral standards, or anything evil, since evil requires moral intention formation. Psychopaths therefore have no moral obligations to violate since they lack sufficient access to the moral universe to be deeply and truly part of a moral community.

3. Moral Internalism vs. Externalism

When referring to internalism and externalism above, remember that this is with respect to the promulgation of divine commands. This debate is closely related to the overall moral internalism vs. moral externalism debate—indeed, it is inevitable and provides another way of understanding where Wielenberg, and those of kin, are coming from. This also presents another way one might respond to Wielenberg's argument. One combination of views, reasons externalism—the view that moral judgments do not have a necessary connection to motivating or justifying reasons—a view held by Shafer-Landau, and moral rationalism—the view that moral obligations either are or entail reasons for action—which is held by both Shafer-Landau and Wielenberg, forces one to conclude that there are some people who will be completely blind to their moral obligations. Notice that both of these—reasons externalism and moral rationalism—are forms of externalism. The moral obligations of psychopaths can be affirmed either by saying that (1) psychopaths can reason sufficiently for moral agency and, therefore, moral obligations or (2) argue that even perfect reasoning is irrelevant or unnecessary for one having moral obligations. Wielenberg argues the former, while Shafer-Landau argues the latter. Let us assume that Wielenberg grants what I have said so far and moves to the next step by arguing for (2) alongside Shafer-Landau. Shafer-Landau himself does this by saying that psychopaths " ... will fail to see what they must do, even were they to reason perfectly from their psychological standpoint. Theirs is a make-up so morally askew that nothing therein is rationally related to moral demands". He argues that they have a possibly ineliminable blindness to moral reasons that still apply to them. These contexts, both the blindness and the reasons for the blindness, are tragic but still exist. These persons are completely blind to moral reasons and moral obligations and are not blameworthy for being as such, yet there are still standards of correct moral behavior that they can violate (Shafer-Landau 2003, pp. 213–14).

Now, in order to make this work, assuming that we are referring to the culpable failure to meet moral standards, one would have to argue that one could lack the relevant internal rational and affective capacities—lacking all access to the moral realm—and still have moral obligations and be morally blameworthy for violating something that one ought not to have violated even though one could not have refrained. It then turns into a defense of premise 1, but now premise 4 is implausible since then the ought–implies–can principle, even weaker forms of it, would be violated. Like Wielenberg's defense of the argument, one's understanding of moral obligations will have consequences for how we should understand the argument. We risk talking past one another if one presents an internal critique of an internalist view from an externalist perspective. Either way, one must either reject (1) or (2) or reject the argument from psychopathy on this understanding of moral obligations.

If, however, we are referring to the non-culpable failure to meet moral standards of behavior, then premise 2 is false. The DCT-ist, again, accepts moral standards of behavior but can either count such failures as violating moral obligations, which is something that some moral externalists would say, or not, which internalists would argue. We would need a good argument for thinking that these non-culpable failures do count as violating moral obligations to take the argument as significant on this understanding of morality which, at present, is lacking. If such an argument can be presented, this would present, at most, a problem for DCT, but not a *unique* problem for DCT, since on this view, neither communication of divine command nor one's access to the moral realm seems to matter in terms of whether we have obligations. Improper access to the moral realm would only mean that we lack culpability or responsibility for failing to do what we ought to have done. If this is a problem, then it is a problem for moral realism, not just DCT. At this stage, the argument seems to prove too much.

4. The Sword of Damocles

Suppose for the moment that Wielenberg is right that all psychopaths have moral obligations. In that case, it turns out that either 1 is false or RNR is in just as much trouble as DCT. On RNR, moral obligations are defined as "decisive normative reasons", namely "reasons that one ought to be responsive too" (Wielenberg 2014, pp. 7–8). However, given that ought implies can, if one cannot be responsive to such reasons, even with the treatment available, then one is not obligated to be so responsive. As I have argued, psychopaths cannot be so responsive to such reasons. Therefore, moral obligations cannot be decisive normative reasons since they can *never* be decisive for the psychopath, yet all psychopaths have at least some moral obligations. Thus, RNR is false. This argument might take something like the following form:

- 1*. There are some psychopaths who (non-culpably) cannot be responsive to normative or moral reasons, let alone decisive normative reasons, i.e., moral obligations.
- 2*. A person S only has moral obligation M to do action A if and only if S is capable of being responsive to normative/moral reasons to do A. (R*)
- 3*. Therefore, there are some psychopaths who have no moral obligations.
- 4. But there are no psychopaths who have no moral obligations.
- 5*. Therefore, RNR is false.

Wielenberg denies 3*, but this results in a few problems. On the one hand, if *1 is denied, then, for analogous reasons, 3 and 1 above should also be denied. Claiming that psychopaths can be responsive to moral reasons, in the sense perhaps a moral nihilist or immoralist might, is to admit that psychopaths have sufficient access to the moral law, which is all that is required to argue that psychopaths are capable of grasping the authority and force of morality. Unless one wants to reduce moral oughts (or one's access to moral oughts) to rational oughts (or one's access to rational oughts), the arguments are analogously supported or denied. Wielenberg accepts this premise when it comes to young children and those with advanced dementia, and given the psychological data above, he should accept it concerning psychopaths as well.

On the other hand, if 2* is denied, which is as modest as 2 above since it is the *capability* of being responsive to moral reasons, then one would have to say that the fact that some normative/moral reasons can never be decisive for some is not enough to say that they have no moral obligations, which violates the very definition of moral obligations that Wielenberg has provided. This is to go back to moral rationalism and reasons externalism. It is no less absurd to believe that people can have no access to the moral realm yet still have moral obligations than it is to say that psychopaths can do bad or evil things yet not violate moral obligations.

2* can also be reformulated to include a temporal component such that, given a person's developmental history, if such a history (non-culpably) precludes the ability to be responsive to moral reasons, then one has no moral obligations in the sense that Wielenberg stipulates. Thus, 2* would be refashioned as the following: (2**) A person S only has moral obligation M to do action A if and only if S, given S's (non-culpable) developmental history, S is capable of being responsive to normative/moral reasons to do A. (R**)

5. Has God Abandoned Psychopaths?

After all of this, and as a deeply religious person, the question of whether God has abandoned psychopaths is of great interest to me. I think that the answer to this question is similar to the answer that people give when asked if God has abandoned them in their suffering. Of course, the answer is 'no'. However, one difference between suffering and psychopathy is that there are a multitude of successful clinical treatments for the effects of the former, yet there is no such treatment for psychopaths that has been successful. This does not mean that we should give up on treating them, nor does it mean that God has given them up. They will be treated the same as those who have other moral incapacities or deficiencies. They will be judged to the degree that they are morally responsible for their actions. Depending upon what religious tradition one accepts, they will then go through a sanctification process (some call this purgatory) and be assigned a temporary place of residence for the final judgment. A person does not, therefore, live a purposeless and meaningless life simply because he cannot respond to God's commands in this life, as Wielenberg charges. There is more to life than *this* life.

Irrespective of one's religious (or non-religious) tradition, we should think about how a just and/or loving God would treat those of similar rational or affective deficiencies. If no satisfactory answer is forthcoming, then perhaps we should be satisfied with not knowing and simply trust God with the healing and sentencing required for those with psychopathy, dementia, and brain defects. A just God would judge based upon the degree of revelation or light that one has, and the psychopath has admittedly very little to none.

6. Ending Sentiments

At first glance at Wielenberg's argument, it strikes as contradictory since it seems that 1 implied ~4. Although Wielenberg quotes several DCT-ists that seem to suggest they support 1 and 4, my intuition about this implication was further confirmed from correspondence with those same DCT-ists,[13] that if 1 is true, then it makes little sense to argue 4, since ~4 is implied by 1 when one understands moral obligations in the internalist fashion. This is because internalists take moral obligations to imply culpability for failing to perform what one is obligated to perform, even if such responsibility is pushed back to an earlier moral failing. Additionally, as we saw, arguing otherwise brings to light several problems with RNR just as well. This discussion has shown, I think, that in the middle of 1 and 4 lies a wealth of debate concerning moral responsibility and agency that a psychopath might or might not possess. As Sousa and Heinrichs put it, "our response to psychopaths will be only as coherent as our most basic conceptions of evil, guilt, and moral responsibility" (de Sousa and Heinrichs 2010, p. 300). Such discussions are vital to Wielenberg's argument and, for now at least, he has not sufficiently argued for the acceptance of both 1 and 4, nor are such prospects promising.[14]

Funding: This research received no external funding.

Conflicts of Interest: The author declares no conflict of interest.

Notes

[1] For a good discussion of this issue, refer to Matthew Flannagan's 2021 article *The Psychopath* Objection *to Divine Command Theory*.

[2] These are sufficient conditions for moral obligations, according to Evans (personal correspondence), not necessary conditions. Evans believes that proper communication is necessary for one to be culpable, not lack moral obligations.

[3] Some DCT-ists might not be comfortable with 2, objecting that general revelation applies to all, even if it cannot be heard or seen by some. Divine commands constitute moral obligations; however, such commands must be properly communicated for one to be morally responsible for violating such commands. This would mean that moral responsibility is not necessary for moral obligations, even if it is sufficient. There is a difference between having moral obligations and moral obligations applying. Thus, divine commands are issued to every person, and their ability or inability to respond makes a difference in moral responsibility, not moral obligations. The necessity of 2 for the DCT-ist therefore rests on whether it is true that if one is not morally responsible for some action, then moral obligations do not apply to one. Such a view would be one that grants exemption status to the psychopath, while the position that I defend in this paper grants exception status to the psychopath. We would need to know, then, whether the mere presence of general revelation, a natural megaphone issued to everyone by God, including the deaf, is enough to be obligation bestowing. If so, then 2 is false.

[4] This might sound strange since we do not usually have an obligation to prevent others from doing things that are morally permissible. But there are different levels or scopes of moral permissibility, such that it is only permissible for the agent involved given their internal deficiencies, but not morally permissible full stop.

[5] I take all of these terms as synonymous or necessarily coincident in this paper. For now, I see no difference between them, and if there are differences, they must be of a kind that would make them contingently coincident to be relevant.

6   Note that this does not mean that DCT-ists actually construe their own understanding of DCT in these terms. In fact, I am not aware of any that do without being pressed.

7   This opens up a world of discussion on free will, action, and moral responsibility that I will leave at this point in the discussion.

8   This does not mean that psychopaths are, even sometimes, sadists (see Levy 2014).

9   The other way would be that Wielenberg is simply not satisfied with the explanations that have been given by DCT-ists for why God would issue commands to almost everybody but psychopaths. If this were the problem, then it is not appropriately an argument against DCT but rather against what some DCT-ists have said that are not essential to DCT. This is not a charitable way to understand Wielenberg, and so I will go with the more powerful interpretation.

10   Indeed, the 'probably' qualifier is necessary since psychopathy does not actually refer to a specific mental disorder but rather a certain level of behavioral problems and emotional deficits.

11   To give an idea of how far gone one must be to be a psychopath, Jeffrey Dahmer scored a 22/40 on the PCL-R and was diagnosed with Borderline Personality Disorder. Dahmer was well known for eating people and collecting hands. The vast majority of the general population does not even score a 1/40, yet Dahmer would have needed 8 more points for one to conclude that he was *probably* a low psychopath. This is still 4 points short of the set of psychopaths that I am referring to.

12   Haji notes that Cordelia Fine, Kennett, and Levy also argue that psychopaths are not morally responsible for their actions.

13   This list includes J. P. Moreland, Matthew Damore, William L. Craig, and Jerry Walls.

14   This paper was presented at the IPA conference at Illinois State University. I am indebted to Jerry Walls, C. Stephen Evans, David Baggett, J. P. Moreland, Matthew Damore, and anonymous reviewers for comments on earlier drafts of this paper.

References

Adams, Robert M. 1999. *Finite and Infinite Goods*. New York: Oxford University Press.

Adshead, Gwen. 2014. The Words but Not the Music: Empathy, Language Deficits, and Psychopathy. In *Being Amoral: Psychopathy and Moral Incapacity*. Edited by Thomas Schramme. Cambridge: MIT Press, pp. 115–36.

Benn, Piers. 2014. Not Caring: Sociopaths and the Suffering of Others. In *Being Amoral: Psychopathy and Moral Incapacity*. Edited by Thomas Schramme. Cambridge: MIT Press, pp. 167–84.

de Sousa, Ronald B., and Douglas Heinrichs. 2010. Will a stroke of neuroscience ever eradicate evil? In *Responsibility and Psychopathy*. Edited by John McMillan and Luca Malatesti. New York: Oxford University Press, pp. 299–318.

Enoch, David. 2008. Luck Between Morality, Law, and Justic. *Theoretical Inquires in Law* 9: 23–59.

Evans, C. Stephen. 2013. *God and Moral Obligations*. Oxford: Oxford University Press.

Flannagan, Matthew. 2021. The Psychopath Objection to Divine Command Theory. *European Journal for Philosophy of Religion* 13. Available online: https://doi.org/10.24204/ejpr.2021.3171 (accessed on 16 November 2022). [CrossRef]

Gillett, Grant. 2010. Intentional Action, moral responsibility, and psychopaths. In *Responsibility and Psychopathy*. Edited by Luca Malatesti and John McMillian. New York: Oxford University Press, pp. 283–98.

Haji, Ishtiyaque. 2010a. Psychopathy, Ethical Perception, and Moral Culpability. *Neuroethics* 3: 135–50. [CrossRef]

Haji, Ishtiyaque. 2010b. The unauthentic evaluative schemes of psychopaths and culpability. In *Responsibility and Psychopathy*. Edited by Luca Malatesti and John McMillian. New York: Oxford University Press, pp. 261–81.

Hare, Robert. 2011. *Without Conscience: The Disturbing World of the Psychopaths Among Us*. New York: The Guilford Press.

Jacobs, Kerrin. 2014. Psychopathic Comportment and Moral Incapacity. In *Being Amoral: Psychopathy and Moral Incapacity*. Edited by Thomas Schramme. Cambridge: MIT Press, pp. 137–66.

Kennett, Jeanette. 2010. Reasons, emotion, and moral judgement in the psychopath. In *Responsibility and Psychopathy*. Edited by Luca Malatesti and John McMillian. New York: Oxford University Press, pp. 243–59.

Kumar, Victor. 2018. Empirical Vindication of Moral Luck. *Nous* 53: 987–1007. [CrossRef]

Levy, Neil. 2010. Psychopathy, responsibility, and the moral/conventional distinction. In *Responsibility and Psychopathy*. Edited by Luca Malatesti and John McMillian. New York: Oxford University Press, pp. 213–26.

Levy, Neil. 2014. Psychopaths and blame: The argument from content. *Philosophical Psychology* 27: 352–67. [CrossRef] [PubMed]

Maibom, Heidi. 2014. Without Fellow Feeling. In *Being Amoral: Psychopathy and Moral Incapacity*. Edited by Thomas Schramme. Cambridge: MIT Press, pp. 91–114.

Mcmillan, John, and Luca Malatesti. 2010. *Responsibility and Psychopathy*. New York: Oxford University Press.

Ryle, Gilbert. 1971. *Collected Papers 2: Collected Essays 1929–1969*. London: Hutchinson and Co.

Schramme, Thomas. 2014. *Being Amoral: Psychopathy and Moral Incapacity*. Cambridge: MIT Press.

Shafer-Landau, Russ. 2003. *Moral Realism: A Defence*. New York: Oxford University Press.

Swinburne, Richard. 2008. God and Morality. *Think* 7: 7–15. [CrossRef]

Talbert, Matthew. 2014. The significance of Psychopathic Wrongdoing. In *Being Amoral: Psychopathy and Moral Incapacity*. Edited by Thomas Schramme. Cambridge: MIT Press, pp. 275–300.

Wielenberg, Erik. 2014. *Robust Ethics: The Metaphysics and Episemology of Godless Normative Realism*. New York: Oxford University Press.

Wielenberg, Erik. 2018. Divine Command Theory and Psychopathy. *Religious Studies* 56: 542–57. [CrossRef]

 *religions*

Article

Theological Utilitarianism, Supervenience, and Intrinsic Value

Matthew Alexander Flannagan

Faculty of Philosophy and Theology, St Peters College, Auckland 1023, New Zealand;
mflannagan@st-peters.school.nz

Abstract: Erik Wielenberg has argued that robust realism can account for the "common-sense moral belief" that "some things distinct from God are intrinsically good". By contrast, theological stateism cannot account for this belief. Hence, robust realism has a theoretical advantage over all forms of theological stateism. This article criticizes Wielenberg's argument. Wielenberg distinguishes between R and D-supervenience. The coherence of Wielenberg's robust realism depends upon this distinction. I argue that this distinction undermines his critique of theological stateism. I will make three points. First, once you utilize the distinction between R and D-supervenience, his argument for the incompatibility of theological stateism and intrinsic value fails. Second, theological stateism is compatible with intrinsic value. The historical example of theological utilitarianism, expounded by thinkers George Berkeley and William Paley, shows someone can accept that moral properties simultaneously R supervene upon God's will and D supervene upon the natural properties of actions. Third, robust realism and theological stateism are in the same boat regarding intrinsic value once we distinguish between R and D-supervenience.

Keywords: supervenience; intrinsic value; god and morality; theological utilitarianism; Erik Wielenberg; George Berkeley; William Paley; theological voluntarism

1. Introduction

Can objective moral requirements exist independently of God? Wielenberg (2014) defends an affirmative answer to this question. He defends a position called "robust realism", the thesis that the property of being morally required is a sui generis non-natural property that supervenes upon natural properties.

In recent years robust realism has received several important defenses from philosophers such as Shafer-Landau (2003), Parfit (2011), and Enoch (2011). According to Wielenberg, robust realism implies that moral properties do not depend upon God's will. However, this implication has received "very little attention, much less defense from its most prominent defenders". (Wielenberg 2014, p. 41) "Engagement with theistic approaches to morality is almost entirely absent from recent book-length defenses of robust normative realism". (p. 41) This is problematic because "both worthwhile theistic theories of morality and challenging arguments against secular moral realism" (p. 41) exist.

In the last few decades, many contemporary theists have embraced and defended a divine command theory of ethics whereby moral requirements depend immediately upon God's will or commands (See, for example (Adams 1999; Alston 1990; Baggett and Walls 2011; Craig 2003; Evans 2013; Forrest 1989; Flannagan and Copan 2014; Wierenga 1989; Wainwright 2005)). Others, such as Zagzebski (2004), Murphy (2011), and Carson (1990), have developed accounts of central moral concepts such as virtues, rights, and goodness, in which God plays a central ontological role. Wielenberg uses the umbrella term "theological stateism" (TS) to refer to these theories.

The problem is that "to the extent that such theistic theories are plausible, "they constitute a viable alternative to robust normative realism" (Wielenberg 2014, p. 42) and "present a challenge to this view" (p. 42). Consequently, "an important part of providing a full defense of robust normative realism is addressing these theories and challenges (p. 41)".

Citation: Flannagan, Matthew Alexander. 2023. Theological Utilitarianism, Supervenience, and Intrinsic Value. *Religions* 14: 413. https://doi.org/10.3390/rel14030413

Academic Editors: David Baggett and John McDowell

Received: 23 January 2023
Revised: 10 March 2023
Accepted: 14 March 2023
Published: 17 March 2023

Wielenberg (2014) is an attempt to address this problem. Wielenberg contends that robust realism is preferable to TS. This is because, unlike TS, Robust realism is consistent with the intuition that certain things apart from God have intrinsic value.

This paper challenges this contention. I will offer three responses. First, Wielenberg's argument that TS cannot accommodate intrinsic value is unsound. Second, an important historical example of TS, theological utilitarianism, shows that TS is compatible with intrinsic value. Third, robust realism is in no better position regarding intrinsic value than TS.

2. Wielenberg's Metaethical Theory

Before doing this, let me briefly elaborate on Wielenberg's metaethical theory. Wielenberg contends that moral properties are sui generis. They are not identical with or reducible to any natural property, such as the property of causing pain. Nor are they supernatural properties, such as being commanded or willed by God. However, moral properties supervene upon natural properties, and acts have the moral properties they have "because" of their natural properties.

Consider Francis of Assisi;[1] if we judge him to be a good person, it will be because of the natural features of his actions. He has refrained from killing and lying, avoided harming others, and devoted himself to benefiting them. He is good because his actions have consistently had these properties. Suppose Francis's twin Dominic of Milan, performs the same kinds of actions as Francis. Dominic also refrains from killing and lying, has avoided harming others, and has devoted himself to benefiting them. He does so with the same motives and intentions, and his actions have the same consequences. Francis and Dominic do not differ in any other way. In such a situation, judging Dominic as not a good person but a bad person would be incomprehensible.

This example illustrates a feature deeply ingrained in our moral thought and practice. Even if moral properties are not identical to natural properties, the former supervene upon the latter: Two actions can't have the same non-moral or descriptive properties and not have the same moral properties. Actions have the moral properties they do because of their natural descriptive properties.

The supervenience relationship between natural and moral properties has seemed to some philosophers to be obscure. Mackie (1977) states:

> Another way of bringing out this queerness is to ask, about anything that is supposed to have some objective moral quality, how this is linked with its natural features. What is the connection between the natural fact that an action is a piece of deliberate cruelty—say, causing pain just for fun—and the moral fact that it is wrong? It cannot be an entailment, a logical or semantic necessity. Yet it is not merely that the two features occur together. The wrongness must somehow be 'consequential' or 'supervenient'; it is wrong because it is a piece of deliberate cruelty. But just what in the world is signified by this 'because'? And how do we know the relation that it signifies (Mackie 1977, p. 41)

Mackie's concern is not just that moral and natural features are modally co-variant: any action with the same natural properties necessarily has the same moral ones. It is that there is some "because" relationship that holds between them. Actions have the moral properties they do *because* they have certain natural properties. But what is the nature of this sort of explanatory relationship? It isn't the kind of physical causation that occurs when an apple falls to the ground, and it isn't a logical or analytic entailment. What is it?[2]

Wielenberg answers that the supervenience relationship consists of what he calls "robust causation". Natural properties directly cause moral properties to be instantiated unmediated by any laws of nature. This causal relationship is metaphysically necessary, so it holds in all possible worlds. He explicates robust causation by noting the relationship theists believe holds between God and the created world. His proposal is that:

[O]n the theistic view, there is a distinctive and robust causal relation that holds between divine willing and its effects, and that *this same sort of causal relation holds between non-moral and moral properties* . . . Secular views often ascribe to the natural world powers that theists are inclined to ascribe to God. By ascribing to non-moral properties rather than God the power to make moral properties be instantiated, *my view does this as well.* (Wielenberg 2014, p. 20) (emphasis added)

3. Wielenberg's Argument

Having clarified Wielenberg's metaethics, I turn to his argument against TS. Wielenberg argues that robust realism is preferable to TS. Why? Because, unlike TS, robust realism is consistent with the intuition that certain things have intrinsic value:

I suggest that among our common-sense moral beliefs are the belief that some things distinct from God are intrinsically good: for example, the pleasure of an innocent back rub, or the love between parent and child", . . . "[B]ecause non-theistic robust normative realism allows for the intrinsic goodness of things distinct from God, that theory fares better in this respect than its theistic alternatives". (Wielenberg 2014, p. 84)

By "the intrinsic value of a given thing", Wielenberg means the "value it has, if any, in virtue of its intrinsic properties". Something's extrinsic value "is the value it has in virtue of how it is related to things apart from itself (p. 2)".

Why can't TS accommodate the commonsense view that some things have intrinsic value? Because theological stateists make the moral value of finite objects depend upon their relationship with God:

A second noteworthy aspect of Adams's view is its implication that no finite thing is intrinsically good (or evil) *since the goodness (and badness) of all finite things is dependent upon their relationship to God.* Craig follows Adams in holding that finite goodness = resemblance to the necessarily existing divine nature. (Wielenberg 2014, p. 44) (Emphasis mine)

Later he refers to (Murphy 2011);

Back in Section 2.2, I noted that Adams's theory implies that no finite thing is intrinsically good (or evil) since, on Adams's view, the goodness (and badness) of all finite things is partly determined by how they are related to God. Consequently, Adams's view entails that nothing distinct from God is intrinsically good. Murphy also holds that the goodness of things distinct from God consists in their standing in a certain relationship to God; their goodness is thus extrinsic rather than intrinsic because it is explained not merely by their intrinsic properties but also by certain properties of God. (Wielenberg 2014, pp. 83–84)

Wielenberg's argument then is as follows: Something has intrinsic value if it is valuable "*in virtue* of its intrinsic properties" and not "*in virtue* of how it is related to things apart from itself". However, TS entails that "the value of all finite things is *dependent* upon their relationship to God" (emphasis mine) (p. 44). Consequently, TS entails "nothing distinct from God is intrinsically good".

Below, I will make three responses to this argument.

4. Is the Argument Sound?

My first response is that the argument is unsound. For Wielenberg's argument to be valid, the phrase "in virtue" in Wielenberg's definition of intrinsic value must refer to the same kind of dependence relationship that theological stateists postulate holds between God and the value of finite things. However, this is not the case.[3]

Wielenberg spends some time elaborating on what he means when he says that intrinsic value is the value something has *in virtue* of its intrinsic properties. In doing so, he distinguishes between two different kinds of supervenience relationship. One is "reductive supervenience" (or R-supervenience). This is where a moral property M supervenes upon a base property B because the moral property is *identical* to the base property. The second is "De-Paul supervenience" (D-supervenience). If a moral property M D-supervenes upon a base property B, then "M is not identical with, reducible to or entirely constituted by B"; instead, "B's instantiation makes M be instantiated". (Wielenberg 2014, pp. 9–15)

D-supervenience and R-supervenience are distinct relationships. A person can consistently deny that moral properties R supervene upon a base property and affirm they do D supervene upon that property. This is implicit in the thesis of Robust Realism itself. Robust realists deny that moral properties R-supervene upon natural properties and hold that moral properties are sui generis. So, Moral properties are not identical or reducible to any natural property. However, moral properties do D-supervene upon natural properties. In Wielenberg's view, natural properties make or "robustly cause" moral properties to be instantiated.[4]

When Wielenberg says something's intrinsic value is its value *in virtue of its* intrinsic properties and its extrinsic value "is the value it has *in virtue* of how it is related to things apart from itself", the phrase "in virtue" is shorthand for a relationship of D-supervenience.

> If there are entities distinct from God that possess intrinsic value, then Craig's claim is mistaken. I think that there are such entities. As I suggested in chapter one, some finite things pass the isolation and annihilation tests, which suggests that such things are intrinsically valuable. *The intrinsic value of such entities D-supervenes upon some set of their intrinsic properties and not on how they are related to other things.* (Wielenberg 2014, p. 44) ... I will call the supervenience of M upon the base properties due to the fact that the base properties being instantiated makes M be instantiated D-supervenience ("D" for "DePaul"). In my view, the most plausible way of understanding the "in virtue of" relation that I earlier claimed holds between the intrinsic properties of certain things and their intrinsic value is as making. To claim that a given thing is intrinsically valuable is to claim that some of that thing's intrinsic properties make it valuable, and the intrinsic value of a given thing is whatever value it has that is explained by its intrinsic properties. More generally, I think that moral properties—indeed all normative properties—D-supervene upon non-normative properties. (Wielenberg 2014, p. 13) (Emphasis mine)

The problem is that proponents of TS do not deny that moral properties *D supervene* upon the intrinsic properties of finite objects. Nor are they committed to this claim. When theological stateists like Murphy, Adams, or Craig contend that the goodness of all finite things depends upon their relationship with God, they claim only that goodness *R supervenes* upon this relationship. Consider what Wielenberg said when he criticized Craig and Adams:

> A noteworthy feature of Adams's view is its implication that no finite thing is intrinsically good (or evil) since the goodness (and badness of things) of all finite things is dependent upon their relationship to God. Craig follows Adams in holding *that finite goodness = resemblance to the necessarily existing divine nature...* (Emphasis mine) (Wielenberg 2014, p. 44)

Wielenberg points out that Adams and Craig hold that the goodness of finite things *depends* on their relationship with God. This is correct. However, in the highlighted sentence, Wielenberg spells out the kind of dependence relationship they are referring to. A relationship whereby "finite goodness = resemblance to the necessarily existing divine nature". Adams believes goodness is identical to this relationship.

Wielenberg makes this explicit when he offers further criticism of Craig and Adams:

> It might be thought that Adams's theory provides a foundation for such ethical facts; doesn't the theory tell us, for instance, that the fact that the Good exists is grounded in the fact that God exists? The answer is no; since the Good just is God, the existence of God cannot explain or ground the existence of the Good. In the context of Adams's view, the claim that God serves as the foundation of

the Good is no more sensible than the claim that H2O serves as the foundation of water. Indeed, once we see that, on Adams's view the Good = God, we see that Adams's theory entails that the Good has no external foundation, since God has no external foundation. (Wielenberg 2014, p. 43)

Here Wielenberg explains that Adams's (and Craig's) position is that goodness *just is* a relationship between finite objects and God. The relationship between God and the good is the kind of relationship that holds between water and H20, a relationship of synthetic identity. Consequently, their position is the goodness of finite objects *R-supervenes* upon their relationship with God.

The upshot is this: If we use the word "in virtue" in the way that Wielenberg does, then TS does not entail that things distinct from God cannot have value *in virtue* of their intrinsic properties. TS entails the goodness of created things R supervenes upon their relationship to God. However, this does not entail that their goodness D supervenes upon God. Consequently, Wielenberg has not shown that TS is incompatible with the commonsense intuition that finite objects can have intrinsic value.

5. Is Theological Stateism Compatible with Intrinsic Value?

If the above argument succeeds, Wielenberg has failed to demonstrate an incompatibility between TS and the commonsense idea that some things have intrinsic value. My second response is to argue that the two are logically compatible.

The method here is like that used by Plantinga regarding the problem of evil. Mackie (1955) argued that the existence of God is logically inconsistent with the existence of evil. In response, Plantinga pointed out that to prove two propositions are consistent, one needs only to come up with a logically possible situation where both would be true. (Plantinga 1986, pp. 122–23). I will follow a similar method. I suggest a logically possible or coherent model which–if true, would entail both that TS is true and actions can be good, bad, right, or wrong in virtue of their intrinsic properties. While I do believe something like the model I sketch is correct. I will assume only that it is possible and that this model of the relationship between God's commands and morality is coherent. If I am correct, a theological stateist can consistently accept the commonsense belief that some things distinct from God have intrinsic value.

5.1. Theological Utilitarianism

The model I will utilize is known to intellectual historians as theological utilitarianism[5]. Hayry (2012) defines theological utilitarianism as: "a doctrine according to which we must promote the good of humanity because God, our universally benevolent creator, wants us to do so". (p. 3). It represents a standard way theists thought about God's commands and morality in the 18th and 19th centuries. I will look at two representative examples.

5.1.1. George Berkeley's Passive Obedience

Berkeley (1712) gives an early exposition of theological utilitarianism in his sermons on *Passive Obedience*. Berkeley states that we "denominate" things "*Good or Evil*". as they are fitted to augment or impair our Happiness". By contrast, "moral goodness" consists "in conformity to the laws of God". Berkeley appears to use the phrase "good or evil" to refer to the concept of "wellbeing" or "prudential value": what is good or an individual. By "moral goodness", Berkeley had a deontological concept in mind. The term is used synonymously with doing one's "duty" following "natural law", following "moral rules", or "precepts" by which actions are praised or blamed. When Berkeley contends that "Moral Goodness" consists of "Conformity to the Laws of God". He identifies himself as a divine command theorist about deontological properties. (Berkeley 1712).[6]

Berkeley articulated the relationship between moral and non-moral goodness in a dense passage:

Now, as God is a Being of Infinite Goodness, it is plain the end he proposes is *Good*. But God enjoying in himself all possible Perfection, it follows that it is not his own good, but that of his Creatures. Again, the Moral Actions of Men are entirely terminated within themselves, so as to have no influence on the other orders of Intelligences or reasonable Creatures: The end therefore to be procured by them, can be no other than the good of Men. But as nothing in a natural State can entitle one Man more than another to the favour of God, except only Moral Goodness, which consisting in a Conformity to the Laws of God, doth presuppose the being of such Laws, and Law ever supposing an end, to which it guides our actions, it follows that Antecedent to the end proposed by God, no distinction can be conceived between Men; that end therefore itself or general design of Providence is not determined or limited by any Respect of Persons: It is not therefore the private Good of this or that Man, Nation or Age, but the general wellbeing of all Men, of all Nations, of all Ages of the World, which God designs should be procured by the concurring Actions of each individual. (Berkeley 1712)

Because God is impartial[7] and benevolent,[8] his goal in issuing the commands he does is that human beings will collectively promote the happiness of his creatures impartially considered. Berkeley proceeded to identify two ways God could promote this goal. One would be to command that "everyone upon each particular Occasion, to consult the Publick Good" directly "and always to do that, which to him shall seem in the present time and circumstances, most to conduce to it. Without the injunction of any specific universal Rules of Morality" The second is to command "the Observation of some determinate, established Laws, which, if Universally practised, have from the Nature of things an Essential fitness to procure the wellbeing of Mankind".

Berkeley raised several objections to the first of these options. In doing so, he anticipated the distinction between rule and act utilitarianism and standard self-effacing objections to act utilitarianism. Berkeley argued that anyone committed to promoting the happiness of others would not command people to accept act utilitarianism as a rule or decision procedure. Public endorsement and acceptance of the rule "do whatever maximizes utility" would probably not maximize utility. If fallible people like us attempted to determine what to do on a case-by-case basis based on our assessment of the consequences, we would fail to maximize utility. For this reason, Berkeley concluded that God followed the second method. God promulgated a *deontological* code that would maximize welfare if fallible agents like us attempted to follow and internalize it.

Stephen Darwall (2006) argues that the best way to interpret Berkeley is to distinguish between his metaethical and normative theories. His metaethical theory attempts "to answer metaphysical questions of what goodness and rightness, respectively, are". (p 314). On the other hand, his normative theory "concerns "what is good and right, respectively". (p 314). Berkeley proposed a divine command *metaethical* theory; "moral goodness consists" in "Conformity to the Laws of God". However, Berkeley's *normative* theory was rule-utilitarian. The property of being morally required is identical to the property of being commanded by God. God commands us to follow a code of rules, the widespread acceptance of which would promote happiness.

5.1.2. William Paley's Principles of Moral and Political Philosophy

Berkeley had intended to write a systematic defense of his moral theory in Part II of *A Treatise Concerning the Principles of Human Knowledge*. But the manuscript of this was lost, and he never re-wrote it (Broad 1953, p. 72). For this reason, we do not get a systematic presentation of theological utilitarianism theory until much later. William Paley's ([1785] 1998) *Principles of Moral and Political Philosophy* is the most famous and systematic exposition of theological utilitarianism. Each of the features I just attributed to Berkeley can be found in Paley's *Principles*.

First, Paley describes virtue as doing "good to mankind" (p. 221). Elsewhere he talks of promoting the "public good" (p. 226). He used these terms to refer to aggregate well-being. Like Berkeley, Paley's account of well-being is hedonist.

In strictness, any condition may be denominated happy, in which the amount or aggregate of pleasure exceeds that of pain, and the degree of happiness depends upon the quantity of this excess. And the greatest quantity of it ordinarily attainable in human life, is what we mean by happiness when we inquire or pronounce what human happiness consists in (p. 213)

Second, Like Berkeley, Paley defended a divine command account of moral obligation.[9] In book II, Paley asks, "what do we mean when we say someone is obliged to do something? He identifies a paradigmatic case; to say someone is obliged to act is to say they are compelled to act by a "violent motive" resulting "from the command of another" (p. 227). (By violent motive, Paley means something like "decisive reason").[10] Paley argued that the property of being commanded by God fits this description. We are obliged to keep our word "[b]ecause I am urged to do so 'by a violent motive' (namely, the expectation of being after this life rewarded, if I do, or punished for it, if I do not), "resulting from the command of another" (namely, of God)". (p. 228)

Paley also combined these two ideas in a manner analogous to Berkeley. He concluded a chapter on God's benevolence as follows:

We conclude, therefore, that God wills and wishes the happiness of his creatures. And this conclusion being once established, we are at liberty to go on with the rule built upon it, namely, "that the method of coming at the will of God, concerning any action, by the light of nature, is to inquire into the tendency of that action to promote or diminish the general happiness. (p. 232)

Like Berkeley, Paley is a rule utilitarian.[11] In response to the objection that there are cases where assassinating an innocent person would promote utility Paley distinguished between the "general" and "particular consequences" (p. 233) of acts. The particular consequence "is the mischief which that single action directly and immediately occasions. (p. 233)" However, "The general consequence of any action may be estimated by asking what the consequence would be if the same sort of actions were generally permitted" (p. 235). Paley clarified that his theory assesses the morality of actions by the general, not the particular consequences of those actions. The particular consequences of assassinating an innocent person on a given occasion might be beneficial. However, the consequences of adopting a rule permitting "every man to kill anyone he meets, whom he thinks noxious or useless" would be pernicious. (p. 233) For this reason God condemns it.

Paley illustrates this distinction through several examples. Consider counterfeiting money. Paley states that a counterfeiting case's "particular consequence" is the loss of "a single guinea to the person who receives the counterfeit money" that appears trivial. However, "the general consequence", i.e., "the consequence that would ensue if the same practice were generally permitted) is to abolish the use of money". This is much more serious. The immorality of counterfeiting is based on the general consequences, not the particular consequences.

Similarly, the "particular consequence" of horse theft is "a loss to the owner, to the amount horse stolen". The general consequence is that "the land could not be occupied, nor the market supplied, with this kind of stock". (p. 235). Paley's theory is that God commands certain acts because those acts have good *general* consequences. If human beings generally adopted a rule requiring such acts to guide their conduct, good consequences would ensue.

The same distinction is evident in Paley's answers to several moral questions. Consider Paley's discussion of religious tolerance. In addressing this question, Paley states that we should not consider whether a particular act of suppressing false religion has good results on a particular occasion. Instead, we should consider what the results would be if "the kind of interference which he [the magistrate] is about to exercise...were adopted as a common maxim amongst states and princes or received as a general rule for the conduct of government in matters of religion". Paley made a similar argument on the question of sexual morality. In examining the traditional Christian condemnation of fornication,

Paley contended that the question is not whether fornicating on a particular occasion "diminishes marriage". Instead, the question is what the consequences would be "if the same licentiousness were universal? Or what should hinder it's becoming universal if it is innocent or allowable in him?"

In both these cases, it is not the consequences of individual actions that determine the rightness or wrongness of an action. Instead, the overall long-term consequences of the general adoption of a rule permitting everyone to perform these actions are determinative.

For these reasons, it is reasonable to construe Paley as offering a divine command metaethical theory and a rule utilitarian normative theory. Paley offers the definition of virtue provided by his associate Edmund Law ([1758] 1998). According to this definition, "the good of mankind is the subject, the will of God the rule" of all virtue. Law thinks moral rules are expressions of God's will. By contrast, doing good is the "material" part of virtue: what the will of God requires". So, while moral rules are divine commands or rules laid down by God, those rules direct us to the performance of acts that have good general consequences.

5.1.3. The Implications of Theological Utilitarianism

The positions of Berkeley and Paley are of considerable interest. Both wrote before Bentham. Bothanticipated the distinction between rule and act utilitarianism before Richard Brandt made it famous in the 1950s[12]. However, for our purposes, two things are noteworthy.

First, as I have read both Paley and Berkeley, their position entails that moral properties R supervene upon God's will or commands. For Berkeley, "Moral Goodness" consists of "Conformity to the Laws of God". For Paley being morally obligated to do an action just is being commanded or induced by God to do it.

Second, moral properties D *supervene* upon various natural properties of acts. Theological utilitarianism implies that the property of being morally good modally co-varies with an action's natural or descriptive properties. Because God is essentially impartial and benevolent, he promulgates rules that promote general happiness. Acts that God prohibits will co-vary with acts with natural or descriptive features that violate those rules. Moreover, these properties do not just co-vary; the instantiation of the latter *depends upon* and is brought about because of the existence of the former. God commands certain acts because of their general consequences. Because the property of being commanded by God is the property of being morally required, it follows that acts are right and wrong *because* of the natural and descriptive features they possess.

This also appears to be a case of "robust causation". For Wielenberg, God's bringing about something by willing is a paradigm of the robust causal relationship that holds when something D supervenes upon another thing. Is not this what occurs here? God's commanding or prohibiting are expressions of God's will. God perceives that an action has certain utilitarian natural properties. He expresses his will that it be done or not be done, and this expression of his will brings a moral property into existence.

One might object as follows: rule utilitarianism cannot account for the intrinsic value of acts. Because the property of being in conformity with a rule whose universal acceptance would maximize well-being is not an intrinsic property of a *singular* action. However, it is not clear to me if this is correct. According to Nathanson, the basic idea of rule utilitarianism has two parts. ""A moral rule is justified if its inclusion into our moral code would create more utility than other possible rules (or no rule at all)." And "a specific action is morally justified if it conforms to a justified moral rule" (emphasis added). (Nathanson 2010, p. 194) If this is correct, then conformity with a rule whose acceptance would maximize well-being is a property of singular actions. God requires certain actions because they fall under a particular description specified by a moral rule. The rule is justified by the consequences, of general acceptance. The act however is not.[13]

Consequently, theological Utilitarianism provides an example of a version of theological Stateism whereby moral properties do D-supervene upon the intrinsic natural features of finite things.

5.1.4. The Influence of Theological Utilitarianism

Nor is this an unrepresentative idiosyncratic position. Paley and Berkley's combination of a divine command meta-ethic with a rule utilitarian normative theory was highly influential. It represents a standard way theists thought about God's commands and morality in the 18th century. (Brogan 1959) argues that this is the position of John Locke. (Louden 1995) finds elements of it in Butler's writings.

Paley published *The Principles* in 1785. However, he based them on lectures he delivered during his tenure at Cambridge between 1766 and 1776. The ideas in these lectures were not original to him. In the preface, Paley describes himself as a compiler of previous writers.[14] His lectures synthesized the work of earlier writers such as Waterland ([1730] 2011), Gay ([1731] 1998), Rutherford ([1744] 2018), Brown ([1751] 1998), and Jenyns (Jenyns [1757] 1998). Law ([1758] 1998), Tucker ([1768] 1998). Paley synthesized and expounded a widespread understanding of the relationship between God's commands and happiness that had been dominant at Cambridge[15] for several decades *before* Bentham. It continued to be expounded in the 19th century by people like Austin ([1832] 1995).

The Principles was a required text in moral philosophy at Cambridge from 1787 until the 1840s. Required reading at Durham and Sydney Universities until the middle of the nineteenth century and required reading at Manitoba University until the late nineteenth century (Francis 1989). Smith (1954) argues that Paley's writings were once as well known in American colleges as were the readers and spellers of William McGuffey and Noah Webster in elementary schools. For these reasons, *The principles* became the most widely read and cited textbook on moral philosophy in the early nineteenth century. Theological utilitarianism was a significant philosophical undermining of many of the conservative responses to the French revolution, offering a theoretical basis to critique ideas of social contract theory and abstract natural rights of man. (Scofield 1986). *The Principles* were also frequently cited in moral and political debates over the corn law and the poor laws of the nineteenth-century era. (Horne 1985) Schneewind (1977) contends, "utilitarianism first became widely known in England through the work of William Paley" (p. 122). Paley, not Bentham being its most well-known exponent.

This means some of the most paradigmatic influential examples of divine command metaethics entailed both that moral properties R supervene upon God's commands and D supervene upon the natural properties of acts. Divine command metaethics is a form of theological stateism. Consequently, theological stateism is not inconsistent with the existence of intrinsic value.

6. Does Robust Realism Provide a Better Account of Intrinsic Value?

This brings me to my third and last response. Once we understand Wielenberg's distinction between R and D-supervenience, robust realism and theological stateism are in the same boat regarding the existence of intrinsically valuable things.

I noted that Wielenberg defines intrinsic value as the value something has "in virtue of its intrinsic properties. We saw that Wielenberg's definition of this locution is in terms of D-supervenience. Let's assume this is correct. Suppose the phrase "in virtue" refers to D-supervenience. In that case, *both* TS and Robust realism can account for intrinsic value. Robust realism holds that actions have sui generis non-natural properties *because* they have natural properties. By contrast, TS contends that God has certain relationships to actions *because* they have certain natural properties. God has the power to issue commands. If God commands that an action be performed, he immediately and directly brings it about that the action in question has been commanded by God. According to Robust realism, natural properties can directly and immediately bring about that non-natural properties exist. The kind of robust causation in each case is the same, even though one is attributed to God and the other to nature.

Perhaps someone could revise Wielenberg's objection, and they could contend that it can be rerun in a context where the phrase "in virtue" refers instead to R supervenience. If intrinsic value is understood this way, then TS will be incompatible with intrinsic values. TS entails that moral properties are reducible to theological properties or relationships between finite things and God. If they are identical to a theological property, then they are not identical to a natural property distinct from God.

One could rerun Wielenberg's argument this way. The problem is that one can also rerun the same argument to show that Robust realism is incompatible with intrinsic value. Robust realism holds that moral properties are "real and *sui-generis*; they are *non-natural and not reducible to any other sort of property*" (Emphasis added). If moral properties are not reducible to other properties, then they also do not R supervene upon the intrinsic properties of distinct finite things. Robust realism will imply that every finite thing R supervenes, not upon its intrinsic properties, but on its relationship to distinct sui generis non-natural properties. No finite thing will have intrinsic value, and everything has extrinsic value.

One might interpret my argument above in the following way. Theological stateism can give an explanation of the D supervenience of moral properties upon non-moral or descriptive properties of action. Robust Realism al la Wielenberg cannot. We might ask why do moral properties D supervene upon these non-moral properties? Why do these descriptive or non-moral properties of the action make it the case that these moral properties are instantiated? Theological utilitarianism answers this question; God links them this way. But this is vague and needs more elaboration. We need to answer the question as to why God would establish this relationship, and defences of theological statism would also need to answer the Euthyphro dilemma.[16]

However, one should not interpret the argument this way. Wielenberg does give an explanation of the D supervenience of moral properties upon non-moral properties. He contends the former "Robustly" causes the latter, and his understanding of Robust causation is modelled on the kind of answer theists provide when they claim God conserves the universe in being. My argument in this section is that the kind of answer he gives and the answer the theological utilitarian both account for the data. Wielenberg cannot claim that Robust realism has an advantage on this point.

More to the point, however, that theological utilitarianism doesn't simply state that "God links" these properties. It gives an account of why he does this. God is essentially impartial and benevolent. For this reason, he promulgates a moral code that promotes his creatures' well-being (impartially considered). Actions are prohibited because they have descriptive features, which means they violate such rules. This explanation contains much more substantive content than simply saying, "God links them". It also explains why God links them the way he does.

As to the Euthyphro dilemma, a complete defence of theological statism would have to say something about the Euthyphro dilemma. However, this article is not a complete defence of theological statism. It is an attempt to rebut one argument against such theories. To address every objection to these theories or even give a rebuttal of various versions of the Euthyphro dilemma would require a separate paper or papers.[17]

7. Conclusions

Wielenberg's thesis is that while moral properties are not identical to natural properties, they do supervene upon these properties. This thesis depends crucially on a distinction between R and D-supervenience. I have argued that this distinction enables a defender of theological stateism to coherently evade the criticisms Wielenberg makes. Theological stateists can maintain that moral properties R supervene upon theological properties. The property of being morally required or morally good is identical to the property of being related to God's commands, nature, or will in a relevant way. However, moral properties

D supervene upon the natural properties of finite things. God relates to those things in virtue of or because they have certain properties, such as promoting human flourishing and happiness. There is no incompatibility between theological stateism and the common-sense moral belief that some things have intrinsic value.

Funding: This research received no external funding.

Institutional Review Board Statement: Not applicable.

Informed Consent Statement: Not applicable.

Data Availability Statement: Not applicable.

Conflicts of Interest: The authors declare no conflict of interest.

Notes

1. Hare (1952, p. 145) inspires this example.
2. See (Moberger 2019) for an explanation and clarification about Mackie's challenge.
3. This section will recap the argument of made in (Flannagan 2017).
4. Given, Wielenberg's definitions D-supervenience and R supervenience are mutually exclusive relationships. Something R supervenes upon a base property when it is identical to that property. It D supervenes upon it when it is not identical with that property, but its instantiation causes the base property to be instantiated. Obviously, if something is not identical with a base property, then it does not R supervene upon it. Moreover, if something is identical to a base property, then its instantiation t "cause" the base property to exist. That would be a case of self-causation.
5. The term "theological utilitarianism" originates with (Stephen 1881). See also (Albee 1901) for an early discussion of theological utilitarianism. More recent studies include (Crimmins 1998) (Wainwright 2005) (Cole 1987, 1991) and (O'Flaherty 2018). Heydt (2014) suggests the term "Anglican utilitarianism".
6. In distinguishing non-moral and moral goodness the way he did, Berkeley was following Locke (Locke 1689).
7. Berkeley's reference to God showing no "respect of persons" alludes to how the kings James Bible describes God's impartiality. See, for example, Deuteronomy 1:17, Deuteronomy 16:19, Chronicles 19:7, Proverbs 24:23, Proverbs 28:21, Acts 10:34, Romans 2:11, Ephesians 6:9, Colossians 3:25, James 2:1, James 2:9, 1 Peter 1:17.
8. The phrase "infinite goodness" is from the 39 articles of the church of England. It is how articles summarize the doctrine of God's essential goodness. (Louden 1995) points out that God's "infinite" goodness was typically understood as "benevolence", a disposition or desire to communicate happiness to his creatures. This understanding of what it means to call God good is found in several seventeenth and eighteenth-century writers such as Locke, William King, Clarke, Edmund Law, John Gay, Butler, Paley, and Adam Smith. In some cases, these authors offer the same line of argument Berkeley makes in this passage when they do so.
9. Strictly speaking, Berkeley claims that moral goodness consists in conformity with God's commands. However, Paley offers a divine command theory of moral obligation. However, if I am correct that when Berkeley uses the term "moral goodness", he has a deontological concept in mind, then this difference is largely verbal.
10. (Tucker [1768] 1998) whom Paley closely followed, used the phrase "violent motive" to refer to a motive, the resistance of which was painful. In other words, a motive is strong compared to any alternative motives to the contrary. (Paley [1785] 1998) earlier (BK I.5) rejected the idea that the "remorse of conscience" and approval of one moral sense was sufficient to ground the authority of morality because " But this remorse may be borne with: and if the sinner choose to bear with it, for the sake of the pleasure or the profit which he expects from his wickedness; or finds the pleasure of the sin to exceed the remorse of conscience, of which he alone is the judge", In (Bk II: 2) He also noted that "gratitude" was not a "violent enough" motive to ground obligation "because the inducement does not rise high enough". He goes on to respond to Hume's account of morality without God with the comment "let them consider, whether any motives there proposed are likely to be found sufficient to withhold men from the gratification of lust, revenge, envy, ambition, avarice; or to prevent the existence of these passions. Unless they rise up from this celebrated essay, with stronger impressions upon their minds than it ever left upon mine, they will acknowledge the necessity of additional sanctions".(Bk II.4). This all suggests that, for Paley, one needed to find a demand that obliged people with motives or reason strong or "violent" enough that the reasons in favor of following the demand were always greater or stronger than the reasons or motives one had for non-compliance.
11. (Crisp 2019, pp. 97–98) argues that Paley was an act utilitarian, who held that rules function as a good way to assess what is right and wrong, but that wrongness does not consist in being in accordance with a rule. Given that Paley understood moral rules as divine laws that God held one accountable for following and defined obligation in terms of God's will, I think this conclusion is doubtful. A good defense of the alternative view, which goes into more detail on rules in Paley's system, is Tuckness (2021, pp. 85–92).

[12] (Nathanson 2014) expresses the common wisdom "The contrast between act and rule utilitarianism, though previously noted by some philosophers, was not sharply drawn until the late 1950s when Richard Brandt introduced this terminology. (Other terms that have been used to make this contrast are "direct" and "extreme" for act utilitarianism and "indirect" and "restricted" for rule utilitarianism.) Because the contrast had not been sharply drawn, earlier utilitarians like Bentham and Mill sometimes apply the principle of utility to actions and sometimes apply it to the choice of rules for evaluating action". Whether or not the distinction is clear in Bentham and Mill, Berkeley explicitly drew the distinction in 1712 and rejected the act utilitarian position.

[13] An anonymous reviewer brought this objection to my attention.

[14] Schneewind (2002) states that Paley's theory was: "an assemblage of ideas developed by others and is presented to be learned by students rather than debated by colleagues". (p. 446).

[15] Waterland, Gay, Jenyns, Law, Rutherford, and Brown were all associated with Cambridge University.

[16] I owe an anonymous reviewer for this objection.

[17] See (Flannagan 2019, 2022) for a recent response to the Euthyphro dilemma.

References

Adams, Robert. 1999. *Finite and Infinite Goods: A Framework for Ethics*. Oxford: Oxford University Press.

Albee, Ernest. 1901. *A History of English Utilitarianism*. London: Swan Sonnenschein, Macmillan.

Alston, William. 1990. Some Suggestions for Divine Command Theorists. In *Christian Theism and the Problems of Philosophy*. Edited by Michael Beaty. Notre Dame: University of Notre Dame Press, pp. 303–26.

Austin, John. 1995. *The Province of Jurisprudence Determined*. Edited by Willard Rumble. Cambridge: Cambridge University Press. First published in 1832.

Baggett, David, and Jerry Walls. 2011. *Good God: The Theistic Foundations of Morality*. Oxford: Oxford University Press.

Berkeley, George. 1712. "A Discourse on Passive Obedience". Eighteenth Century Collections Online. Available online: https://quod.lib.umich.edu/e/ecco/004899015.0001.000/1:3?rgn=div1;view=fulltext (accessed on 15 September 2021).

Broad, C. D. 1953. Berkeley's Theory of Morals. *Revue Internationale de Philosophie* 23–24: 72–86.

Brogan, A. P. 1959. John Locke and Utilitarianism. *Ethics* 69: 79–93. [CrossRef]

Brown, John. 1998. 'On Motives to Virtue, The Necessity of Religious Principle' From the Essays on the Characteristics of the Earl of Shaftesbury. In *Utilitarianism and Religion*. Edited by James Crimmins. Bristol: Theommes Press, pp. 54–106. First published in 1751.

Carson, Thomas L. 1990. *Value and the Good Life*. Notre Dame: Notre Dame University Press.

Cole, Graham. 1987. A Note on Paley and His School—Was Sir Leslie Stephen Mistaken? *Tyndale Bulletin* 38: 151–56. [CrossRef]

Cole, Graham. 1991. Theological Utilitarianism and The Eclipse of the Theistic Sanction. *Tyndale Bulletin* 42: 226–44. [CrossRef]

Craig, William Lane. 2003. *Philosophical Foundations of a Christian World View*. Downers Grover: Intervarsity Press.

Crimmins, James E. 1998. *Utilitarians and Religion*. Bristol: Theommes Press.

Crisp, Roger. 2019. *Sacrifice Regained: Morality and Self-Interest in British Moral Philosophy from Hobbes to Bentham*. Oxford: Clarendon Press.

Darwall, Stephen. 2006. Berkeley's Moral and Political Philosophy. In *Cambridge Companion to Berkeley*. Edited by Kenneth Winkler. New York: Cambridge University Press, pp. 311–98.

Enoch, David. 2011. *Taking Morality Seriously: A Defense of Robust Realism*. Oxford: Oxford University Press.

Evans, C. Stephen. 2013. *God and Moral Obligation*. Oxford: Oxford University Press. [CrossRef]

Flannagan, Matthew Alexander. 2017. Robust Ethics and The Autonomy Thesis. *Philosophia Christi* 19: 345–62. [CrossRef]

Flannagan, Matthew Alexander. 2019. Divine Commands, Duties and Euthyphro: Theism and Naturalist Misunderstandings. In *The Naturalness of Belief: New Essays on Theism's Rationality*. Edited by Charles Taliaferro and Paul Copan. London: Lexington Books, pp. 123–36.

Flannagan, Matthew Alexander. 2022. "Why the Horrendous Deeds Objection Is Still a Bad Argument". *Sophia* 61: 399–418. [CrossRef]

Flannagan, Matthew, and Paul Copan. 2014. *Did God Really Command Genocide: Coming to Terms with the Justice of God*. Grand Rapids: Baker Books.

Forrest, Peter. 1989. An argument for the Divine Command Theory of Right Action. *Sophia* 28: 2–19. [CrossRef]

Francis. 1989. Naturalism and William Paley. *History of European Ideas* 10: 203–20. [CrossRef]

Gay, John. 1998. Preliminary Dissertation on the Fundamental Principle of Virtue or Morality. In *Utilitarians and Religion*. Edited by James E. Crimmins. Bristol: Theommes Press, pp. 31–33. First published in 1731.

Hare, Richard Mervyn. 1952. *The Language of Morals*. Oxford: Clarendon Press.

Hayry, Matti. 2012. Passive Obedience and Berkley's Moral Philosophy. *Berkeley's Studies* 23: 3–14.

Heydt, Colin. 2014. Utilitarianism before Bentham. In *The Cambridge Companion to Utilitarianism*. Edited by Ben Eggleston and Dale E. Miller. Cambridge: Cambridge University Press, pp. 16–37. [CrossRef]

Horne, Thomas. 1985. "The Poor have a claim founded in the law of nature" William Paley and the rights of the poor. *Journal of the History of Philosophy* 23: 51–70. [CrossRef]

Jenyns, Soame. 1998. A Free Inquiry into the Nature of Evil. In *Utilitarians and Religion*. Edited by James Crimmins. Bristol: Theommes Press, pp. 111–34. First published in 1757.

Law, Edmund. 1998. On Morality and Religion. In *Utilitarians and Religion*. Edited by James Crimmins. Bristol: Theommes Press, pp. 135–41. First published in1758.

Locke, John. 1689. Essay Concerning Human Understanding. *Project Gutenberg*. Available online: https://www.gutenberg.org/files/10615/10615-h/10615-h.htm (accessed on 13 March 2023).

Louden, Robert. 1995. Butler's Divine Utilitarianism. *History of Philosophy Quarterly* 12: 265–80.

Mackie, John L. 1955. Evil and Omnipotence. *Mind* 64: 200–12. [CrossRef]

Mackie, John L. 1977. *Inventing Right and Wrong*. Harmondsworth: Penguin Publishing.

Moberger, Victor. 2019. The Mackiean Supervenience Challenge. *Ethical Theory and Moral Practice* 22: 219–36. [CrossRef]

Murphy, Mark. 2011. *God and the Moral Law: A Theistic Explanation of Morality*. Oxford: Oxford University Press.

Nathanson, Stephen. 2010. *Terrorism and the Ethics of War*. New York: Cambridge University Press.

Nathanson, Stephen. 2014. Act and Rule Utilitarianism. *Internet Encyclopedia of Philosophy*. Available online: http://www.iep.utm.edu/util-a-r/ (accessed on 13 March 2023).

O'Flaherty, Niall. 2018. *Utilitarianism in the Age of Enlightenment: The Moral and Political thought of William Paley*. Cambridge: Cambridge University. [CrossRef]

Paley, William. 1998. Principles of Moral and Political Philosophy. In *Utilitarians and Religion*. Edited by James E. Crimmins. Bristol: Thoemmes Press, pp. 207–11. First published in1785.

Parfit, Derek. 2011. *On What Matters*. Oxford: Oxford University Press.

Plantinga, Alvin. 1986. Is Theism Really a Miracle? *Faith and Philosophy* 3: 109–34. [CrossRef]

Rutherford, Thomas. 2018. *An Essay on the Nature and Obligations of Virtue*. Gale Ecco, Print Editions. Available online: https://onlinebooks.library.upenn.edu/webbin/book/lookupid?key=ha001920975 (accessed on 13 March 2023). First published in1744.

Schneewind, Jerome B. 1977. *Sidgwick's Ethics and Victorian Moral Philosophy*. Oxford: Oxford University Press.

Schneewind, Jerome B. 2002. *Moral Philosophy from Montaigne to Kant*. Cambridge: Cambridge University Press.

Scofield, Philip Thomas. 1986. Conservative Political Thought in Britain in Response to the French Revolution. *The Historical Journal* 29: 601–22. [CrossRef]

Shafer-Landau, Russ. 2003. *Moral Realism: A Defense*. Oxford: Oxford University Press.

Smith, Wilson. 1954. William Paley's Theological Utilitarianism in America. *The William and Mary Quarterly Third Series* 11: 402–224. [CrossRef]

Stephen, Leslie. 1881. *History of English thought in the Eighteenth Century*. London: Smith, Elder.

Tucker, Abraham. 1998. The Light of Nature Pursued. In *Utilitarians and Religion*. Edited by James Crimmins. Bristol: Thoemmes Press, pp. 158–206. First published in1768.

Tuckness, Alex. 2021. *Morality and Legislation: Rules and Consequences*. Cambridge: Cambridge University Press.

Wainwright, William J. 2005. *Religion and Morality*. Aldershot: Ashgate.

Waterland, Daniel. 2011. *The Nature, Obligation, and Efficacy, of the Christian Sacraments, Considered*. Charleston: Nabu Press. First published in1730.

Wielenberg, Erik J. 2014. *Robust Ethics: The Metaphysics and Epistemology of Godless Normative Realism*. Oxford: Oxford University Press.

Wierenga, Edward. 1989. *The Nature of God: An Enquiry into the Divine Attributes*. Ithaca: Cornell University Press.

Zagzebski, Linda. 2004. *Divine Motivation Theory*. Cambridge: Cambridge University Press.

 *religions*

Article

The Secular Moral Project and the Moral Argument for God: A Brief Synopsis History

Dale Eugene Kratt

Rawlings School of Divinity, Liberty University, Lynchburg, VA 24515, USA; dekratt@liberty.edu

Abstract: This article provides an overview of the history of what is termed the secular moral project by providing a synopsis of the history of the moral argument for God's existence and the various historical processes that have contributed to the secularization of ethics. I argue that three key thinkers propel the secular moral project forward from the middle of the 19th century into the 20th century: John Stuart Mill, whose ethical thinking in *Utilitarianism* serves as the background to all late 19th century secular ethical thinking, Henry Sidgwick, who, in the *Methods*, indisputably establishes the secular autonomy of ethics as a distinctive discipline (metaethics), and finally, G.E. Moore, whose work, the *Principia Ethica*, stands at the forefront of virtually all secular metaethical debates concerning naturalism and non-naturalism in the first half of the 20th century. Although secular metaethics continues to be the dominant ethical view of the academy, it is shown that theistic metaethics is a strong reemerging position in the early 21st century.

Keywords: secular ethics; metaethics; Mill; Sidgwick; Moore; moral argument for God

Citation: Kratt, Dale Eugene. 2023. The Secular Moral Project and the Moral Argument for God: A Brief Synopsis History. *Religions* 14: 982. https://doi.org/10.3390/rel14080982

Academic Editor: Roberto Di Ceglie

Received: 1 May 2023
Revised: 25 June 2023
Accepted: 11 July 2023
Published: 29 July 2023

1. The Moral Argument for God: A Brief Synopsis

In considering the moral argument for the existence of God, it is only appropriate to have a sense of the background and history of this particular argument in the historical debates of normative ethics and metaethics. Dave Baggett and Jerry Walls have written an excellent overview and analysis of the history of the moral argument for God's existence entitled *The Moral Argument: A History* (Baggett and Walls 2019). The history of this particular argument, rarely thoroughly considered, is interesting and impressive. Consider the following quick synopsis. The modern form of the moral argument proper is usually traced back to Immanuel Kant {1724–1804}, (Kant [1785] 2012 Groundwork of the Metaphysics of Morals; Kant [1788] 2015; Critique of Practical Reason; Kant [1797] 2017 The Metaphysics of Morals).[1] Among other notable thinkers who advanced a positive form of the moral argument are John Henry Newman (1801–1890) in his *Aid to a Grammar of Ascent* (1870), Arthur Balfour {1848–1930} (Balfour 1915, in Theism and Humanism; Balfour 1923, Theism and Thought),[2] William Sorley {1885–1935} in his *On The Ethics of Naturalism*, (Sorley [1884] 2015); also *Moral Values and the Idea of God*, (Sorley 1918).[3] Hastings Rashdall {1858–1924} also made unique contributions in his *The Theory of Good and Evil: A Treatise on Moral Philosophy* (Rashdall 1907, vol. 1&2), Clement Webb {1865–1954} in his *God and Personality*, (Webb 1918), W.G. de Burgh {1866–1942}, From Morality to Religion, (De Burgh [1938] 1970),[4] A.E. Taylor {1869–1945}, in his *The Faith of a Moralist* (Taylor 1930), W.R. Matthews {1881–1973} in his *God in Christian Thought and Experience*, (Matthews 1947), A.C. Ewing {1899–1973} in his *Values and Reality: The Philosophical Case for Theism*, (Ewing 1973), C.S. Lewis {1898–1963} in his well-known *Mere Christianity*, (Lewis 1978; *The Abolition of Man*, (Lewis 1978),[5] and finally H.P. Owen ({1926–1996}, The Moral Argument for Christian Theism, (Owen 1965) and Basil Mitchell {1917–2011} *Morality, Religious and Secular: The Dilemma of the Traditional Conscience*, (Mitchell 2000; *Law, Morality, and Religion in a Secular Society*), (Mitchell 1967).

In the period since C.S. Lewis's writings, there has been a resurgence in Theistic philosophy and ethics and a resurgence specifically in the moral argument for God's existence. A brief sample of works will illustrate this point. Take for example Robert Merrihew Adams, *Finite and Infinite Goods: A Framework for Ethics* (1999); Robert Merrihew Adams, "Moral Arguments for Theistic Belief" (1987); John Hare, *God's Command* (2015); John Hare, "Naturalism and Morality", (2002); "Naturalism's Incapacity to Capture the Good Will", (Willard 2011); *The Disappearance of Moral Knowledge.* (Willard 2018); Mark Linville, "The Moral Argument", (Linville 2012); William Lane Craig, *Reasonable Faith: Christian Truth and Apologetics,* (Craig 2008); Angus Ritchie, *From Morality to Metaphysics: The Theistic Implications of Our Ethical Commitments* (Ritchie 2012); David Baggett and Jerry Walls, *Good God: The Theistic Foundations of Morality* (Baggett and Walls 2011) as well as their *God and Cosmos: Moral Truth and Human Meaning* (Baggett and Walls 2016); Paul Copan, "The Moral Argument", (2005); Paul Copan. "Hume and the Moral Argument" (2005); *Atheism?: A Critical Analysis* (Parrish 2019); Stephen Parrish (forthcoming), *The Nature of Moral Necessity; Natural Signs and Knowledge of God: A New Look at Theistic Arguments* (Evans 2010); *God and Moral Obligation* (Evans 2014). (Baggett 2018; Jakobsen 2020); "The Moral Argument", (Evans and O'Neill 2021); Matthew Carey Jordan, "Some Metaethical Desiderata and the Conceptual Resources of Theism", (Jordan 2011); *The Recalcitrant Imago Dei: Human Persons and the Failure of Naturalism* (Moreland 2009); *Body & Soul: Human Nature & the Crisis in Ethics* (Moreland and Rae 2000); William Lane Craig et al., *A Debate on God and Morality: What Is the Best Account of Objective Moral Values and Duties?* (Craig et al. 2020); Adam (2023). *Divine Love Theory: How the Trinity Is the Source and Foundation of Morality.*; Dale Kratt, "A Theistic Critique of Secular Moral Nonnaturalism" (Kratt 2023).

Several notable features stand out as one considers the history of the moral argument. First, it is interesting that the moral argument does not take definite form and shape as a distinct evidential argument for God until the connections from the human moral domain to God become, in some sense, problematic. David Hume (1711–1776) and others, during the period dubbed the Enlightenment, directly challenged prevailing arguments for natural theology, various religious beliefs, and the Theistic basis for morality (see Hume [1739] 1984, [1779] 1998). Hume's work was quite effective at the time, and his efforts have had a continuing and lasting influence and continue to generate strong assessments for and against (see Sennett and Groothuis 2005).

Today, the questions and challenges to the God-and-moral-order connection persist. However, many current secular thinkers refuse to engage with the theistic arguments or even to acknowledge the history of the moral argument that we briefly reviewed above.[6] They remain fully committed to what will be termed here the *secular moral project*. Nevertheless, the sophistication of contemporary theistic-centered philosophy, theistic metaethics, various developments in natural theology, and the moral argument are notable. Next, from the history of the moral argument, it is also instructive to consider how the differing arguments proceed and which particular facets of the multifaceted phenomena of the moral order each thinker has chosen to focus on. From this, it can be seen that the moral domain, and consequently the moral argument, is a very deep, wide, and rich area that continues to present new opportunities and challenges for Christian thinkers.[7]

The moral argument for God's existence can legitimately take many forms that focus both on distinct features of the moral domain and differing aspects of the 'God side' of the equation. Furthermore, we are incorrigibly moral, since human beings are inescapably immersed in the moral domain. If the God of Theism exists, then the existence of this God is not only relevant to how we understand the normative order of Reality, but an account of this order will most certainly be misunderstood if the Living God is not taken into consideration (MacIntyre 2011).[8]

Finally, the moral argument for God's existence is not only in good intellectual company, with a venerable history, but also remains profoundly relevant in today's world, on multiple fronts. To be sure, naturalism continues to be a primary challenge. However, from William Sorley onward (Sorley 1904, 1905, 1918), various Christian thinkers have successfully met the challenges of naturalism and naturalistic ethics. But there is now also the ascending challenge of secular non-naturalist metaethics (moral Platonism)[9] as well as the various and sundry versions of realism, non-realism, constructivism, error theory, and others. It is important to note, however, that there is a long lineage of Christian moral thinkers who have done good work in the past, as well as contemporary Christian thinkers, and so what I am calling the *theistic moral project* is also once again in the ascendency. But this project does not start from scratch; it just needs to be creatively reworked and expanded to meet the array of contemporary challenges.

2. The Cultural Processes of Secularization

The Historical Opening for Secular Ethics

In this paper, "secular" simply refers to God-excluding ethical thinking. This need not involve active hostility to Theism but only that God is not considered in relation to any particular moral project.[10] However, secularism, as part of secularization, involves much more than excluding God. The interest of this section is to briefly understand the broader and more encompassing story of secularization as it unfolds and to situate the development of ethical thinking and metaethics in the 21st century.

The 19th-century context of British moral philosophy is vital for an understanding the historical background of the rise of the discipline of metaethics. For example, almost all thinkers reviewed in our synopsis of the moral argument for God's existence worked in this broader context of British moral philosophy.[11] This broader context is vital for understanding G.E. Moore and his predecessors. Given his influential work *Principia Ethica*, Moore is considered a pivotal thinker who bridges late 19th and early 20th century ethical philosophy. If one examines the field of contemporary metaethics, it is evident that most contemporary metaethical thinkers view their work as part of the more comprehensive secular moral project (see Bourget and Chalmers 2014). Of course, the secular need not necessarily exclude God, and it need not entail wholesale atheism. For example, while metaphysical naturalism entails atheism, moral non-naturalism does not. Secular moral naturalism and secular moral non-naturalism disagree on the wider metaphysics of normative Reality. However, they generally agree that there is no God, or that God is of no account in systematically thinking through the moral, the ethical, the normative,[12] the prescriptive, the obligatory (categorical), the aesthetic, or the axiological, and just as importantly, the scientific. A more careful look at secularism and secularization is then in order. Charles Taylor in his (Taylor 2007) eminent work entitled *A Secular Age*, begins his wide-ranging study of secularization in Western society with this incisive question.

One way to put the question that I want to answer here is this: why was it virtually impossible not to believe in God in, say, 1500 in our Western society, while in 2000 many of us find this not only easy, but even inescapable?[13]

The secular moral project we are interested in occurs in this broader opening of secularization in Western society. Few would dispute the claim that today's Western culture is secular in a considerable measure and some general sense. But what precisely is secularization, and how is it to be understood? How did secularization of the culture occur historically, and what are its implications and impact? A brief examination of these questions is essential to establish a broader context for our understanding of the secular moral project. As is common knowledge, the details are disputed. Overall, secularization is a historically complex, fully multi-dimensional, socio-cultural process that occurs over time and ranges from a given society's macro-level institutions, middle-level organizations, the family–household, and micro-level personal experiences of the lifeworld. The personal lifeworld is a part of this broader process of secularization. The lifeworld involves the whole taken-for-granted practical world of a person's day-to-day life embedded within a wider umbrella of organizations and institutions. It is the dimension of personal, taken-for-granted beliefs, experiences, sensibilities, and everyday practices. The embedded individual's day-to-day lifeworld and wider embedding macro context makes up the full range of the story of secularization.

A full account of secularization would deal with this full scope. But this scope is obviously too broad and complex to be examined here. Yet awareness of this broader scope helps us point out a few common misconceptions about secularization. Clearly, secularization involves more than a mere change of ideas and beliefs. Also, it is more than simply a change of beliefs; it is a wholesale change of life practice and worldview. The material conditions of secularization are deep and diffuse. Sometimes, the secularization of society is caricatured as the advancement of reason and science that results in the inevitable decline of irrational belief in God and religion. This sort of activist characterization is much too quick and involves a particular vested spin on how secularization is to be understood. Charles Taylor convincingly argues against the idea that secularization is a one-sided story of the loss of God, the inevitable outcome of modernization, and a coming of age that has thrown God off. He calls this view the subtraction thesis.

Most importantly, the subtraction thesis cannot explain the persistence of religious belief and practice in the West and outside the Western world. But neither can it readily explain the optimistic side of secularization—a positive humanist belief in and total commitment to unbridled human powers of self-determination, human autonomy, rationality, general human flourishing as an ultimate good, and a fully human-sourced morality (ibid. pp. 253, 572). Clearly, this moral repertoire is more than mere subtraction of God.

A brief survey of some of the broader and deeper dimensional changes is helpful to situate our analysis. Historically at the macro level from the top-down, secularization involves a complex process of institutional transformation, separation, and differentiation over time. The economic dimension and the rise of capitalism involve new technologies of production, transportation, finance, energy, mechanization, architecture, warfare, and communication. In part, this is the industrial revolution. The economic order becomes rationally objectified and differentiated as a distinct order of production, consumption, commodification, and wealth; this also requires the innovative birth of modern finance. The economic order also shapes both the bottom-up content and practice of personal disciplinary virtue at the micro level that capitalism requires; workers must be disciplined and specialized to be productive and contribute to the civil and economic order. Next, it is important to consider the unfolding political dimension and the rise of the nation-state that involves new forms of the political structuring of power, social ordering, and law.

Constitutionalism is born, and its notion of political rights comes to the fore. Along with this, political, military, and economic power can be projected across the globe as never before by various competing nation-states, hence the global Western colonialist legacy and the continued inertia regarding globalization. Commodities can be sourced and extracted from across the globe. The late 20th century and early 21st century see the continued rise of multinationals. Then add the religious dimension—in particular, the reformation.

The reformation becomes a constant force for radical religious reform that generates religious institutional differentiation and religious organizational pluralization. The secular order comes to encompass and embed the religious order. Some view this religious and political separation as the heart of the secularization process. The transformation of religious practice and pluralization also occur from the bottom up at the individual practice level within middle-range organizations. The reformation thinkers challenge and attenuate a sacred/secular distinction of practice and vocation. With the ascendance of the physical sciences, new forms of knowledge in the sciences, mathematics, and the arts proliferate and accumulate. These transform our understanding of the physical world, from astronomy, physics, chemistry, biology, medicine, and the arts—all contributing to developing new technologies and accounts of human nature and the physical world. Evolutionary theory becomes central to the sciences from the middle of the 19th century onward. Additionally, the sciences transform the dimension of education; the Academy shifts from a classical educational format to a more science and technical-based format. The human-centered place in the cosmos gives way to the peripheral human place in the more expansive but finite universe.

Of course, Taylor understands that the material conditions of modernity are important. But these conditions do not cause secularization, explain secularization, or explain the numerous changes associated with secularism (Taylor 1989, pp. 310–13, 393–418). His analysis of secularization is a wide and detailed interdisciplinary account. It is strongly interpretive. The analysis here will build upon Taylor's analysis to further clarify the subject matter. He identifies several significant transformations in his work that are important to recognize clearly. There is a transition from a fulsome transcendent theism to a much thinner and remote providential deism (Taylor 2007, pp. 221–69).[14] The personal God of theism is no longer seen as an agent that speaks and acts in history (ibid., pp. 274–75). In this shift in belief, the broadest horizon of Reality and humanity's relationship to it is transformed. The relation of God and the created world and the relation of God to the human order of things are reconceived and reconstituted in different ways (ibid., p. 43). In part, this results from what Taylor calls the "great disembedding" in which the social and ritual facets of religious practice and experience are transformed and broken up by decisively shifting towards the individual (ibid., pp. 146–58). The reformation contributes to this shift. In many ways, this is a positive shift. However, with the eclipse of a personal God, the new order in many ways also becomes a complex, impersonal order; a vast sea of governing cosmic natural laws, impersonal causes and mechanisms, formulas and functions, impersonal social and historical laws, impersonal moral ideals, codes, and requirements. (ibid., pp. 270–93). However, that the world was made for human beneficence remains central to both theism and deism. In addition, religion becomes narrowed to a diffuse but rather thin moralism in deism (ibid., p. 225).

From the shift to providential deism, only one step away from atheism, there is the related transition to seeing the world in which one lives as disenchanted instead of enchanted. I describe these changes this way. A "disenchanted world" is a world in which a barrier exists between the lifeworld and what is referred to here as World2. By World2 is meant the immaterial world that includes God, who is Spirit, the gods, spirits, angels, demons, invisible powers, and even the dead, including the world of the afterlife (ibid., p. 147).[15] It is obvious that, in different cultures, World2 is conceived in different ways. An "enchanted world" means that whatever powers are taken to occupy World2 can influence World1 (the physical world) and the lifeworld of individuals. As part of this shift to disenchantment, there is a transformation towards seeing the self, the lifeworld, as "buffered" rather than "porous". In describing the lifeworld as "porous", Taylor means that there is an open connection, penetration, and interchange between World2 and the lifeworld (ibid., pp. 35–43). By "buffered", he means that an open porous interchange is closed off (ibid., pp. 135–42).[16] There is outright denial that World2 exists in disenchantment, or the lifeworld is isolated or buffered from World2.

Secularization also involves a transformation in one's sense of time and history. Without a transcendent God, the broader temporal horizon is still considered as linear, but the sense of time becomes flattened, a strictly horizontal flow of time. The lifeworld is only situated within real World1 time (ibid., pp. 54–59). But this horizontal flow of time is still defined by a linear notion of historical progress on all fronts. These combined changes contribute to what Taylor further describes as a developing crystallization of an "immanent frame" of experience and thinking (ibid., pp. 542–57). By this, he means that the totality of human life and thought become enframed within this-worldly immanence instead of an other-worldly transcendence. Central to the immanent frame is "exclusive humanism", (ibid., pp. 242–69).[17] Humanism of this sort is a radical shift, an intra-human, "inward turn in the form of disengaged reason", (ibid., p. 257).[18] Exclusive humanism becomes a fully rational and moral vision in which human nature is valorized (ibid., p. 256).[19] It is thought possible to utilize exclusive humanly sourced powers of reason, morality, values, and the sciences to achieve exclusively human ends of progress and human flourishing. Associated with this is a transition from a universal ethic grounded in Christian *agape* to a universal and idealized commitment focused exclusively on human beneficence in this world. The key is that all of this is God-excluding, either actively or passively. It is a distinctively anthropocentric moral ideal and commitment (ibid., p. 247). Humanity alone becomes the locus of a positive and exclusive humanist belief in, and total commitment to, unconstrained human powers of self-determination, human autonomy, rationality, political freedom, universal justice, generalized human flourishing as an ultimate good, and an exclusively human-sourced morality and scheme of values. Taylor convincingly argues that none of this would have been possible without the prior groundwork laid by Christian theism. He states,

> ... all present issues around secularism and belief are affected by a double historicity, a two-tiered perfecttensedness. On one hand, unbelief and exclusive humanism defined itself in relation to earlier modes of belief, both orthodox theism and enchanted understandings of the world; and this definition remains inseparable from unbelief today. On the other hand, later-arising forms of unbelief, as well as all attempts to redefine and recover belief, define themselves in relation to this first path-breaking humanism of freedom, discipline, and order. (ibid., p. 269)

As regards religion, after the reformation, an unending and continuous pluralism of both belief and unbelief unfolds (ibid., p. 437; see also MacIntyre 1998).[20] In many respects, this development is positive. Over time, both belief and unbelief are subjected to tremendous cross-pressures and what Taylor calls fragilization (ibid., pp. 303–4). He has dubbed this contentious explosion and proliferation of religious and spiritual options beyond orthodoxy a "nova effect". The pluralized world of today lives in the aftermath of this nova effect.

3. Mill, Sidgwick and Moore

This section will explore more specific historical developments while taking the preceding as a general context for understanding the secular moral project. By the middle of the 19th century, when our analysis will now pick up, the full opening of secularization is firmly in play and continuing to unfold. Into this broader opening, the secular moral project develops. Three specific thinkers, John Stuart Mill, Henry Sidgwick, and G.E Moore, are relevant to our analysis. Here is the logic behind selecting these three successive thinkers as decisive for the development of the secular moral project. Moore is the transitional thinker leading into the modern period who set the debates for early 20th century metaethics. These debates continue into the present. But, prior to Moore, Sidgwick is the critical thinker that sets the table for Moore by 'doing ethics' differently, by doing metaethics. Sidgwick, along with Mill, laid the groundwork for the modern period by laboring to work out the basis and details for a new and fully adequate secular ethics. Hence, these three thinkers are decisive for understanding the development of the secular moral project.

Theism has always provided a natural and unproblematic placement within which the moral order of things is fittingly nested (Parfit 1987, pp. 452–54).[21] If God exists, then the moral order is grounded. To be sure, the details of this are worked out in different ways in Christian, Jewish, Islamic, and other versions of Theism. But all Theists agree that God, who is personal, who is fundamentally a moral, spiritual being, by virtue of being God, must somehow be the ultimate source of the normative order. In a Theistic world, all credible, ethical sources involve God and are intimately linked to God. They must depend upon God in some fundamental way. This dependence on God also has profound practical implications. In this sense, historically, a God-given moral order not only structured and guided the whole of life in thinking and practice but also indirectly showed God's undeniability (Taylor 1989, pp. 303–4). This order of human life needed God. However, once the deniability of God becomes broadly plausible, the very foundations of the moral order are also questioned. Secularization then forces a rethinking of the moral order down to the foundations. Once there is a total commitment to an exclusive humanism that is optimistic about rationally elaborating a fully humanly sourced moral vision, the gauntlet is laid down for fully engaging and developing the secular moral project. This need must be filled and hammered out by serious secular moral thinkers.

Otherwise, the secular project will morally flounder. Secular thinkers are forced to squarely face a whole host of thorny questions and problems concerning the moral order, given the premise and conditions of secularization. Mere reactionary critiques of Theism will no longer suffice in this regard. Secular worldview logic has a straightforward premise; since God does not exist, this fact must be squarely faced on all fronts. The big questions still loom very large indeed. For example, how should we think and live? Why should we believe and live this way or that way, and how can this thinking and living be systematically formulated in a strictly secular view of Reality? The secular moral project becomes central to this broader set of pressing questions and concerns.

4. John Stuart Mill

John Stuart Mill (1806–1873) not only feels the need for such an account but also takes up the challenge of trying to develop one adequately. Mill's writings are prolific, and his impact was significant.[22] Several aspects of his thinking will be briefly discussed before moving on to the work of Sidgwick and Moore.[23] Mill was raised by his father in the tradition of *philosophical radicalism* to become the ultimate Victorian intellectual and utilitarian reformer (Brink 2018, p. 3).[24] It is significant that as a young man, between the years 1826–1830, Mill suffered from a severe period of depression. He experienced a deep intellectual and emotional crisis (ibid., p.4). In the period that Mill writes, he pens not only his classic work on the ethics of utilitarianism (1861)[25] but also philosophical works arguing against various elements of Theism and natural theology by critiquing the standard pieces of evidence put forward in favor of Theism (Mill [1874] 1998).[26] Mill was an exclusive humanist who advocated what Auguste Comte called the religion of humanity (Raeder 2001, 2002).[27] In this religion surrogate, humanity becomes a kind of object of devotion, as both the source and object of moral good and endeavor. Two additional things should be noted about the context in which Mill writes. First, Paley's work on natural theology (Paley [1802] 2017[28]) was still highly influential at the time, so much so that Mill felt compelled to respond to the prevailing arguments of Paley.[29] Frederick Rosen takes Paley's natural theology as the spiritual core of the metaphysics of the British Enlightenment (Rosen 2005, p. 113). But Paley's work in moral and political philosophy (1785) was also highly influential (Schneewind 1977, p. 177).[30] Paley was a proponent of a version of Theistic utilitarianism (Paley [1785] 2017).[31] Both of Paley's works were commonly used as textbooks for years in the first half of the 19th century (Fyfe 1997).[32] Second, Mill fully recognized that an adequate and complete secular ethics had yet to be worked out. In 1847 Mill urged John Austin to write a systematic treatise on morals, without which the kind of moral reform Mill, Austin, and others were hoping for could not be achieved (Schneewind 1977, p. 178).[33] Mill also shared his views in 1854 that "ethics as a branch of philosophy is still to be created" (ibid.)[34] This year, 1854, was the same year that *Utilitarianism* was drafted; after some 30 years of thought, his final revisions came in 1859, and it was finally published in 1861 (Irwin 2011, p. 364). Initially, it was only marginally impactful. Only gradually was it noticed and given critical attention (Schneewind 1977, pp. 178–88). It is now the best-known account of classical utilitarianism to date. But Mill was no staunch atheist. He was a Theist of sorts, a believer in a finite Theistic God, what some have referred to as a "probable Theist". This can be seen both from the practical side of his life and his posthumously published essay entitled "Theism". (Settanni 1991; Devigne 2006; Carr 1962).[35] Although Mill worked to contribute to the secular moral project, he also recognized that it was far from complete. He saw it as just beginning. But clearly Mill believed that there was a comprehensive moral answer, though he could not provide it fully. This point is significant. Mill is not committed to anything like moral skepticism or moral nihilism.

Moreover, he developed his utilitarian account after a long line of previous thinkers, both secular and religious, had espoused some form of utilitarianism.[36] He attempted to remedy previous problems and misconceptions throughout his argument, which sought to develop a convincing account of utilitarianism and provide a kind of "proof" of utilitarianism.[37] Most agree that his proof is less than successful. Nevertheless, Mill was a highly influential political and moral reformer, philosopher, and statesman; his moral philosophy was worked out toward these larger ends. He believed philosophy could change how people thought and lived regarding moral good and that this could have a positive social, political, and economic impact. This project is in complete agreement with Mill in this regard. How important, then, is Mill? Given his work, David O. Brink takes Mill as the most influential philosopher of the 19th century in British moral philosophy.[38]

5. Henry Sidgwick

While Mill's work leaves the secular moral project unfinished, still to be created, it also overlaps and leads into the work of Henry Sidgwick (1838–1900), author of *The Methods of Ethics* (1907, 7th edition).[39] Schneewind comments on this monumental work of Sidgwick.

> It was not until Sidgwick's *Methods*, which tried to reconcile these two schools (intuitionism and utilitarianism), that all the characteristics of a modern treatment of ethics were fully and deliberately brought together in a single work. Sidgwick is often described as the last of the classical utilitarian's. He may with as much accuracy be viewed as the first of the modern moralists. (1997, p. 122)

In what ways might Sidgwick be considered the first of the modern moralists? It has mostly to do with the way that Sidgwick went about the task of ethical philosophy, and the reasons why he did it.[40] A lot of this can be gleaned from his introduction to the *Methods*. Sidgwick completed the first edition of the *Methods* when he was 36 years old in 1874. The final seventh edition was completed and published after his death in 1907. He spent his entire academic life revising the *Methods*. His influence is clearly seen in that the dominant forms of the problems of later British and American moral philosophy were, in many important ways, shaped by his work.[41] (Harrison 1996). In the very first sentence of the *Methods*, Sidgwick points out that the boundaries of ethics have been variously and vaguely conceived. Deliberately and clearly establishing the boundaries of ethics was thus a major part of what Sidgwick set out to do in the Methods (1907, pp. 11–12).[42] Throughout the *Methods*, he works to clearly differentiate ethics from other disciplines, such as politics, economics, philosophical metaphysics, or theology (ibid., pp. 78–80). Sidgwick also shows how ethics must be distinct from psychology and sociology (1907, p. 2).[43] When Sidgwick writes, moral philosophy includes these various disciplines within its scope. According to Sidgwick, ethics is an autonomous discipline standing on its own (ibid., 507). Its aims, sources, and boundaries should have clear limits while not borrowing fundamental premises from other sources (ibid.).

Sidgwick thus establishes the autonomy of ethics, a significant achievement in the secular moral project. Establishing the autonomy of ethics also helps to further distinguish between first order ethics and second-order metaethics. This distinction is central to 20th and 21st-century ethical theory and had much to do with Sidgwick's work.[44] For example, first order ethics might discuss what our various duties are. Second-order metaethics seeks to understand the nature of duty itself—what duty itself fundamentally consists of. Much of Sidgwick's discussion in the *Methods* is worked out at the level of the metaethical, as one can see in his analysis of what is "good", "right", the notions of "ought", "virtue", "duty", and so on. In the wake of the *Methods*, ethical analysis at the abstract level of metaethics has become commonplace, an independent specialty in ethics. According to Sidgwick, a related claim follows from his analysis that there is a fundamental distinction between "is" and "ought". This means that a truly categorical "ought" cannot be derived from an existing particular thing or an infinite collection of particular things (1907, pp. 25, 396; see also Phillips 2011, pp. 55–57). Next, Sidgwick fully recognizes that the situation within which the ethical theorist works is pluralistic. Sidgwick seeks to understand and explain why and how this is so. The major ethical viewpoints in British moral philosophy at the time that Sidgwick wrote were egoism, intuitionism, and utilitarianism. This pluralism is the starting point for the *Methods*, analyzing its character and working out ethical theory to cut through various confusions induced by conflicting viewpoints.[45] The *Methods* seeks to work out a unique synthesis in this regard. By and large, Sidgwick accomplishes this. He ends up synthesizing an intuitionally grounded utilitarianism.[46]

Notwithstanding Sidgwick's efforts, however, ethical pluralism since the *Methods* has only increased. Next, theoretical ethics for Sidgwick is a fully human undertaking. This is key. Fundamentally, ethics is a task undertaken by human beings for human beings, and it is basically about human beings. The task of ethical thinking excludes anything above and beyond the human, even if such might exist (1907, pp. 114–15). Sidgwick's exclusive humanism is evident here. Ethics is a fallible human project and mostly a secular moral project. But this does not mean, as will be further seen, that Sidgwick subscribes to atheism. He does not. Nevertheless, after Sidgwick, the secular moral project is in full swing. So then, for Sidgwick, the project of ethics is progressive given that first order ethical views will change over time. The ethical views of the future will probably differ from those of the present in the same way that the views of the ancients differ from those of the moderns. What "ought" consists of will not change (the metaethical), whereas what we take to be our specific "oughts" may very well change over time (Sidgwick and Sidgwick 1906, pp. 607–8).

By a *method* of ethics, Sidgwick means "any rational procedure by which we determine what individual human beings 'ought'—or what is 'right' for them—to do, or to seek to realize by voluntary action" (Sidgwick 1962, p. 1). He recognizes a diversity of methods in ordinary practical ethical thinking (ibid., p. 6; see also Brink 1994, pp. 179–201). In this, Sidgwick identifies three primary methods: egoism, utilitarianism, and intuitionism. According to Sidgwick, the study of the methods of ethics should involve "systematic and precise general knowledge of what ought to be". (Ibid., p. 1). Ethics is thus clearly focused on the categorical, on oughtness. Sidgwick is an "all-purpose" rationalist in that ethics must be worked out and made precise through human reason. He is not an extreme rationalist believing that reason is all there is.

Sidgwick believes that this kind of rational study of ethics can be carried out in a somewhat "neutral" fashion, in the sense that one need not be rationally pre-committed to a particular outcome in the analysis. But there is a conflict here. Any supposed neutrality can never be complete because it will conflict with the practical requirement that compels us to ethical thinking and action (ibid., p. 14). After all, a method, according to Sidgwick, is how to think about what is right (and wrong) to do. While Sidgwick believes that common sense morality has practical value and provides a bedrock for moral truth and practice, it is nevertheless imprecise and unclear in many respects. Rational analysis of ethics, therefore, must give precision and clarity to common sense morality so that ethics attains the position of a rational science. It must transcend common-sense moral thinking.[47] Here, the notion of science, as Sidgwick is using the term, is the looser 19th-century sense that was common at the time. But he did see the natural sciences as a paradigm case of how progress is achieved. Since Sidgwick works to delineate "fundamental principles" of ethics along intuitionist and utilitarian lines, and rejects both logical and systemic contradictions as negative tests for truth, his epistemology is appropriately classed as moderately foundationalist and coherentist (1907, p. 509). Sidgwick sometimes compares ethics to how geometry is worked out with axioms and derivations (ibid.). Sidgwick is moderate, given that the Methods focus on practical reason, what one "ought" to do, and how to determine right conduct. Finally, Sidgwick aims overall toward a "harmonious system" in his exposition of the methods of ethics, but he explicitly warns that he is not striving to forge a single, unified, harmonious systematic method (ibid., pp. 13–14, 496).

It is generally agreed that Sidgwick is accurately described as an ethical non-naturalist (Crisp 2015). But Sidgwick is no moral Platonist. He does not use the language of moral properties or ontology and does not refer to any Third Realm or the like to elaborate his version of ethics. He is what today is termed a moral realist of the cognitivist sort (Sayre-McCord 1988b).[48] He rejects the notion that the "natural" can furnish an ethical first principle to work out a consistent metaethical system (Sidgwick 1962, p. 83).[49] He also rejects the notion that the ideal of Ultimate Good or Universal Happiness can be established naturalistically (1907, p. 396). Sidgwick takes naturalistic ethics to be inadequate in at least two respects. First, all versions run afoul of what he takes to be the fundamental is/ought distinction. The categorical "ought" cannot be derived from any collection of natural particulars, nor can ethical ideals be similarly established. Second, the various naturalistic proposals each have their particular problems that lead Sidgwick to reject them (Phillips 2011, pp. 14–15; Crisp 2015, p. 11, nt. 18).[50]

However, Sidgwick also rejects Theistically grounded ethics but for different reasons (1907, pp. 504–7). Sidgwick's relation to Theism is intriguing and ambivalent and merits a closer look. As is well known of Sidgwick, he resigned his fellowship at Cambridge in 1869 because of reservations concerning the requirement to assent to the 39 Articles of the Anglican Church in order to teach (Tribe 2017; Medema 2008).[51] The 39 Articles were expressly orthodox in content and practice. Sidgwick's resignation is often referred to as his turbulent "crises of faith".[52] But Sidgwick does not become an atheist, although he fits the profile of a secularist rather well.[53] He might best be described as an agnostic with leanings toward Theism, or a weak Theist with agnostic leanings.

On the one hand, Sidgwick concludes in the *Methods* that Theism cannot be established "on ethical grounds alone" (1907, pp. 506–7). Most theists would agree. On the other hand, Sidgwick writes in personal correspondence in 1898 that "the need of Theism—or at least some doctrine establishing the moral order of the world—seems clear to me".[54] Again, most Theists would agree. Sidgwick seems to be gesturing toward a version of Providential Theism.

Along with rejecting orthodoxy, he also saw that Paley's natural theology and moral philosophy had pretty much exhausted itself by the mid to late 19th century. It was no longer interesting and compelling for many thinkers. Again, most theists would agree. So Sidgwick is fully committed to and engaged in the secular moral project. We previously noted that Sidgwick sought to establish ethics as an autonomous discipline with distinctive non-theological first principles rationally derived. This goal partly forms the basis for his acceptance of intuitionism (Skelton 2010).[55] Sidgwick concluded that intuitionism and utilitarianism, thought by most to be in conflict, could be reconciled. But he also sought to reconcile individual personal happiness (egoistic hedonism/self-interest) with ultimate collective happiness (utilitarianism/duty to others) as an ideal of ethics.[56] However, he finally concluded that these two methods of ethics could not be rationally reconciled. If a person acts in self-interest, this might be rational. If a person acts for the greater happiness of others, this, too, might be rational. Sidgwick concluded that no unified universal, categorical "ought" could be synthesized between these two principles. Though not always, but sometimes, these two methods will necessarily conflict. For Sidgwick, this is more than a moral conflict, intellectual tension, moral difficulty, or philosophical paradox. He describes it as an "ultimate and fundamental contradiction" of intuition and judgment that informs practical reason and, along with such a contradiction, the attendant failure of a non-contradictory, rational ethical theory.[57] This was a final and severe blow to Sidgwick's systematic aspirations. Sidgwick's conception of practical rationality is that it provides complete and conflict-free guidance (Holley 2002).[58] Therefore, as is Sidgwick's notoriety, he ends up with the contradictory and intractable "dualism of practical reason". This dualism he takes to be a rational contradiction at the heart of his ethical system that he cannot resolve within his exclusive humanist and rationalist commitments. Sidgwick judges the implications of this to be severe. He even admits that this contradiction threatens to open "the door to universal skepticism" (1907, p. 509). He never gave in to such skepticism. He concludes the final edition of the *Methods* this way:

I do not mean that if we gave up the hope of attaining a practical solution of this fundamental contradiction, through any legitimately obtained conclusion or postulate as to the moral order of the world, it would become reasonable for us to abandon morality altogether: but it would seem necessary to abandon the idea of rationalizing it completely.... If then the reconciliation of duty and self-interest is to be regarded as a hypothesis logically necessary to avoid a fundamental contradiction in one chief department of our thought, it remains to ask how far this necessity constitutes a sufficient reason for accepting this hypothesis. This, however, is a profoundly difficult and controverted question, the discussion of which belongs rather to a treatise on General Philosophy than to a work on the Methods of Ethics: as it could not be satisfactorily answered, without a general examination of the criteria of true and false beliefs.[59]

We must bear in mind that this is the mature Sidgwick writing here and not the Sidgwick of the oft-quoted concluding passage of the first edition of the *Methods* of 1864 that was effectively revised out of subsequent editions and never to reappear.[60] We can see in these final words that all of the things that have done good work for Sidgwick throughout the *Methods* now seem to work against him: his exclusive humanism, his rationalism, his utilitarianism, the autonomy of ethics, his quest for a unified and perfect ethical ideal, his inveterate precisionism, his thin providential Theism, and finally his sidelining of full-orbed Theism as integral to a completed metaethics. But in these final thoughts, he clearly states that, for ethics to be rational, there must be a reconciliation of the "fundamental contradiction" as a "logically necessary" hypothesis. In other words, reconciliation is achievable, but he does not know how. His gesture toward a solution from "General Philosophy" is hardly optimistic. The language of logical necessity here is strong indeed. Most contemporary Sidgwick interpreters think it is too strong[61] and demurred on Sidgwick's precisionist and perfectionist tendencies and how he frames the problem (Crisp 2015; Parfit 2011, vol. 1).[62] But there is another way to see things.

Ironically, what Sidgwick actually discovered in his trek through the moral trees as he exits out of the moral forest was a version of the moral argument for the existence of God. So argue Baggett and Walls.[63] Notice how Sidgwick looks to the world's moral order for a possible resolution. Theism could provide the basis for this order. Sidgwick saw this, as he stated in personal correspondence. Not, of course, the thin and exhausted Theism of Paley's natural theology or the Victorian moralism of the day. "Full moral rationality requires an ontological ground of morality that, among other things, 'guarantees' an unbreakable connection between morality and the ultimate self-interest of all rational beings".[64] This rationality must involve *both* God and reconciliation of the moral order in life after death, that is, in a world to come.[65] Can a full account of Theistic metaethics provide for such rationality? Ironically, Sidgwick's *Methods* create an opening for just such a moral argument for God, but Sidgwick himself did not see a way to solidify the connections and ideas. While a Theistic relation to the moral order seemed intuitively evident to him, he could never work out a rationally clear account of the nature of that order within either a dogmatic Anglican orthodoxy or an exhausted Paleyan natural theology, both of which he rejected. But he also could not work out a final reconciliation of the dualism of practical reason within an entirely secular moral logic. For if such a logic failed of logical necessity, it thus failed of moral necessity.

For Sidgwick, there was nowhere else to go. He had come to an end of his resources. But clearly, Sidgwick still believed there was an objectively right and true answer to his quest. Yes, Sidgwick, who some consider the most significant moral philosopher of the 19th century, was fully committed to the secular moral project (Broad 1930).[66] But the methods of ethics could not be fully rationalized as Sidgwick had hoped. We can see then that this left his task unfinished and unfinishable, given his array of secular commitments and his particular formulation of ethics methods. As the generations invariably shifted toward the young and optimistic thinkers of the early 20th century, "old Sidg", as Bertrand Russell and other of his young students called him, died in 1900.[67] Much of his labor fades into obscurity.[68]

6. G.E. Moore

One of these students was the young G. E. Moore (1873–1958). Moore was a student of Sidgwick's, and Moore's impact on 20th-century ethical thought beyond Sidgwick is indisputable. Contrary to popular belief, the publication of Moore's most well-known work, the *Principia Ethica*, did not rock the world of ethical philosophy in 1903 when it was first released (Moore [1903] 1993).[69] It wasn't until the 1930s that the influence and importance of Moore's primary work were widely recognized.[70] It is one of his earliest articles that gave him early fame—"The Refutation of Idealism", also published in 1903.[71] Sidgwick's influence on Moore is evident throughout Moore's work.[72] In the *Principia*, Moore trod well-worn paths, and many of his ideas were shared by his contemporaries.[73] However, this diminishes neither Moore's originality nor his impact. But it is important to put that impact in proper context regarding the history and thought that concerns us (Hurka 2003).[74]

Moore's work was highly impactful for several reasons. The first is Moore's rhetorical style. The Principia first strikes one as crisp, succinct, to the point, laser-like, and exudes rhetorical confidence. It is laid out in what appears to be a powerfully logical format, and he looks to be proceeding succinctly and rigorously. This style is very different from other writing in philosophy at the time. For example, it contrasts sharply with Sidgwick's expositional, wandering, wordy, heavy, and unconcise style (Eddy 2004; MacIntyre 1998).[75] In the preface of the first 1903 edition of the *Principia*, Moore asserts that the problem with virtually *all* past philosophies, and ethics in particular, is their need for more clarity in questions, answers, and analysis. Moore set out to rectify *all* these confusions of the past in the *Principia* (Moore [1903] 1993, pp. 33–37). Who would not be interested in a serious philosophical work that genuinely set all previous philosophers straight? The turn of the 20th century was rife with this kind of visionary optimism.

Secondly, like Sidgwick, Moore claims to be developing a "scientific ethics" in the sense of science common in the late 19th century (Moore [1903] 1993, p. 55). According to Moore, all previous ethical systems of thought before his work failed to achieve this status of a rigorous science of ethics (Willard 2018, p. 113). Moore spent much effort detecting errors and fallacies, defining terms, analyzing the language of ethics, and parsing the words being used, as well as the sentences, concepts, and ideas. This way of doing philosophy was part of the beginnings of the analytic tradition, with its linguistic turn, that still pervades much of technical philosophy today.[76] One can agree with Moore that the muddled use of language leads to muddled philosophy. But the analysis of language itself cannot yield a complete understanding of the moral domain, in whatever ways this domain is conceived. Ethics and values are more than language use. The central strategy was to get at the meaning of the ethical by analyzing the language of the ethical, which then, it was hoped, would enable one to clarify the concepts and content of ethics and thereby forge a science of ethics. For Moore, the central factor around which all ethical thinking revolved was that of intrinsic good (Moore [1903] 1993, p. 55). His central question was, "what is good?" Moore is not asking the question, "what is *the* good?", that is, the highest good in Plato's sense of the summum bonum, but rather, what is the nature of good itself as we use the term in our everyday moral language?[77] Put more precisely, how is good to be defined? And then how is this definition to be applied to the things we refer to as good and understand to be good? (Moore [1903] 1993, p. 57)[78] Moore believed that a science of ethics would be based on a precise and accurate conception of intrinsic good. He also carried forward the commitment to British utilitarianism as well as intuitionism, but he argued that good is the fundamental principle of ethics, and the definition of good is the central question of ethics. So then, according to Moore, the notion of right is derivative from that of good. Good makes an action right and not the reverse. In Moore's day, the analysis of properties had not been developed thoroughly in philosophy, so Moore's analysis of moral properties and ontology is very limited in scope. He also never technically deploys the notion of supervenience, a development that later ethical thinkers will find almost indispensable to conceptualize the metaphysics of the moral domain.[79] Nevertheless, he argues that good is not a natural property, nor is it a supernatural property. He thus rejects both ethical naturalism and ethical Theism. He claims instead that good is an indefinable, irreducible, simple, intrinsic, and nonnatural property (Moore [1903] 1993, pp. 60–61; Moore 1962, pp. 89–100). This notion of a nonnatural property was both interesting and intriguing. Strangely, it looked like Platonism but was curiously different than classical Platonism (Moore [1903] 1993, pp. 227–31). Yet precisely how this notion was to be taken became a thorny issue that carried over into subsequent debates and remains disputed in current debates.

Thirdly, Moore utilized two argumentative strategies in particular to make his point that good is a nonnatural property. He dubbed the two centerpiece arguments in the *Principia* the "open question argument" and the "naturalistic fallacy" (Willard 2018, pp. 116–17).[80] These two things and the question of non-naturalism were particularly disputed. Clarifying these matters absorbed much of the efforts of the first half of 20th-century secular moral philosophy (see Prichard 1912; Frankena 1950; Broad 1930; Ross 1930, 1939; Geach 1956).[81] It is generally agreed that the naturalistic fallacy is no formal fallacy (Sinclair 2019),[82] that the open question argument is formally invalid but interesting and sometimes useful,[83] and that Moore's way of conceptualizing a nonnatural property contributed to many unfruitful controversies that plagued 20th century secular moral philosophy (Baldwin 2003; Darwall et al. 1992; Scott Soames 2005; Miller 2013; A Warnock 2007).[84] The issues are still discussed today, and the notion of a secular non-naturalist metaethics has recently been revived with full force (see Enoch 2013; Shafer-Landau 2005; Wielenberg 2014; Huemer 2008; Kulp 2017, 2019, and, critical of this trend, see Baggett and Walls 2016; Kratt 2023; Parrish forthcoming).[85] There are few defenders of the naturalistic fallacy or the classical open question argument as Moore formulated these concepts, but there has been a revival of secular moral non-naturalism (Regan 2003; Tucker 2018).[86]

Fourthly, at the time that Moore wrote, it was believed that Moore had achieved a knockout argument against ethical naturalism, that he had actually refuted it. It indeed appeared so. Moore states his rejection of ethical naturalism in no uncertain terms throughout the *Principia* (Moore [1903] 1993, pp. 70–71). And if Moore had actually achieved a knockout argument against ethical naturalism, then that would have stood as a significant philosophical achievement (Sturgeon 2003).[87] If the naturalistic fallacy and open question argument fail to hold, and nonnatural moral properties remain mysterious, Moore's case against naturalism is greatly diminished.[88]

Finally, what of the legacy of Moore's work (Horgan and Timmons 2006)?[89] Mary Warnock argues convincingly that the *Principia* dealt the final death blow to grand metaphysical theories of ethics, particularly those of Idealism. Moore's rhetorical style also had a significant effect.[90] But he had many second thoughts about the ideas in the *Principia*, as the preface to the second edition (1922; see also Baldwin 2010) shows.[91] Moore reflectively described the *Principia* as "full of mistakes and confusions".[92] But he still held that intrinsic good was not identical to any natural or supernatural property.

Nevertheless, in his well-known "A Reply to My Critics", he acknowledges that his characterization of naturalism seemed to him now (1942) "silly and preposterous". He also admits, "I agree, then that in *Principia* I did not give any tenable explanation of what I meant by saying that 'good' was not a natural property".[93] He also acknowledged that his notion of an intrinsic property was vague and unclear.[94] So then, if the three central theses of the *Principia* do not stand and Moore's characterization of naturalism, against which he is predominantly arguing, is admittedly fuzzy, there is little of Moore's ethical philosophy that remains standing.[95]

But there is another big worry which Dallas Willard points out in Moore's *Principia* that is typically ignored by friend and foe alike.[96] Relating to right conduct, after providing a long list of impossible consequential qualifications to evaluate right conduct, Moore concludes that "(w)e *never* have any reason to suppose that an action is our duty".[97] Willard rightly takes this to be an eye-popping, concussive conclusion. He further points out that Moore never retracts this view; instead, he reinforces it in his summary and conclusion on right conduct that follows.

So then, Moore's vaunted boldness in 1903 in aiming to correct all the philosophical errors of the past is now laid bare in his honest and unpretentious admissions of philosophical incoherence and confusion on key details. If the past of ethical philosophy was fuzzy in 1903, it is even less clear or certain after Moore. In Moore's defense, one must acknowledge that the issues he works through are quite difficult. Nevertheless, after the *Principia,* the secular moral project is reeling, trying to find its footing and sense of direction. The impact of the *Principia* propels the secular moral project in several different directions. God is nowhere an option for Moore or any of the other secularists. Theistic thinkers did not significantly interact with Moore's work. In 1907 Hastings Rashdall, a lucid theistic ethical thinker of the early 20th century, remarks in the preface to *The Theory of Good and Evil: A Treatise on Moral Philosophy* that the work of Moore (1903) came too late for him to incorporate it into his newly published volumes (1907).[98] William Sorley does mention Moore in a couple of places in his work but with no significant interaction, since Moore's work completely ignores the question of God in relation to good, right, and the ethical. In the early 1940s and 50s, a little-known thinker, C.S. Lewis, no technical philosopher, gives his radio lectures in Britain that are later published on the moral argument for the existence of God. Moore is never acknowledged. To this day, Lewis's works remain readable and compelling classics of moral argument and analysis.[99] As a former atheist turned Theist, Lewis clearly perceived his day's intellectual and ethical vacuum and responded to it accordingly.

In the broader academic context of the period, two primary heirs of Moore's ethical thinking are the emotivists and the intuitionists of the 1930s and beyond.[100] Intuitionism breaks some new positive ground, while emotivism devolves into the position that ethical (and theological) propositions contain nothing truly factual but only reflect a person's feelings of approval or disapproval toward ethical matters.[101] By mid-century (1949), Stewart Hampshire laments the fact that moral philosophy has lost its way, (Hampshire 1949). Roderick Firth complains that just about every form of ethical analysis has been tried with no agreement, only more details and fragmentation (Firth 1952), and Elizabeth Anscombe in 1958 demands a halt to all moral theorizing until further developments in the human sciences can accommodate a theoretical moral consensus (Anscombe and Margaret 1958).[102]

At present, the *secularism* of the moral project is the dominant view of the Academy in metaethics. Secularism has institutional clout. However, it is distributed throughout a dizzying cacophony of differing metaethical theories and proposals. The common denominator is the rejection of explicit Theism. Naturalistic ethics continue to have a powerful influence on secular ethics, but new-wave secular moral non-naturalism is certainly in an ascendant position. Theistic metaethics is also a reemerging position, as we have briefly shown, and the moral argument for the existence of God is charting new territory with or without recognition by secularists. However, the secular moral project has not abated since Mill, Sidgwick, Moore, and beyond, and 21st century secular metaethics shows no signs of diminishing. Engaging with this wide and diverse panoply of secular thinkers and the secular moral project is one of the most urgent features of the resurgent Theistic moral project. Theistic moral philosophers are clearly required to undertake their work, given the conditions and challenges of secularization. Going forward, however, both secularist and Theistic thinkers in metaethics will have to develop a more comprehensive metaphysics of Reality that enables them to fill in and adequately support their metaethical thinking. In this author's opinion, for both the secular and Theistic moral projects, this is where the most pressing philosophical and theological challenges lie for metaethics.

Funding: There is no funding source for this article.

Institutional Review Board Statement: Not applicable.

Informed Consent Statement: Not applicable.

Data Availability Statement: Not applicable.

Conflicts of Interest: There is no conflict of interest.

Notes

1. (Baggett and Walls 2019, pp. 8–19) Baggett and Walls point out the contributions to moral thinking from Augustine (354–430), Aquinas (1225–1244), Descartes (1596–1650), Pascal (1632–1662), Locke (1632–1704) and Reid (1710–1796) prior to Kant. They summarize the moral arguments for God that Kant put forward in this way.Better than anyone, Kant recognized the power and authority of the moral law. On that foundation he constructed two variants of the moral argument. 1. His argument from grace pertains to whether or not the moral life is possible. Morality requires us to achieve a stand too demanding to meet on our own. Divine assistance is needed to close the resulting gap. So rationality dictates that we postulate God's existence. 2. Kant's argument from providence pertains to the aforementioned rational need for happiness and virtue to cohere. Full rational commitment to morality requires that morality is a rationally stable enterprise, which entails the ultimate correspondence between virtue and (both individual and corporate) fulfillment. Without God's existence there is no particularly good reason to think such correspondence obtains. So rationality dictates the postulation of God's existence (ibid., p. 33).
2. Baggett and Walls, ibid., pp. 66–71. The focus of Balfour's argument was against ethical naturalism and its inadequacies as contrasted with Theism. C.S. Lewis noted in 1962 that Balfour's *Theism and Humanism* strongly influenced him; see the excellent work, Arthur James Balfour and Michael W. Perry, *Theism and Humanism: The Book That Influenced C.S. Lewis*, New, Enhanced edition. (Balfour and Perry 2000).
3. Sorley's very early critique of the ethics of naturalism is notable. Of the later work of Sorley's, Baggett and Walls comment that it is "...perhaps the most sophisticated development of the moral argument for God's existence before the present time". Ibid., p. 74.
4. De Burgh deploys a cumulative case in which he combines the cosmological and teleological argument with the moral argument for God's existence. See Baggett and Walls. Ibid., p. 133. See also (Sessions 1985). Sessions provides good historical context and analysis for De Burgh's moral argument.
5. Lewis has been the most widely read and influential writer of the moral argument in the 20th and 21st centuries. *Mere Christianity* continues to gain in popularity. It has sold over 3.5 million copies since the early 2000s.
6. Breitenbach is correct in judging the impact of Kant's moral argument. He observes that "Kant's argument made an impact on the landscape of moral philosophy by forcing those who came after him to consider what implications atheism would have for the rationality of following the moral law". Zachary Breitenbach (2021), "Evaluating the Theistic Implications of the Kantian Moral Argument that Postulating God Is Essential to Moral Rationality", *Studies in Christian Ethics* 34, no. 2: 149.
7. See (Dougherty et al. 2018, p. 447) In this interview Alvin Plantinga states that he thinks the moral argument for God's existence to be "the most compelling."
8. As Alastair MacIntyre puts the matter, "To be a theist is to understand every particular as, by reason of its finitude and its contingency, pointing towards God....It is to believe that, if we try to understand finite particulars independently of their relationship to God, we are bound to misunderstand them" (MacIntyre 2011, p. 23).
9. This author has recently completed a PhD dissertation (2023) entitled *A Theistic Critique of Secular Moral Nonnaturalism* © that fully critiques the secular moral Platonism of David Enoch, Russ Shafer-Landau, Eric Wielenberg, Michael Huemer and Christopher Kulp. The dissertation also develops a distinctive version of the moral argument for the existence of God.
10. For that matter, it could also be polytheistic, or pantheistic, to point out some other options. As Dallas Willard rightly points out, "nonnaturalism has been the rule and not the exception in ethical theory". (Willard 2018, p. 114).
11. Many of the books of these thinkers grew out of a presentation of the Gifford lectures. The Gifford Lectures were established in 1887 to focus on issues related to natural theology. God and the moral order has been a central theme in natural theology.
12. The first order moral, ethical and the normative are taken to be roughly equivalent throughout this article.
13. (Taylor 2007, p. 25) Taylor takes almost 900 pages to work out this question.
14. Taylor also notes the move to atheism by the intermediary stage of deism, ibid., p. 293.
15. I am using this as a socio-cultural concept and not a metaphysical possible worlds concept.
16. As Taylor describes this, "(the) buffered self is the agent that no longer fears demons, spirits, magic forces". Ibid., p. 135. See also his discussion on pp. 300–1.
17. This "frame" is part of what he terms "secularity 3", which is "not ususally, or even mainly a set of beliefs which we entertain about our predicament", but instead "the sensed context in which we develop our *beliefs*". p. 549 (emphasis original).

[18] Taylor refers to this as "one of the great achievements of our civilization, and the charter of modern unbelief", p. 257.

[19] Here, Taylor (p. 256) speaks of the "ontic placement" of this moral vision in human nature itself. For his notion of "fullness": see pp. 600–1.

[20] Taylor summarizes this on p. 305. MacIntyre similarly emphasizes this in his last chapter entitled "Contested Justices, Contested Rationalities" in (MacIntyre 1998).

[21] Here, Parfit points out that the secular moral project is in its infancy and that Theism has been the natural home of ethics. As Parfit puts things, "Belief in God, or in many gods, prevented the free development of moral reasoning. Disbelief in God, openly admitted by a majority, is a recent event, not yet completed. Because this event is so recent, Non-Religious Ethics is at a very early stage". Ibid., p. 456.

[22] All of Mill's writing can be accessed in 33 volumes; see Collected Works of John Stuart Mill, in 33 vols. | Online Library of Liberty (libertyfund.org, accessed 7 May 2017).

[23] I have relied heavily in this section on David O. Brink's thorough work on Mill as well as the excellent work by J.B. Schneewind on Mill and Sidgwick. See David O. Brink, "Mill's Moral and Political Philosophy", ed. Edward N. Zalta, *Stanford Encyclopedia of Philosophy* (Stanford, CA, Fall 2022) John Stuart Mill, *The Basic Writings of John Stuart Mill: On Liberty, The Subjection of Women, and Utilitarianism* (NY: Random House, Modern Library, 2002); J.B. Schneewind, *Sidgwick's Ethics and Victorian Moral Philosophy* (Oxford: Clarendon Press, 1977). For excellent overviews and analysis, see the two chapters in (Irwin 2011).

[24] (Brink 2018, p. 3) The three most famous proponents of philosophical radicalism are Jeremy Bentham (1748–1832), John Austin (1790–1859) and Mill's father, James Mill (1773–1836).

[25] (Mill 2002).

[26] (Mill [1874] 1998).

[27] Linda C. Raeder, *John Stuart Mill and the Religion of Humanity* (Columbia, MO: University of Missouri Press, 2002); see also her summary Linda C. Raeder, "Mill's Religion of Humanity: Consequences and Implications", *Humanitas* 14, no. 2 (Mill 2001), pp. 4–34. Mill describes this religion of humanity as "the sense of unity with mankind, and a deep feeling for the general good, may be cultivated into a sentiment and a principle capable of fulfilling every important function of religion and itself justly entitled to the name" (Mill [1874] 1998, p. 109).

[28] William Paley, *Natural Theology* (Miami: HardPress, 2017 [1802]). It should be noted that Paley was not a deist, he was clearly a Theist.

[29] Mill, *Three Essays on Religion*, pp. 167, 174. Here Mill critiques and accepts Paley's argument from design. He argues that knowledge of design is only derived from things we already know as designed. Since we already possess experience of specific designed things, by induction they do serve as evidence for God as a designing intelligence. Schneewind, *Sidgwick's Ethics and Victorian Moral Philosophy*, p. 151 points out that beyond 1830 or so Paley's influence begins to wane.

[30] (Schneewind 1977, p. 177) Schneewind's summary of Paley is quite useful, ibid, pp. 122–29. As Schneewind points out, Paley's work was published in 1785 and was used as a textbook and reprinted many times. Bentham's work on utilitarianism was published in 1789 and William Godwin also published a work in 1793. Neither of these works was as popular as Paley's, Ibid., p. 127. See a more detailed discussion of this in (Rosen 2005, pp. 131–43). Rosen shows that in England there were many religious or theological utilitarians prior to Paley.

[31] See a discussion of this in the section entitled, "William Paley as a Utilitarian", in (Rosen 2005, pp. 131–43). Paley was a hedonist of sorts, but as a theist he placed emphasis on God rather than a strictly natural knowledge of right, wrong, good and evil and consequential good.

[32] Aileen Fyfe, "The Reception of William Paley's "Natural Theology" in the University of Cambridge", *The British Journal for the History of Science* 30, no. 3 (September 1997): 321–35. Even Darwin was influenced by Paley, see (Thorvaldsen and Øhrstrøm 2013).

[33] (Schneewind 1977, p. 178).

[34] Quoted in (Schneewind 1977, p. 178).

[35] The religious side of Mill is thoroughly documented in Timothy Larsen (2018), *John Stuart Mill: A Secular Life* (Oxford: Oxford University Press); see also Mill, *Three Essays on Religion* [Reprint] London, 1874, Prometheus Books, Amherst, NY, 1998. Mill rejected a providential, benevolent deism, p. 242. The only argument that Mill found inductively convincing for God was the argument from design, ibid, p. 174. But God according to Mill was finite as shown by the existence of evil in the world and the constraints of design, pp. 38–39, 177–83. Mill also rejected the notion of miracles, accepting Hume's argument of unalterable natural law as conclusive, but did hold open the possibility that God could creatively intervene in the world, pp. 233, 244. Hence Mill was a Theist of sorts.

[36] Frederick Rosen, *Classical Utilitarianism from Hume to Mill*, p. 131. Rosen lists six thinkers cited by (Crimmins 1998).

[37] John Stuart Mill, *Utilitarianism*, ed. George Sher, 2nd ed. (IN: Hackett, 2001), p. 35. For a careful reconstruction of Mill's argument and solid criticism of it, see (Brink 2018, pp. 34–39). MacIntyre simply calls Mill's proof "unimpressive". He thinks that it flounders on a haziness of the central concept. Alasdair C. MacIntyre, *A Short History of Ethics: A History of Moral Philosophy from the Homeric Age to the Twentieth Century*, 2nd ed. (Notre Dame, IN: University of Notre Dame Press, 1998), pp. 238–40.

[38] Brink, Ibid., p. 1.

39. This work will quote only from the 7th edition of the *Methods*, unless otherwise noted, as is common among interpreters of Sidgwick's work. Henry Sidgwick, *The Methods of Ethics*, 7th ed. [1907] (London: Macmillan & Co, 1962). The work went through five printings and revisions in Sidgwick's lifetime. The last two versions were posthumous. This 7th edition also includes all of the prefaces from editions 1–7. This is very helpful for tracing the changes in Sidgwick's work and thinking.

40. (Harrison 1996) This is an excellent review of Sidgwick's reformist efforts in helping to found a first women's college near Cambridge, and other practical institutional reform efforts he was involved with. For these things, Harrison says of Sidgwick, "But if conventional answers were insufficient, he needed some kind of different and more theoretical guidance. He needed a theory of the "ought". He needed a Method of ethics". p. 427. Harris further describes Sidgwick not only as a reformer but also as a highly scrupulous "resigner", p. 437.

41. Ibid., p. 422.

42. (Sidgwick 1962, pp. 11–12).

43. Note that at this time psychology and sociology are also newly forming disciplines.

44. Parfit says of Sidgwick's *Methods* that it is the "best book on ethics ever written. . . . Sidgwick's book contains the largest number of true and important claims". *On What Matters*, vol. 1:xxxiii.

45. Hence the plural *Methods of Ethics* and not the singular Method of Ethics.

46. (Sidgwick 1962) As Sidgwick puts it describing his intellectual journey away from Mill's utilitarianism toward his own formulation of utilitarianism, "I was then a Utilitarian again, but on an Intuitional basis". Preface to the 6th edition, xx.

47. (Sidgwick 1962) See chapter XI entitled "Review of Common Sense". See especially the conclusion pp. 360–61.

48. Geoffrey Sayre-McCord (1988a), "Introduction: The Many Moral Realisms", in *Essays on Moral Realism*, ed. Geoffrey Sayre-McCord, (Ithaca: Cornell University Press), pp. 1–23.

49. See also (Sidgwick et al. 1892; Sidgwick 1879).

50. Phillips, *Sidgwickian Ethics*, pp. 14–15; Crisp, *The Cosmos of Duty: Henry Sidgwick's Methods of Ethics*, p. 11, note 18.

51. For background to this period and the development of Sidgwick's view on religion see (Schneewind 1977, pp. 17–40). See also (Tribe 2017). Tribe provides additional useful context and background. The 39 Articles requirement was dropped as an academic requirement in 1871. See also (Medema 2008).

52. (Tribe 2017, p. 916) Tribe comments, "The Problem then is that Sidgwick's 'crises of faith' has been assimilated to a narrative of secularization created by intellectuals themselves skeptical of religious faith of any kind; which was certainly not Sidgwick's own position".

53. I disagree with Parfit who too quickly classes Sidgwick as an atheist, *Reasons and Persons*, p. 453).

54. (Sidgwick and Sidgwick 1906, p. 560) See also Sidgwick's discussion of freedom and what he terms "the moral government of the world". (Sidgwick 1962, p. 69).

55. (Anthony Skelton 2010) Skelton argues convincingly that Sidgwick's moral epistemology is intuitionist foundationalism.

56. (Sidgwick 1962, p. 498) Sidgwick defines happiness as "desirable consciousness" and universal happiness as ". . .desirable consciousness or feeling for the innumerable multitude of sentient beings, present and to come". (Sidgwick 1962, p. 404).

57. (Sidgwick 1962, p. 508) Sidgwick repeats this notion of "fundamental contradiction".

58. (Holley 2002, p. 51).

59. (Sidgwick 1962, pp. 508–9).

60. In this first edition of the *Methods*, Sidgwick concludes, "But the Cosmos of Duty is thus really reduced to a Chaos: and the prolonged effort of the human intellect to frame a perfect ideal of rational conduct is seen to have been foredoomed to inevitable failure". M1, p. 473. See also "Sidgwick's Pessimism", *Philosophical Quarterly* 26, no. 105 (Mackie 1976): pp. 317–27. This passage is quoted in full by Mackie and thoroughly discussed. In some respects Mackie finds in Sidgwick an ally to his own error theory. For a full account see (Mackie 1990).

61. I note that a reviewer questioned this assessment that Sidgwick's requirement of "logical necessity" is taken to be to strong. Indeed, this is the case. The footnote that follows documents this to be case for modern interpreters of Sidgwick.

62. (Crisp 2015; Parfit 2011; Phillips 2011; Holley 2002).

63. Baggett and Walls, *The Moral Argument: A History*; pp. 58–59; Baggett and Walls, *God and Cosmos*, pp. 243–69. In the first citation see the entire section on Sidgwick; in the second citation see chapter 8 entitled "Moral Rationality" that deals with C.S. Lewis, Sidgwick and Kant.

64. (Baggett and Walls 2016, p. 269) In this vein, Bart Schultz (2004) says of Sidgwick that he could not bear the idea that we lived in a universe where ". . .the wages of virtue might 'be dust'". *Henry Sidgwick, Eye of the Universe: An Intellectual Biography* (New York: Cambridge University Press), p. 15.

65. Breitenbach, "Evaluating the Theistic Implications of the Kantian Moral Argument that Postulating God Is Essential to Moral Rationality", p. 151.

66   C.D. Broad describes the *Methods* as "the best treatise on moral philosophy that has ever been written". C.D. Broad, *Five Types of Ethical Theory* (London: Kegan Paul, Trench, Tubner, 1930), p. 143; Parfit echoes this stating that the *Methods* is "the best book on ethics ever written". Parfit, *On What Matters*, vol. 1, pxxxiii. Both, however, register the common complaint about its lack of conciseness.

67   The words that Sidgwick wanted to have said over his grave were, "Let us commend to the love of God with silent prayer the soul of a sinful man who partly tried to do his duty. It is by his wish that I say over his grave these words and no more". (Sidgwick and Sidgwick 1906, pp. 598–99). He was instead given the traditional Anglican funeral with all its ritual and pronouncements. Bertrand Russell and others referred to Sidgwick as "old Sidg" and regarded him as a product of a bygone era. They regarded themselves as initiating a new era in thought and ideas.

68   Of course, we have the advantage of hindsight in evaluating Sidgwick's thinking. We can see better where things go, where things end up and from where new things start. I think there are at least two important take aways from Sidgwick's *Methods*. First, if moral/ethical debate occurs at the level of what we might call the middle range, the strictly practical range, applied ethics, there will be a great deal of consensus on matters, unless our practicality is informed by radically different metaphysics. Secondly, at some point, all practicality must link up with and be informed by a larger, even Ultimate metaphysics; that is, how all things Ultimately hang together in relation to fundamental ethical principles. It is here where the most substantive and difficult, but also, the most important. debates will be carried out. This is also the level of metaethics. It is here where the "why" and "how" of the moral/ethical is fundamentally grounded and worked out.

69   I will be quoting only from this edition of *Principia* unless otherwise noted. (Moore [1903] 1993) This is the standard work with additional notes and commentary.

70   (Baldwin 2003, p. 4) Much of this seems to be due to the detailed discussion of Moore in the works of W. D. Ross, *The Right and the Good*, ed. Philip Stratton-Lake, New edition. (Oxford, New York: Clarendon Press, 1930); see also W. D. Ross, *Foundations of Ethics* (New York: Oxford University Press, 1939).

71   (Moore 1903) Baldwin also points out the importance of this early article of Moore's, see Baldwin, ibid. See also Thomas Baldwin's excellent account of Moore's early dissertation work and the developmet of his ideas in "George Edward Moore". In *Stanford Encyclopedia of Philosophy*, edited by Edward N. Zalta, pp. 1–16. Stanford, CA: The Metaphysics Research Lab, Summer 2010.

72   The *Principia* cites Sidgwick's *Methods* more than any other work.

73   Even Rashdall complains in a footnote on the nature of the good. He details the fact that Moore's way of seeing things is not at all new. In particular he references Plato. See Hastings Rashdall, *The Theory of Good and Evil a Treatise on Moral Philosophy*, (Clarendon Press, Oxford, Britian, 1907), vol. 1: 135–36.

74   Hurka's exposition of the history and thinking shows many, if not most, of the ideas that Moore develops were put in place by earlier thinkers; especially Sidgwick (Hurka 2003).

75   (Eddy 2004) This rhetorical style harkens back to an earlier style of Newton, as opposed to Hume's or Sidgwick's style. This style Alasdair MacIntyre refers to as Moore's "...method of calm assertion". He continues, "More unwarranted and unwarrantable assertions are perhaps made in *Principia Ethica* than in any other single book of moral philosophy, but they are made with such well-mannered, although slightly browbeating certitude, that it seems almost gross to disagree. But what then is Moore's case?" MacIntyre, *A Short History of Ethics: A History of Moral Philosophy from the Homeric Age to the Twentieth Century*, p. 250.

76   The beginnings of analytic philosophy are generally attributed to Gottlieb Frege (1848–1925), Bertrand Russell (1872–1970), G.E. Moore (1873–1958) and Ludwig Wittgenstein (1889–1951). Early on, Moore and Russell were collaboraters but there seems to have been little to no interaction between Frege and Moore, although Moore acknowledged the influence of Wittgenstein; see Moore's autobiography in (Schlipp 1968a, vol. 1, pp. 33–34).

77   It should be noted that Moore does include a discussion of ethical ideals that touches on the concpt of good as an ethical ideal in the final chapter of the *Principia*. Moore and Baldwin, *Principia Ethica*, pp. 232–73.

78   As Moore states things, he says that "(t)he most important sense of 'definition' is that in which a definition states what are the parts which invariably compose a certain whole; and in this sense 'good' has no definition because it is simple and has no parts". (Moore [1903] 1993, p. 61). Given this, it is widely recognized that Moore deploys a highly peculiar notion of the term definition throughout the *Principia* but also that this strategy of analyzing parts and wholes, today known as mereology, is really the strategy that Moore deploys throughout his work to analyze the concept of good.

79   Much more discussion on the subject of moral supervenience can be found in this author's dissertation (Kratt 2023).

80   Willard, I think correctly and succinctly, identifies what Moore meant by the naturalistic fallacy, namely, the mistake of identifying one property with a property that is not identical to it. The open question argument specifies that all correct definitions of good do not create open questions, or a remaining question about goodness not specified in associated non-moral properties. For example, is pleasure good? This is an open question. If pleasure is good, then the question reduces to this—is good (pleasure) good? This open question shows that good is something other than pleasure. Good and pleasure are then not identical. Hence, Moore argued, "Good" is a distinguishable, intrinsic and non-natural property.

81   The article by (Prichard 1912; Frankena 1950; Broad 1930).

For a book length treatment on various aspects of the naturalistic fallacy, see (Sinclair 2019) The issue is still of some philosophical interest.

(Horgan and Timmons 2006, p. 7) Horgan notes that toward "...the end of the twentieth century, we find that the open question argument is alive and well". For example, he points to its use in T.M. Scanlon's "buck passing" account of value. See (Scanlon 1998, pp. 95–100) Susana Nuccetelli and Gary Seay, "What's Right About the Open Question Argument", in *Themes from G. E. Moore: New Essays in Epistemology and Ethics*, ed. Susana Nuccetelli and Gary Seay (New York: Oxford University Press, 2008), 261–82. (Nuccetelli and Seay 2008).

(Darwall et al. 1992; Baldwin 2003) For an excellent overview and analysis of Moore, see the section on Moore in Dallas Willard's, *The Disappearance of Moral Knowledge*. See also (Soames 2005; Irwin 2011) See also the relevant sections in Alexander Miller, *Contemporary Metaethics: An Introduction*, Second edition. (Malden: Polity Press, 2013); Mary Warnock, Ethics Since 1900 (Mount Jackson, VA: Axios Press: Distributed by National Book Network, 2007).

See also this author's critical analysis of all these thinkers *A Theistic Critique of Secular Moral Nonnaturalism* © (2023) PhD dissertation, Liberty University.

The open question argument is still appealed to as refuting naturalistic forms of reductionism; see for example (Huemer 2008, pp. 67–72) Shafer-Landau defends the open question argument as "relevant". See also (Shafer-Landau 2005, pp. 57–58).

See also Nicholas L. Sturgeon (2016) "Naturalism in Ethics", in *Routledge Encyclopedia of Philosophy* (London: Routledge). For a useful exposition of how Moore uses the notion of the naturalistic fallacy see (Gauthier 1967).

(Irwin 2011, p. 633) Here Irwin makes an important point as it relates to Moore's open question argument. He observes, ". . . if the appeal to an open question is legitimate, it shows that Good is not only indefinable, but also inexplicable". This leaves us effectively with no moral knowledge. See Irwin's excellent entire discussion.

The many debates spinning off from Moore's work can be sampled in (Horgan and Timmons 2006).

(Warnock 2007).

(Irwin 2011, pp. 639–41) See also (Moore 1962, p. 98).

(Moore [1903] 1993, p. 2). Moore stated in the same preface that a rewrite of the entire book was needed but that he was not able to undertake such a task.

(Schlipp 1968b, 2:582) See both volumes in this series for many well-known critical essays on Moore's ethics.

(Schlipp 1968b, 2:591).

Soames provides the most technical and detailed criticism of Moore's thinking. *Philosophical Analysis in the Twentieth Century. 1: The Dawn of Analysis*: 3–90.

(Willard 2018, p. 159) Emphasis original.

(Moore [1903] 1993, p. 199) Emphasis mine. This view is also reaffirmed in Moore's summary of his views on right conduct, ibid, pp. 229–31. Moore later states, ". . . an action ought to be done or is our duty, only where it produces *more* pleasure than any which we could have done instead". (Moore 2005, p. 15) Emphasis is the author's. The problems with this again seem obvious. See also ibid, p. 120 for a version of Sidgwick's dualism of practical reason juggernaut.

Hastings Rashdall, *The Theory of Good and Evil a Treatise on Moral Philosophy*, (Clarendon Press, Oxford, Britain, 1907) vii. (Sorley 1918).

(C.S. Lewis 1978, 2001; Baggett et al. 2008).

Intuitionism is most strongly represented by the work of W.D. (Ross 1930, 1939) Curent versions of intuitionist nonnaturalism are discussed and criticized in detail in the authors Dissertation *A Theistic Critique of Secular Moral Nonnaturalism* ©.

Ayer (1936), *Language, Truth and Logic* (New York: Dover Publications) 107. Ayer represents the movement known as logical positivism. Theological propositions are "meaningless" according to Ayer. The term emotivism is used by C.L. Stevenson (1937). By this term, Stevenson meant that ethical propositions expressed emotional attitudes that involved personal influence directed towards ethical matters. C.L. Stevenson (1944), "The Emotive Meaning of Ethical Terms", *Mind* 46, no. 181 (1937): 14–31; C.L. Stevenson, *Ethics and Language* (Oxford: Oxford University Press). Emotivism is part of a larger turn in ethics that occurred after Moore and is referred to as ethical non-cognitivism. For a good introduction to this, see (Schroeder 2010).

Stuart Hampshire, "Fallacies in Moral Philosophy", *Mind*, 58, no. 232 (October 1949): 466-82; (Firth 1952; Anscombe and Margaret 1958; Hampshire 1949).

References

Adam, Lloyd Johnson. 2023. *Divine Love Theory: How the Trinity Is the Source and Foundation of Morality*. Grand Rapids: Kregel Academic.

Anscombe, Gertude, and Elizabeth Margaret. 1958. Modern Moral Philosophy. *The Journal of the Royal Institute of Philosophy* 33: 1–19.

Ayer, A. J. 1936. *Language, Truth and Logic*. New York: Dover Publications.

Baggett, David. 2018. Moral Arguments (Actually R1 to Rn): An Abductive Moral Argument for God. In *Two Dozen (or so) Arguments for God: The Plantinga Project*. Edited by Trent Dougherty, Jerry L. Walls and Alvin Plantinga. New York: Oxford University Press.

Baggett, David, and Jerry L. Walls. 2011. *Good God: The Theistic Foundations of Morality*. New York: Oxford University Press.

Baggett, David, and Jerry L. Walls. 2016. *God and Cosmos: Moral Truth and Human Meaning*. New York: Oxford University Press.

Baggett, David, and Jerry L. Walls. 2019. *The Moral Argument: A History.* New York: Oxford University Press.

Baggett, David, Gary R. Habermas, and Jerry L. Walls, eds. 2008. *C.S. Lewis as Philosopher: Truth, Goodness and Beauty.* Downers Grove: IVP Academic.

Baldwin, Thomas. 2003. A Hundred Years of Principia Ethica: Interview with Thomas Baldwin. *Florianopolis* 2: 3–13.

Baldwin, Thomas. 2010. George Edward Moore. In *Stanford Encyclopedia of Philosophy.* Edited by Edward N. Zalta. Stanford: The Metaphysics Research Lab., pp. 1–16.

Balfour, Arthur. 1915. *Theism and Humanism.* London: Hodder and Stoughton.

Balfour, Arthur. 1923. *Theism and Thought.* London: Hodder and Stoughton.

Balfour, Arthur James, and Michael W. Perry. 2000. *Theism and Humanism: The Book That Influenced C.S. Lewis.* Seattle: Inkling Books.

Bourget, David, and David J. Chalmers. 2014. What Do Philosophers Believe? *Philosophical Studies* 170: 465–500. [CrossRef]

Breitenbach, Zachary. 2021. Evaluating the Theistic Implications of the Kantian Moral Argument That Postulating God Is Essential to Moral Rationality. *Studies in Christian Ethics* 34: 143–57. [CrossRef]

Brink, David O. 1994. Common Sense and First Principles in Sidgwick's Methods. *Social Philosophy and Policy* 11: 179–201.

Brink, David O. 2018. Mill's Moral and Political Philosophy. In *Stanford Encyclopedia of Philosophy.* Edited by Edward N. Zalta. Stanford: Metaphysics Research Lab., pp. 1–55.

Broad, C. D. 1930. *Five Types of Ethical Theory.* New York: Routledge, Taylor & Francis Group.

Carr, Robert. 1962. The Religious Thought of John Stuart Mill: A Study in Reluctant Scepticism. *Journal of the History of Ideas* 23: 495.

Craig, William Lane. 2008. *Reasonable Faith: Christian Truth and Apologetics,* 3rd ed. Wheaton: Crossway Books.

Craig, William Lane, Erik J. Wielenberg, Adam Lloyd Johnson, and J. P. Moreland. 2020. *A Debate on God and Morality: What Is the Best Account of Objective Moral Values and Duties?* New York: Routledge, pp. 93–114.

Crimmins, J. 1998. *Utilitarian's and Religion.* Bristol: Thoemmes Press.

Crisp, Roger. 2015. *The Cosmos of Duty: Henry Sidgwick's Methods of Ethics.* Oxford: Clarendon Press.

Darwall, Stephen, Allan Gibbard, and Peter Railton. 1992. Toward Fin de Siecle Ethics: Some Trends. *The Philosophical Review* 101: 115.

De Burgh, W. G. 1970. *From Morality to Religion.* Gifford Lectures 1938. New York: Kennikat Press. First published 1938.

Devigne, Robert. 2006. Reforming Reformed Religion: J. S. Mill's Critique of the Enlightenment's Natural Religion. *American Political Science Review* 100: 15–27.

Dougherty, Trent, Jerry L. Walls, and Alvin Plantinga, eds. 2018. *Two Dozen (or So) Arguments for God: The Plantinga Project.* New York: Oxford University Press.

Eddy, M. D. 2004. The Rhetoric and Science of William Paley's Natural Theology. *Literature and Theology* 18: 1–22. [CrossRef]

Enoch, David. 2013. *Taking Morality Seriously: A Defense of Robust Realism.* Oxford: Oxford University Press.

Evans, C. Stephen. 2010. *Natural Signs and Knowledge of God: A New Look at Theistic Arguments.* Oxford: Oxford University Press.

Evans, C. Stephen. 2014. *God and Moral Obligation.* Oxford: Oxford University Press.

Evans, C. Stephen, and Trinity O'Neill. 2021. The Moral Argument. In *Contemporary Arguments in Natural Theology: God and Rational Belief.* Edited by C. P. Ruloff and Peter Horban. New York: Bloomsbury Academic.

Ewing, A. C. 1973. *Values and Reality: The Philosophical Case for Theism.* Hyattsville: Alphaville Books.

Firth, Roderick. 1952. Ethical Absolutism and the Ideal Observer. *Philosophy and Phenomenological Research* 12: 317.

Frankena, William K. 1950. Some Arguments for Non-Naturalism About Intrinsic Value. *Philosophical Studies* 1: 56–60. [CrossRef]

Fyfe, Aileen. 1997. The Reception of William Paley's 'Natural Theology' in the University of Cambridge. *The British Journal for the History of Science* 30: 321–35. [CrossRef]

Gauthier, David P. 1967. Moore's Naturalistic Fallacy. *American Philosophical Quarterly* 4: 315–20.

Geach, P. T. 1956. Good and Evil. *Analysis* 17: 33–42. [CrossRef]

Hampshire, Stuart. 1949. Fallacies in Moral Philosophy. *Mind* 58: 466–82. [CrossRef]

Harrison, Ross. 1996. Cambridge Philosophers VI: Henry Sidgwick. *Philosophy* 71: 423–38.

Holley, David M. 2002. Sidgwick's Problem. *Ethical Theory and Moral Practice* 5: 45–65.

Horgan, Terry, and Mark Timmons, eds. 2006. *Metaethics after Moore.* New York: Clarendon Press; Oxford: Oxford University Press.

Huemer, Michael. 2008. *Ethical Intuitionism.* New York: Palgrave Macmillan.

Hume, David. 1984. *A Treatise of Human Nature.* Edited by Ernest C. Mossner. New York: Penguin Books. First published 1739.

Hume, David. 1998. *Dialogues Concerning Natural Religion, the Posthumous Essays, of the Immortality of the Soul, and of Suicide, from an Enquiry Concerning Human Understanding of Miracles,* 2nd ed. Edited by Richard H. Popkin. Indianapolis: Hackett Publishing. First published 1779.

Hurka, Thomas. 2003. Moore in the Middle. *Ethics* 113: 599–628. [CrossRef]

Irwin, Terence. 2011. *The Development of Ethics: A Historical and Critical Study. Vol. 3: From Kant to Rawls.* Oxford: Oxford University Press.

Jakobsen, Martin. 2020. *Moral Realism and the Existence of God: Improving Parfit's Metaethics.* Leuven and Paris: Peeters.

Jordan, Matthew Carey. 2011. Some Metaethical Desiderata and the Conceptual Resources of Theism. *Sophia* 50: 39–55.

Kant, Immanuel. 2012. *Groundwork of the Metaphysics of Morals,* Revised ed. Edited by Jens Timmermann. Translated by Mary J. Gregor. Cambridge: Cambridge University Press. First published 1785.

Kant, Immanuel. 2015. *Critique of Practical Reason,* Revised ed. Translated by Mary J. Gregor. Cambridge Texts in the History of Philosophy. Cambridge: Cambridge University Press. First published 1788.

Kant, Immanuel. 2017. *The Metaphysics of Morals*, 2nd ed. Edited by Denis Lara. Translated by Mary J. Gregor. Cambridge: Cambridge University Press. First published 1797.

Kratt, Dale E. 2023. A Theistic Critique of Secular Moral Nonnaturalism. Ph.D. dissertation, Liberty University, Lynchburg, VA, USA.

Kulp, Christopher B. 2017. *Knowing Moral Truth: A Theory of Metaethics and Moral Knowledge*. New York: Lexington Books.

Kulp, Christopher B. 2019. *Metaphysics of Morality*. Switzerland: Palgrave Macmillan.

Larsen, Timothy. 2018. *John Stuart Mill: A Secular Life*. Oxford: Oxford University Press.

Lewis, C. S. 1978. *The Abolition of Man*. New York: Macmillan.

Lewis, C. S. 2001. *Mere Christianity: A Revised and Amplified Edition, with a New Introduction*. San Francisco: HarperSanFrancisco.

Linville, Mark D. 2012. The Moral Argument. In *The Blackwell Companion to Natural Theology*. Edited by William Lane Craig and J. P. Moreland. Oxford: Wiley-Blackwell, pp. 391–448.

MacIntyre, Alasdair C. 1998. *A Short History of Ethics: A History of Moral Philosophy from the Homeric Age to the Twentieth Century*, 2nd ed. Notre Dame: University of Notre Dame Press.

MacIntyre, Alasdair C. 2011. On Being A Theistic Philosopher in a Secularized Culture. *Proceedings of the American Catholic Philosophical Association* 84: 23–32. [CrossRef]

Mackie, J. L. 1976. Sidgwick's Pessimism. *Philosophical Quarterly* 26: 317–27. [CrossRef]

Mackie, J. L. 1990. *Ethics: Inventing Right and Wrong*. New York: Penguin.

Matthews, W. R. 1947. *God in Christian Thought and Experience*. London: James Nisbet.

Medema, Steven G. 2008. 'Losing My Religion': Sidgwick, Theism, and the Struggle for Utilitarian Ethics in Economic Analysis. *History of Political Economy, Annual Supplement* 40: 189–211.

Miller, Alexander. 2013. *Contemporary Metaethics: An Introduction*, 2nd ed. Malden: Polity Press.

Mill, John Stuart. 1998. *Three Essays on Religion*. Amherst: Prometheus Books. First published 1874.

Mill, John Stuart. 2001. Utilitarianism, 2nd ed. Edited by George Sher. Chandigarh: Hackett.

Mill, John Stuart. 2002. *The Basic Writings of John Stuart Mill: On Liberty, The Subjection of Women, and Utilitarianism*. New York: Random House, Modern Library.

Mitchell, Basil. 1967. *Law, Morality, and Religion in a Secular Society*. Oxford: Oxford University Press.

Mitchell, Basil. 2000. *Morality, Religious and Secular: The Dilemma of the Traditional Conscience*. New York: Clarendon Press.

Moore, G. E. 1903. The Refutation of Idealism. *Mind* 12: 433–53. [CrossRef]

Moore, G. E. 1962. Is Goodness a Quality? In *Philosophical Papers*. New York: Collier Books, pp. 89–100.

Moore, G. E. 1993. *Principia Ethica*, Rev. ed. with Pref. to the 2nd ed. and Other Papers. Edited by Thomas Baldwin. New York: Cambridge University Press. First published 1903.

Moore, G. E. 2005. *Ethics: The Nature of Moral Philosophy*. Edited by William H. Shaw. Oxford: Clarendon Press.

Moreland, James Porter, and Scott B. Rae. 2000. *Body & Soul: Human Nature & the Crisis in Ethics*. Downers Grove: InterVarsity Press.

Moreland, J. P. 2009. *The Recalcitrant Imago Dei: Human Persons and the Failure of Naturalism*. London: SCM Press.

Nuccetelli, Susana, and Gary Seay. 2008. What's Right About the Open Question Argument. In *Themes from G. E. Moore: New Essays in Epistemology and Ethics*. Edited by Susana Nuccetelli and Gary Seay. New York: Oxford University Press, pp. 261–82.

Owen, H. P. 1965. *The Moral Argument for Christian Theism*. London: George Allen & Unwin Ltd.

Paley, William. 2017. *Natural Theology*. Miami: HardPress. First published 1802.

Paley, William. 2017. *Principles of Moral and Political Philosophy*. Miami: HardPress. First published 1785.

Parfit, Derek. 1987. *Reasons and Persons*. Oxford: Clarendon Press.

Parfit, Derek. 2011. *On What Matters*. 3 vols. The Berkeley Tanner Lectures. New York: Oxford University Press, vol. 1.

Parrish, Stephen E. 2019. *Atheism?: A Critical Analysis*. Eugene: Wipf & Stock.

Parrish, Stephen. *The Nature of Moral Necessity*, forthcoming.

Phillips, David. 2011. *Sidgwickian Ethics*. New York: Oxford University Press.

Prichard, H. A. 1912. Does Moral Philosophy Rest on a Mistake? *Mind, New Series* 21: 21–37.

Raeder, Linda C. 2001. Mill's Religion of Humanity: Consequences and Implications. *Humanitas* 14: 4–34.

Raeder, Linda C. 2002. *John Stuart Mill and the Religion of Humanity*. Columbia: University of Missouri Press.

Rashdall, Hastings. 1907. *The Theory of Good and Evil: A Treatise on Moral Philosophy*. vols. 1 and 2. Oxford: Clarendon Press.

Regan, Donald H. 2003. How to Be a Moorean. *Ethics* 113: 651–77. [CrossRef]

Ritchie, Angus. 2012. *From Morality to Metaphysics: The Theistic Implications of Our Ethical Commitments*. Oxford: Oxford University Press.

Rosen, Frederick. 2005. *Classical Utilitarianism from Hume to Mill*. London and New York: Routledge.

Ross, W. D. 1930. *The Right and the Good, New edition*. Edited by Philip Stratton-Lake. Oxford and New York: Clarendon Press.

Ross, W. D. 1939. *Foundations of Ethics*. New York: Oxford University Press.

Sayre-McCord, Geoffrey. 1988a. Introduction: The Many Moral Realisms. In *Essays on Moral Realism*. Edited by Geoffrey Sayre-McCord. Ithaca: Cornell University Press, pp. 1–23.

Sayre-McCord, Geoffrey, ed. 1988b. *Essays on Moral Realism*. Ithaca: Cornell University Press.

Scanlon, Thomas. 1998. *What We Owe to Each Other*. Cambridge: Belknap Press of Harvard University Press.

Schlipp, Paul Arthur. 1968a. *The Philosophy of G.E. Moore*, 3rd ed. The Library of Living Philosophers. London: Cambridge University Press, vol. 1.

Schlipp, Paul Arthur. 1968b. *The Philosophy of G.E. Moore*, 3rd ed. The Library of Living Philosophers. London: Cambridge University Press, vol. 2.

Schneewind, J. B. 1977. *Sidgwick's Ethics and Victorian Moral Philosophy*. Oxford: Clarendon Press.

Schroeder, Mark Andrew. 2010. *Noncognitivism in Ethics*. New York: Routledge.

Schultz, Bart. 2004. *Henry Sidgwick, Eye of the Universe: An Intellectual Biography*. New York: Cambridge University Press.

Sennett, James F., and Douglas R. Groothuis, eds. 2005. *In Defense of Natural Theology: A Post-Humean Assessment*. Downers Grove: InterVarsity Press.

Sessions, William Lad. 1985. A New Look at Moral Arguments for Theism. *International Journal for Philosophy of Religion* 18: 51–67. [CrossRef]

Settanni, Harry. 1991. *The Probabilist Theism of John Stuart Mill*. New York: Peter Lang Publishing.

Shafer-Landau, Russ. 2005. *Moral Realism: A Defense*. Oxford: Clarendon Press.

Sidgwick, E. M, and A. Sidgwick. 1906. *Henry Sidgwick: A Memoir*. London: Macmillan & Co.

Sidgwick, Henry. 1879. The Establishment of Ethical First Principles. *Mind* 13: 106–11. [CrossRef]

Sidgwick, Henry. 1962. *The Methods of Ethics*, 7th ed. London: Macmillan & Co.

Sidgwick, Henry, J. H. Muirhead, G. F. Stout, and S. Alexander. 1892. Symposium: Is the Distinction between 'Is' and 'Ought' Ultimate and Irreducible? *Proceedings of the Aristotelian Society* 2: 88–107.

Sinclair, Neil, ed. 2019. *The Naturalistic Fallacy*. Cambridge: Cambridge University Press.

Skelton, Anthony. 2010. Henry Sidgwick's Moral Epistemology. *Journal of the History of Philosophy* 48: 491–519. [CrossRef]

Soames, Scott. 2005. *Philosophical Analysis in the Twentieth Century. 1: The Dawn of Analysis*. Princeton Paperbacks. Princeton: Princeton University Press.

Sorley, W. R. 1904. *On The Ethics of Naturalism*. Shaw Fellowship Lectures 1884. London: William Blackwood and Sons.

Sorley, W. R. 1918. *Moral Values and the Idea of God*. Cambridge: Cambridge University Press.

Sorley, William. 1905. The Method of a Metaphysic of Ethics. *The Philosophical Review* 14: 521–634.

Sorley, W. R. 2015. *On The Ethics of Naturalism, Shaw Fellowship Lectures*. London: William Blackwood and Sons. First published 1884.

Stevenson, Charles Leslie. 1937. The Emotive Meaning of Ethical Terms. *Mind* 46: 14–31. [CrossRef]

Stevenson, C. L. 1944. *Ethics and Language*. Oxford: Oxford University Press.

Sturgeon, Nicholas L. 2003. Moore on Ethical Naturalism. *Ethics* 113: 528–56.

Sturgeon, Nicholas L. 2016. Naturalism in Ethics. In *Routledge Encyclopedia of Philosophy*. London: Routledge.

Taylor, A. E. 1930. *The Faith of a Moralist*. London: Macmillan & Co.

Taylor, Charles. 1989. *Sources of the Self: The Making of the Modern Identity*. Cambridge: Harvard University Press.

Taylor, Charles. 2007. *A Secular Age*. Cambridge: Belknap Press of Harvard University Press.

Thorvaldsen, Steinar, and Peter Øhrstrøm. 2013. Darwin's Perplexing Paradox: Intelligent Design in Nature. *Perspectives in Biology and Medicine* 56: 78–98. [PubMed]

Tribe, Keith. 2017. Henry Sidgwick, Moral Order, and Utilitarianism. *The European Journal of the History of Economic Thought* 24: 907–30. [CrossRef]

Tucker, Miles. 2018. Simply Good: A Defence of the Principia. *Utilitas* 30: 253–70. [CrossRef]

Warnock, Mary. 2007. *Ethics Since 1900*. Mount Jackson: Axios Press, Distributed by National Book Network.

Webb, Clement C. J. 1918. *God and Personality*. New York: Macmillan & Co.

Wielenberg, Erik J. 2014. *Robust Ethics: The Metaphysics and Epistemology of Godless Normative Realism*. Oxford: Oxford University Press.

Willard, Dallas. 2011. Naturalism's Incapacity to Capture the Good Will. In *The Nature of Nature: Examining the Role of Naturalism in Science*. Edited by Bruce Gordon and William A. Dembski. Wilmington: ISI Books, pp. 865–78.

Willard, Dallas. 2018. *The Disappearance of Moral Knowledge*. Edited by Gregg Ten Elshof, Steven L. Porter and Aaron Preston. New York: Routledge.

Article

Might Beauty Bolster the Moral Argument for God?

David Baggett

Department of Philosophy, School of Christian Thought Apologetics, Houston Christian University, Houston, TX 77074, USA; dbaggett@hbu.edu

Abstract: John Hare argues that Kant, in his *Third Critique*, offers an aesthetic argument for God's existence that shares premises with his famous moral argument. Karl Ameriks demurs, expressing skepticism that this is so. In this paper, I stake out an intermediate position, arguing that the resources of Kant provide ingredients for an aesthetic argument, but one distinctly less than a transcendental argument for God or an entailment relation. Whether the argument is best thought of as abductive in nature, a C-inductive argument, or a Pascalian natural sign, prospects for its formulation are strong. And such an argument, for its resonances with the moral argument(s), can work well in tandem with it (them), a fact not surprising at all if Kant was right that beauty—in accordance with an ancient Greek tradition—exists in close organic relation to the good. More generally, along the way, I argue that the sea change in Kant's studies over the last decade or so should help us see that Kant is an ally, rather than foe, to aesthetic theodicists.

Keywords: kalon; good; beauty; sublime; Immanuel Kant; John Hare; Karl Ameriks; aesthetic argument; moral argument; Critique of Judgment; transcendentals

Citation: Baggett, David. 2023. Might Beauty Bolster the Moral Argument for God? . *Religions* 14: 1029. https:// doi.org/10.3390/rel14081029

Academic Editor: Roberto Di Ceglie

Received: 28 June 2023
Revised: 1 August 2023
Accepted: 7 August 2023
Published: 10 August 2023

1. Introduction

This exploratory essay wishes to broach the connection between two sorts of evidence for God's existence, namely, that from beauty and that from goodness. Both sets of considerations are experiential in nature because they tend to be predicated on a certain sort of phenomenological appeal—of beauty, in the first instance, and of goodness (or oughtness or human value or justice or some other important axiological or deontic moral reality) in the second instance.[1]

Rather than thinking of the evidential significance of the two sets of considerations as altogether independent, it might be worthwhile to explore whether their juxtaposition, if not their integration, might enhance their cumulative power. What animates the study is the traditional view in the history of Christianity, not to mention other important philosophies and religions, that the so-called "transcendentals" (truth, goodness, beauty, unity, etc.) are ultimately, in some sense, of a piece. Iris Murdoch, to mention just one among a plethora of examples that could be adduced, wrote in *The Sovereignty of the Good*, echoing a central claim of the Platonic tradition regarding the unity of the transcendentals, "Goodness and beauty are not to be contrasted, but are largely part of the same structure. Plato, who tells us that beauty is the only spiritual thing that we love immediately by nature, treats the beautiful as an introductory section of the good. So that aesthetic situations are not so much analogies of morals as cases of morals" (Murdoch 1989, p. 40).

We will take the general logical schema of moral arguments for God's existence, whatever their specific content, to go something like this:

(P1) There are various moral phenomena that stand in need of explanation.
(P2) The only or best explanation of such phenomena is God.
(C) So, these moral phenomena give us reasons to believe in God.

We will not take a position on whether instances of such a form are sound, nor on how much evidence such arguments may provide, besides mentioning a spectrum of possibilities. Our concerns lie elsewhere, in what might be called overall dialectic features of the resultant discursive structure. Among the moral phenomena that the first premise might adduce include moral goodness, intrinsic human value, moral rights or duties, or other putative moral facts. Obviously, a defense of the moral realism of the first premise would require offering positive reasons in its favor and a critique of various meta-ethical alternatives like constructivism, expressivism, and nihilism. This essay will not be doing such work, vitally important as it is. (Jerry Walls and I are finishing a book on this topic.)

The second premise would require positive reasons for thinking that theism provides a good explanation of the moral phenomena in question. Accomplishing this task requires two goals to be achieved: providing those reasons, along with reasons for thinking that nontheistic alternative explanations do not explain the moral phenomena just as well or better. The sort of theism we have in mind is the usual suspect: something in the neighborhood of classical theism or theistic personalism, according to which God is the possessor of the various omni-qualities, the maximally compossible set of great-making properties. There are of course less ambitious ways to formulate the second premise, some of which will be mentioned later, but this suffices to get our discussion underway.

Now, among the moral phenomena in the world are not just duties and rights and values, but conspicuous disvalues, discordant ethical realities, grave injustices, horrific tragedies, and heinous evils. So, it is incumbent on proponents of the moral argument, at some point, to provide explanations of these moral realities as well. This creates a shared space for moral apologists and theodicists.

When William Sorley was writing his Gifford lectures on God and ethics, he received news of the death of his son Charles, who had been fighting in the First World War. The whole tenor of his subsequent lectures seems tinged with tragedy, a poignant recognition that he somehow could not just discuss moral goodness, but also the tragedy and evil that we encounter in this world (Sorley 1935).

How might beauty—and aesthetic considerations more generally—inform our understanding of the tragedies of this world? And might doing so help bolster the moral argument for God's existence?

2. Misguided Efforts and Kant's Aesthetic Judgments

One reason that many might be skeptical about aesthetic insights making important contributions to a discussion of theodicy owes to what amounts to painfully bad and patently superficial efforts to do so. Terence Penulhum argues at length against thinking that, as he puts it, "minor aesthetic advantages could outweigh major moral and physical disadvantages". He uses as a rhetorical example the "charming pink flush" of a tuberculosis patient (Penulhum 1992). Timothy O'Connor and Philip Quinn, without denying the reality of aesthetic values, agree, echoing similar skepticism over aesthetic considerations having much to offer theodicy. Eleonore Stump is more open to what nonmoral values might contribute to the discussion, but she remains tentative and provisional (O'Connor 2002; Quinn 1992; Stump 1985).

Among the several reasons why many retain skepticism about contributions of aesthetics to theodicy is the formidable influence of Immanuel Kant, because a common reading of his *Third Critique* is that aesthetics is a largely subjectivist matter. Marilyn Adams cites this volume of Kant's—his *Critique of Judgment*—as a significant explanation why thinkers like those just mentioned enforce a compartmentalization of aesthetics and ethics (Adams 1999). Philip Tallon, in his brilliant and erudite *Poetics of Evil*, gravitates toward such a reading of Kant, even while lamenting that such a reading lends itself to divorcing aesthetics and theodicy. Tallon assigns quite a bit of primacy to what Kant has to say in the *Third Critique* about a rigid distinction between aesthetic judgments on one hand and recognition of something's purpose or function on the other.

The crux of this point pertains to the role of *concepts*. In concert with a common reading of Kant, Tallon discerns "a sharp break between Kant's theory and the mimetically driven accounts of Plato and Aristotle. Further, Kant is keen to break with the Medieval emphasis on formal properties and principles of the kind frequently described by Augustine as proportion or order (to which Aquinas adds luminosity and integrity)" (Tallon 2012, p. 52). Tallon takes the import of Kant's denial that there is an empirical ground of proof that would force a judgment of taste on anyone to be tantamount to arguing that aesthetic judgments are largely devoid of cognitive content, a reading that lends itself to a strongly subjectivist understanding of beauty that bears little relevance to ethics (and thus theodicy).

This reading of Kant resonates with a great deal of Kantian exegesis and the way Kant has often been historically understood. Even Kant himself, in the Transcendental Aesthetic of the first edition of the *Critique of Pure Reason*, began with a note indicating that the sensory character of taste disqualifies it from being characterizable as pure and objective. Subjectivist readings of Kant's philosophy still abound (sometimes not just in aesthetics, but also in ethics and metaphysics). As Karl Ameriks puts it, "Ever since the interpretive tradition of Hegel to Gadamer and then beyond to the deconstructionists, Kant's aesthetics has been interpreted–sometimes favorably, but often for dismissive purposes–as the inauguration of a subjectivist turn in aesthetics" (Ameriks forthcoming). Such readings are understandable. Kant himself even often characterized items like space, time, and empirical knowledge in subjective terms, not to mention various moral and religious experiences.

While conceding Roger Scruton's point that Kant did not altogether separate aesthetics and morality, Tallon seeks out more points of contact between them than he thinks Kant's subjectivism allows. Kant's dismissal of the deliverances of art critics suggests to Tallon that there is no room, to Kant's thinking, for adjudicating between divergent aesthetical appraisals. Even worse, Kant affirms the autonomy of aesthetic objects qua aesthetic objects, rendering their use for other purposes impossible. As Tallon puts it, "On Kant's conception, perception of beauty and perception of purpose must exist in alternate dimensions of thinking and cannot mutually inform one another. While beauty and other aesthetic categories can be affirmed under this model, its value for theodicy will likely be minimal to nonexistent" (Tallon 2012, p. 53).[2]

Even among those who have neither the time nor inclination to read Kant can often be found a subjectivist construal of aesthetics. The notion that beauty resides in the eye of the beholder is ubiquitous nowadays, even among a range of art critics, a loss of nerve that Tallon dubs a "near-Kantian philosophy". Assuming objectivist ethics are often tacitly presumed verboten. Tallon concludes, "Thus, it seems probable that, though the modern aesthetic attitude may not be held to dogmatically, the Kantian legacy remains widely influential among everyday consumers of culture, eloquent critics, and theodicists as well" (Tallon 2012, p. 54).

3. Kant in Context

Hans Urs von Balthasar famously argued that Kant's arrival at beauty only in his *Third Critique* (after truth in the *First* and goodness in the *Second*) represents the way philosophers tend to privilege truth and goodness over beauty. Balthasar argued that this is a mistake. He thought that beauty paves the way to thinking of goodness and finally truth in the right sort of way, making beauty the appropriate place to begin. It can offer an enrapturing vision of how the world ought to be, something that includes our will within God's animating providence. Whether or not he was right about this claim is not our present concern, but this essay is definitely predicated on the intriguing possibility that aesthetic considerations, including evidential ones, can augment and supplement the dialectic forging a vital connection between God and ethics.

Perhaps even more indicting was von Balthasar's critique of those strands of Enlightenment thought that relegate aesthetic considerations to the realm of the subjective, with Kant's approach being the most pre-eminent among them. He read Kant in saying that aesthetic realities are confined to the world as it appears to us rather than the world as it is in itself as suggesting that beauty is delimited to psychic states of imagination and empathy rather than as one of the transcendental aspects of Being as such (von Balthasar 1982). Following various church fathers, as mentioned, Balthasar opposed how Kant merely concluded his trilogy with beauty and suggested instead that beauty should be our proper starting point. Gadamer's *Truth and Method*, similarly, argued that art puts us in touch with the "other", in opposition to the "radical subjectivization of aesthetics" that followed Kant's *Critique of Judgment* (Gadamer 2004).

Such readings of Kant are common. Still, a serious case can be made, and has been made, that subjectivist readings of Kant's aesthetics, though eminently understandable and quite widespread, are nevertheless quite mistaken. In just the last few decades there has been quite a sea change in Kant studies, with scholars like John Hare, Stephen Palmquist, and Karl Ameriks playing leading roles.[3] If this fresh set of interpretations of Kant is on the right track, then Kant may actually be a powerful ally to aesthetic theodicists, even if not all Kantian exegetes are as cordial or amenable to the enterprise.

Although it is true that early on Kant thought aesthetic judgments are, of necessity, subjective for being tied to pleasure and the faculty of feeling, he quickly nuanced his view and struck a different note. In an edition of the *First Critique* published several years before the *Third Critique*, Kant turned to the view that aesthetic feeling has a more than merely sensory significance, for there is a *pure* judgment of taste that can be distinguished from mere sensory reactions and impersonal empirical observations.

Feelings, of course, are easily and notoriously construed in contingent and subjectivist terms, but here, Kant's mention of "disinterested pleasure" in quality is relevant. Tallon and others take the import of such disinterestedness to preclude looking to the aesthetic with an eye for application to religious concerns, including that of theodicy. But Ameriks and Hare, among others, see its import differently: Kant's point lifts taste above the acquisitive contingencies of our sensory nature and also differentiates it from the concern with actualization essential to the moral will (Ameriks forthcoming). It is instructive, indeed striking, that Kant's first *positive* depiction of aesthetic taste comes with the claim of *universal validity*, a conception rife with objective significance. Indeed, that a judgment of taste rightfully makes a claim of validity for *all* other human perceivers is about as objective as it can be. And as Ameriks puts it, "Taste is not disadvantaged by not providing a direct access to things in themselves, or by an inability to rest its claims on deductions from mere concepts in pure theoretical arguments" (Ameriks forthcoming).

While acknowledging the brilliance of Kant's effort to solve the antinomy of subjectivity and universality, Tallon focuses inordinately on the subjective component. In the process, he potentially misses out on seeing that Kant may be more friend than foe in the effort at constructing an aesthetic theodicy. In truth, we can find in Kant's work more organic connections between beauty and goodness than Tallon thinks. This will become increasingly clear, especially as we explore the possibility that Kant aimed to provide not just a moral argument for God's existence, but an aesthetic one. First, let us address a few lingering points from earlier.

What about the critique that Kant's aesthetics leave little to no room for discussion about art with a philosopher? Here, recall that the antinomy of judgment with which Kant struggled involves the thesis that aesthetic judgments are personal and subjective and the antithesis that we argue, and rightly so, about those judgments. The former suggests that aesthetics lacks guiding concepts, and the latter that it does not. By turns, both seem true, thus the antinomy.

Kant's solution, which we will have occasion to discuss more in a moment, aimed to effect a rapprochement between objective and subjective elements, not vitiate the former altogether. Of course, the challenge of generating such a synthesis is real, as anyone can attest who has tried to convince someone not already convinced of or, worse, dead set on rejecting the beauty of something. If someone wishes to deny the sublime and transcendent qualities of the most beautiful of sunsets or orchestral movement, she is at liberty to do so, and powers of persuasion quickly reach their limits. No logical demonstration is available like we find in geometry. But just as a good argument need not be found to be universally persuasive, the limitations of rational efforts at aesthetic adjudication are no evidence against objective beauty.

This is arguably related to Kant's refusal to listen to arguments and reasoning when an alleged art critic is invoked as a definitive authority. Perhaps on occasion such resistance is attributable to a sort of obstinacy or recalcitrance, incorrigibility or hubris, but on other occasions it is eminently justified. If an art critic, in the spirit of Oscar Wilde, divorces beauty and goodness, and heaps accolades on (say) Andres Serrano's *Piss Christ*, a 1987 photograph depicting a small plastic crucifix submerged in the artist's urine, we remain skeptical. Art critic Lucy R. Lippard has presented a constructive case for the formal value of the artwork that she thinks ineffably mysterious, "a darkly beautiful photographic image . . . the small wood and plastic crucifix becomes virtually monumental as it floats, photographically enlarged, in a deep rosy glow that is both ominous and glorious" (Lippard 1990). With Kant, we are rather unapologetically inclined to stop our ears and to demur from rather than defer to the "expert".

Lastly, for now, does Kant's aesthetic theory preclude consideration of what a piece of artwork or beautiful scene objectively provides? Ameriks does not think so, writing:

> [T]here is something significantly objective about an aesthetic judgment's being rooted even in a feature of the first moment of taste, its involving pleasure in the specific way that it does as a matter of sensory *givenness*. This is because pleasure in taste is not a mere internal event but is the result of a *special* kind of positive *reaction* to a general feature of something that is originally given to us from *outside*. As with other reactions to the impact of external objects, it is only appropriate to presume that taste rests on some kind of objective causal features that make talk of "universally valid" judgment possible. The special significance of the *Faktum* of *natural* beauty for Kant depends on the fact that the pleasure involved here is not to be understood as initially a mere reverie but as a response to an *appropriate external form* (Ameriks forthcoming).

If this recent shift in Kantian exegesis rightly tracks strongly objectivist elements in his aesthetic analysis, it is good news for an aesthetic theodicy because it means that, rather than Kant being a detractor, he might instead be a staunch ally. We can see this perhaps more clearly as we look at what may well be something of an aesthetic argument for God's existence in Kant's *Third Critique*.

4. Kant's Aesthetic Argument

Earlier, we briefly sketched a general schema for moral arguments. Kant is well known for offering a moral argument. A word is in order by way of quickly capturing its gist and concrete flavor because, if John Hare is right, Kant also provided an aesthetic argument that is closely related to it. If Hare is even close to being right, it will show that Kant may help rather than hurt or hinder an aesthetic theodicy.

Kant is well known for writing in the preface to the second edition of the *First Critique* that he found it necessary to deny knowledge in order to make room for faith. There is a moral argument from grace found in Kant, but here the focus will be on an argument from providence.[4] The argument, with a gloss from Hare, goes something like this: we have to postulate that God exists, even though this goes beyond our knowledge, in order to believe with rational stability in the real possibility of the highest good, which is the end that morality gives to us and which is made possible by the will of the supersensible author of nature (Hare 2023).

A key question is how to rank the priorities of happiness and virtue, and Kant thought that though duty should come first, we still retain both incentives. We need to believe rationally they do not, in the end, conflict, and this is how morality naturally leads to religion. We are not the authors of the moral law ourselves, but, owing to the experiential element of morality, we have to appropriate its truths for ourselves. This is the meaning of how we make morality a law for ourselves, and part of that procedure is recognizing our duties as God's commands. For only in this way can we reasonably believe in the real possibility of the highest good, right and good coming together, happiness and virtue reconciled. A loving and providential God is what ensures that righteousness and peace kiss. (Again, this is not the place to anticipate or try to answer some or all of the objections that could be raised to the argument.)

A central problem that emerges, which Kant hoped to address, is how to sustain the moral life. Respect for the moral law is important and deeply animating, but what happens when respect wanes, especially when the demands of the moral law become onerous and demanding? This is where, Hare argues, Kant introduced aesthetic considerations to fit the bill. What we need in those moments of temptation and weakness of will is a supplement not explicitly connected with the moral law. Recall that Kant spoke of beauty as a symbol of morality. Tallon is less than impressed with the image, writing that while the beautiful, for Kant, may be the mascot of the moral, it cannot play on the team, inhibiting its usefulness in theodicy. Hare would disagree, arguing that, in Kant's view, beauty makes moral ideas perceptible by a kind of analogy. The relationship between goodness and beauty is an intimate one, and the way to understand Kant on beauty is first to get clear on what he said about goodness.

The *Third Critique* came after the *Second*, where Kant accorded to the practical a kind of primacy. It is true that in the *First Critique* Kant eschewed theoretical efforts to demonstrate God's existence, but the *Second Critique* augmented the picture. Taking the inference to God as merely regulative merely warrants acting as if God exists; but taking it as constitutive, as Kant thought his practical argument made possible, warrants believing that God actually exists. The aesthetic argument of the *Third Critique* is constructed only after and in tandem with the moral argument of the *Second Critique*. Arguably, it is less an independent argument than an extension of the first, which was an adumbration of the second.[5]

Aesthetic pleasure, for Kant, provides a foretaste of the ultimate unity between nature and freedom, the unity to come that we will enjoy between our moral purposes and the world. We will experience this fully when our highest good is realized, which is God's purpose for us. This is why Ameriks thinks the most important locution of Kant's famous phrase "the starry heavens above and the moral law within" is the conjunction *and*. It is their ultimate union—nature and morality—that is the most breathtaking of all.

So, Hare argues that when Kant spoke of beauty as a symbol of morality, he spoke of a symbol because a symbol features structural similarity to that which is symbolized. Beauty is a symbol of morality because there is an analogy by which something true of morality is presented by a perceptible vehicle: the beautiful object. Herein lies Kant's solution to the antinomy of taste. When we experience harmony between the world and our faculties, we are encouraged to think the same supersensible author of nature is producing the analogous harmony that is our destination.

And thus, the beauty of various sensuous and finite things can and rightly should point us beyond those things to the deepest source of beauty itself. Aesthetic taste declares certain pleasures rightly valid for all humans as such, and not just for each person's private feeling. Kant's suggestion was that there is something all humans should value that the aesthetic enjoyment connects with and depends on. Because of differing tastes, what is universal is the highest good, of which aesthetic pleasure gives us a foretaste. This rationally requires, writes Hare, that we believe in God as the ground for the union of our happiness and our virtue and as the ground for the analogous fit between the aesthetic object and our faculties (Hare 2023).

If Kant intended to provide an aesthetic argument, overlapping considerably with his moral argument from providence, then the notion that his aesthetic theory has little to add to theodicy is deeply misguided. The aesthetic argument is largely predicated on aspects of the moral argument and is inextricably tied to it, and as such constitutes additional reasons to take value considerations into account in figuring out the nature of reality. The moral argument and the problem of evil are locked in a zero-sum game, each vying for primacy on how best to pronounce a verdict on the moral evidence of this world. The aesthetic argument, if Hare is right, provides additional reason to think not just that God exists, but that God is good. And this, once more, stands in diametric opposition to the notion that aesthetic judgment adds nothing to our stock of knowledge about the world, nor asserts that there is order and purpose in the world, nor is relevant to making judgments about God's goodness.

5. Some Thoughts on Explanation

We will not provide an assessment of Kant's argument at this point, but we would like to focus a bit of attention on Hare's claim that Kant advanced such an aesthetic argument for God's existence. Some might be dubious about it. Adjudicating this point of difference would require a fine-grained exegetical analysis of Kant's *Third Critique*, which we will not be conducting. Rather, we intend to take the occasion to discuss a few matters in the vicinity of this potential disagreement. (Readers uninterested in this digression are free to proceed to the final section).

Although we will not presume to try to settle this disagreement, we do find ourselves drawn to staking out something of an intermediate position between them. Not that we are suggesting that the right interpretation of Kant is this middle ground, but rather that we find ourselves gravitating to something in between these two claims: first, that aesthetics for Kant provide a compelling and altogether distinct argument for God's existence and, second, Ameriks' weaker assertion that "the phenomena of taste, as Kant construes them, can be given an especially good religious explanation *if* one *already* has a warrant on other grounds for making reference to a divine power" (Ameriks forthcoming).

Even if we are persuaded that there is a robust religious explanation of various aesthetic phenomena, we harbor the suspicion that we can push for a bit more than that. But why harbor any misgivings about the stronger claim that the beautiful and sublime, for Kant, can provide an argument for God's existence?[6] Here our reticence owes to Ameriks' characterization of the claim. So, let us first provide that characterization, and then we will aim to problematize it a bit and, in the process, push for there being Kantian resources for constructing an aesthetic argument for God's existence after all, though perhaps not one able to satisfy Ameriks' strictures.

So how does Ameriks characterize Hare's claim that Kant provided an aesthetic argument for God? This is not an exhaustive set of characterizations, but first, he quotes Hare himself with these words: "an argument that leads from our aesthetic experience of beauty to the existence of a supersensible ground and thus to God". Then, in turn, Ameriks casts the argument as involving features of our experience sufficient to ground a reference to God, an argument that grounds religion, a positive claim providing a logical or epistemic kind of derivation, a sufficient condition to show that theism is true, and an argument entailing a positive logical connection between aesthetics and religion.

By the way, we do not think any of these characterizations are unfair or uncharitable on Ameriks' part, and indeed we think they are eminently understandable in light of Hare's careful, systematic, and methodical effort to lay out what he takes to be a Kantian aesthetic argument in the *Third Critique*. Hare admits the argument can seem obscure and that it stands in need of careful unpacking and explication. Exactly because of the explicitness and rigor with which Hare does this work, Ameriks, to our thinking, is warranted to identify junctures at which the argument, thus explicated, can be called into question—and indeed whether Hare was right in the first place to think such an argument is even implicitly there. Admittedly, we think the argument construed in certain particular ways—especially when associated with notions of a transcendental argument for God, of logical or epistemic sufficiency, or of entailment—at best is subject to serious scrutiny and at worst can be argued with some plausibility was not intended by Kant.

So why are we drawn to an *intermediate* position here—an aesthetic argument that is less ambitious than a transcendental argument for God or an entailment relation, but more than merely a set of considerations that can fortify belief in God among those who are already theists that the beautiful and sublime evidentially point to God? To explain this, allow us to explore a bit more this idea of *making an argument for God's existence* because such language can be ambiguous in multiple ways.

Kant eventually came to see a conspicuous parallel between ethics and aesthetics, except in the latter the rapprochement, integration, or reconciliation between freedom and nature took a different form, namely, between our higher faculties as human beings, especially our imagination and understanding on the one hand, and an objectivist reading of aesthetic realities in the world on the other. Kant largely presupposed the latter to be there. Certain experiences of (say) the beautiful and sublime have the capacity to confirm within us an aesthetic approval of them as a matter of "universal validity", analogous to the moral law that applies to us all.

For Kant this "should" is not a moral should, but it functions similarly. There is something normatively prescriptive about certain aesthetic experiences that applies to all of us, and these experiences generate a hope within us of the greatest good coming to fruition—the ultimate correspondence of virtue and happiness, of unity between human beings and the world. In this sense, the beautiful and sublime offer a "foretaste" of the glory to come. Kant thought, and Hare and Ameriks agree, that the extraordinary purposiveness of such experiences calls for some kind of special explanation.

Invoking the category of *explanation* is telling here. The question that demands an answer, even if we grant that something supersensible is needed to account for the coordination of the intricately connected aesthetic structures within human beings as well as without, is whether the further inference to God is warranted. Unless God is not just the best or only explanation, but the only possible explanation, a transcendental argument all the way to God does not seem practicable. A transcendental argument can be seen as a sort of deductivism on steroids.

It is similar for more garden-variety entailment relations. Why think that God would be the only explanation for aesthetic union? Ameriks for one explicitly denies it when he writes, "Even if the excess of beauty is astonishing and is not demonstrably necessary for nature to exist at all, there are, as Kant's early work on cosmology stresses, all sorts of natural causes that appear to explain practically all that we know of the impressively complex general organization of the cosmos" (Ameriks forthcoming). If God is one among other explanation candidates, hankering after anything like deductive entailment is bound to disappoint.

That said, we are skeptical that Hare intends to convey something so strong as entailment. For example, consider these words of his: because there is a sense of an extraordinary "fit" in aesthetic experience, just as there is in moral experience, "we are encouraged to think the same supernatural author" is responsible (Hare 2023). "Encouraged to think" is an eminently judicious way to put it, bespeaking a fair bit of epistemic humility, and falling conspicuously short of an entailment relation.

Note Ameriks' conclusion that "it is hardly immediately obvious that we have to move beyond natural explanations and say that aesthetic phenomena *themselves* provide adequate argumentative support for positing a *specific* kind of supersensible ground that has something tantamount to the extraordinary power of a being that can undergird the complex real possibility of the highest good and thereby warrant a belief in God" (Ameriks forthcoming). Yes, but even if true, pointing out that we are *encouraged to think* about a particular possibility falls shy of suggesting we are somehow epistemically obligated to embrace it, that we "have to" gravitate to it on pain of patent irrationality.

Again, the language of explanation is helpful to offer us less ambitious formulations of the aesthetic argument. Ameriks wants to claim that we have little reason to take Kant as providing an aesthetic argument; but we are not so sure Kant is not providing one, even if it is not best construed as a transcendental argument or an entailment relation.[7] So, let us set aside categories like the only possible or even only explanation, and ask this question instead: Might God provide the best explanation of the sort of aesthetic phenomena Kant pointed to? And here, though more work may be required to make the case, we are inclined to think the answer is likely yes.

But this almost certainly requires that we move the discussion into non-deductive sorts of arguments—inductive ones, abductive ones, and perhaps even less ambitious strategies than those. We begin, then, with the more ambitious and then move toward the less ambitious.

Consider an inference to the best explanation. Historically, in one like Peirce or Harman, abduction starts with surprising data points that call for explanation. Finding the instantiation of order and beauty in the world as we do in such resplendent abundance is a good example. A variety of aesthetic phenomena stand in need of serious explanation. God presumably is among the explanation candidates. We then identify other possibilities, including naturalistic ones, and see if God provides the better explanation of the phenomena by applying a principled set of criteria (explanatory scope and power, for example).

Here we would remark that the greater the array of relevant moral phenomena we adduce, the stronger the abductive inference is likely to be. A lesson from Hare and Ameriks when employing Kantian resources is not to be too quick to domesticate the aesthetic evidence and settle for superficial accounts; there is no replacement for close and careful attentiveness to the evidence—a point that also applies to the moral argument(s).

In that connection, we might suggest that in addition to natural beauty and sublime experiences in both nature and human artworks that first humiliate us and then remind us of our dignity (paralleling our moral experience), we should extend the range of relevant aesthetic evidence under consideration. The way aesthetic criteria seem so central to reliable epistemological standards in science and mathematics, to cite but one example, seems quite relevant as well.[8]

We need not reiterate the abductive procedure any more, but what we are doing here has been called by Mark Murphy an explanandum-based approach. One can also take an explanans-centered approach that, in this case, does not start with the aesthetic evidence, but rather with God himself.[9] Then we can point out why God, as traditionally construed as (say) the possessor of the omni-qualities, is such a good candidate for answering the aesthetic questions that our experiences raise. Murphy suggests that this approach, though, carries no apologetic significance, since God's existence is presupposed. This at least superficially reminds us of Ameriks' effort to salvage a connection between aesthetics and God by saying that the theistic hypothesis may well be found compelling, but only to the already committed theist. Again, no argument for God is provided, Ameriks says; or as Murphy says, the explanans-centered approach provides no apologetic value.[10]

But again, we are inclined to think something more ambitious than that is possible. For we are not convinced that an explanans-centered approach lacks evidential significance. And for similar reasons that we retain skepticism that Murphy is right to suggest explanans-driven arguments are bereft of apologetic value, we harbor the suspicion that Ameriks' delimitation of the Kantian-inspired evidential connection of aesthetics to theism to those who are already theists is overstated.[11] Recall where we are in our dialectic: we are considering the question of explanation. If we see that (say) the God of classical theism is powerfully or even uniquely able to provide an impeccable explanation of important aesthetic phenomena, then that can arguably play a part in an evidential case for God's existence, a commitment at the heart of what has been called *explanationism* (McCain and Poston 2018).

Admittedly, this strategy remains rather ambitious, so let us ratchet it down slightly and consider an inductive aesthetic argument, starting with what Swinburne dubs a P-inductive argument, according to which aesthetic evidence shows that theism is more likely than not. Again, an ambitious agenda. Less ambitiously, though, we could construct a C-inductive aesthetic argument, which would merely enhance the likelihood of theism without making it more likely true than not.[12] It would add plausibility points to theism, and it could play a role in a larger case involving other sorts of arguments, the cumulative effect of which might constitute a P-inductive argument. But the basic idea on which such an argument is predicated is that we are more likely to assess the quality and quantity of aesthetic experiences we actually engage in based on theism rather than naturalism.

Note two points here. First, even if the best we can do using aesthetic considerations is to construct a C-inductive argument that but increases the likelihood of theism to some extent (which even atheist Paul Draper accepts), there remains evidence and an argument. A good argument does not always have to render its conclusion likely true. And second, besides the possibility of a cumulative case going beyond aesthetics to include other resources from natural theology, there is also the possibility of a distinctively aesthetic cumulative case, encompassing aesthetic evidence alluded to earlier that exceeds the specific range of that adduced by Kant.

Less ambitious still, we could move the discussion into the arena of Reformed episte-mology, as Plantinga does with design arguments more broadly (Plantinga 2011, pp. 225–48). As a convenient example, take Steve Evans' notion of natural signs, which fulfill the two Pascalian traits of being both widely accessible and easily resistible (Evans 2010). Aesthetic considerations are good candidates. Experiences of beauty and the sublime are ubiquitous, and empirical evidence suggests that such experiences not uncommonly in point of fact do dispose people to become more open to the transcendent and sacred, and on many occasions engender profound doubts about the adequacy of something like materialism, which seems to have the considerably harder time accounting for the texture, depth, and ingression of certain aesthetic experiences. Even on occasion folks have found themselves, either temporarily or permanently, gravitating to theism on their basis. Whether this is purely a naturalistic phenomenon or just the sort of experience one would expect if the beautiful and sublime are indeed natural signs can of course be debated, but again we have another potential example of the evidential significance of aesthetics.[13] For present purposes, this is the sort of modest evidential appeal of most interest to the analysis of this paper.

Lastly, as laudable as is the effort to articulate with care the intricacies and nuances of Kant's analysis, it almost invariably seems to leave something of the existential element out, making it seem on paper less persuasive than it actually may be in practice.[14] Not unlike moral arguments, aesthetic arguments are ineliminably experiential, which is related to Kant thinking them more practical than merely theoretical—and thus their deliverances constitutive rather than merely regulative. But for their essential element of subjectivity and personal appropriation, they remind us of the complicated process of our becoming convinced of anything. Human psychology, and just epistemology for that matter, are richer than what discursive arguments written on the board can always encapsulate.

As John Henry Newman's expansive epistemology would have it, a thousand things typically can and do contribute to our changes of mind; aesthetic considerations (as with ethical ones) are especially germane to deep acquisitions of understanding, as much akin to the catching of a vision as to the deliverances of a discursive analysis. If Kant is right, aesthetic judgments appeal to the whole person—both the head and the heart, the imagination and understanding—lending themselves not just to intellectual assents, but to an existential depth, profound understanding, and attitudes of reverence and awe, inspiration and gratitude.

At any rate, whether the case can be made that theism is not just a possible explanation of aesthetic phenomena but a plausible one, perhaps even the best one, remains to be seen, a work in progress, and is an exciting research agenda, even if we give up the more ambitious deductive or transcendental claims that it is, respectively, the only or the only possible explanation.[15] If Balthasar was right, the experience and enjoyment of beauty might well sensitize one not only to the evidential significance of aesthetics, but also to that of morality, of which beauty, if Kant was right, is a palpable symbol. In this way, Kant harkened back not just to the Hebraic and Christian conception of the transcendentals[16] but also to the ancient Hellenistic and Greek practice of the same word—*kalon*—being used to refer to them both.[17] And if indeed Kant offered an aesthetic argument for God's existence, or even embraced a robustly objective reading of beauty, it puts the lie to the idea his work cannot be deployed in the service of an aesthetic theodicy.

6. Horror and Nothing Buttery

From mathematical equations to sunrises, from paintings to novels, from a woman's hair to a lasting friendship, beauty is multiform. And in various ways, those realities may well open us up to something more—something sacred, something transcendent. But just as there are bad things in this world in addition to good things, requiring explanation all, there are tragic and horrible and ugly things in this world, not just beautiful things. Hare recognizes this, writing, "We have made in Western culture asphalt and concrete wastelands, where we are starved of beauty. The lack of fit between these spaces and our faculties is also something that needs explanation. The experience of ugliness is not merely a personal distaste (like hating horseradish). It is a symbol of what is wrong with our world more deeply, lack of meaning and congruence between what ought to be and what is" (Hare 2023).

The truly tragic is radically bereft of the sorts of traits traditionally associated with beauty—harmony, balance, unity, integrity, and the like. And in the worst cases, it is enough to break our hearts altogether. The most challenging cases of the problem of evil involve unspeakable evils and tragedies featuring no beauty at all. Marilyn Adams takes up the challenge this poses to theodicy. Several features of her work make it stand out: she is opposed to generic sorts of solutions to the problem of evil, she is altogether willing to employ distinctively Christian resources to address the problem, and she considers the worst sorts of evils and most hideously ugly scenarios imaginable—a woman raped whose limbs are then cut off, for example.

Another feature of her work is that she intentionally employs aesthetic considerations. She directs her attention to horrendous evils, those that have the power to *degrade* by being prima facie ruinous of personal meaning. The worst of real-life atrocities rob people of their meaning, making them think their lives can never again be unified and integrated into wholes with positive meaning; note her use of aesthetic categories to cash out this dimension of the discussion and cast the problem in need of a solution.

Adams also departs from much of the theodicy literature by not trying to locate "morally sufficient reasons" for the sufferings people endure. Rather, employing a category of Roderick Chisholm, she prefers to speak of the *defeat* of evils. God must be understood as good to everyone, which includes all of those who experience the most horrendous of sufferings. If there is a great enough good the experience of which can defeat evils of the worst sort—as she thinks there is—then the problem of evil would be solved.

It has been this experiential dimension of beauty, too, that has been the primary focus here. We have resisted formulating the aesthetic argument in a tight discursive format for a few reasons, one of which is that in actual practice it might be less propositional than that. Recall the possibility of a "natural sign" approach instead: what is important is not propositions about the existence or features of beauty that matter most, but rather the transformative power of experiencing beauty itself that can play a critical role in the complicated process of persuasion. Although philosophers tend to privilege the propositional and discursive, many of life's decisions are simply not reducible to such things. The experience of the good and the beautiful may well be an example of something not properly deflated and compartmentalized.

It is no coincidence that among moral skeptics we can often find aesthetic skeptics as well. The emotivist A. J. Ayer, heavily influenced by logical positivism, saw his analysis of morality equally applicable, mutatis mutandis, to aesthetics; and he was hardly alone in this.[18] Ayer wrote that "any attempt to make our use of ethical and aesthetic concepts the basis of a metaphysical theory concerning the existence of a world of values, as distinct from the world of facts, involves a false analysis of these concepts. Our own analysis has shown that the phenomena of moral experience cannot fairly be used to support any rationalist or metaphysical doctrine whatsoever. In particular, they cannot, as Kant hoped, be used to establish the existence of a transcendent god" (Ayer 1952, p. 114).

Now that scientism and logical positivism, naturalism, and classical emotivism have all been roundly subjected to withering critical scrutiny, and metaphysics, cognitivist morality, and even non-naturalism have made a comeback, it is a foregone conclusion that Ayer's view about the prospect of moral (or even aesthetic) arguments for theism leaves much to be desired. If morality and aesthetics were wrongly thought to fall together, perhaps they can rise together, and the time has come for us to reconsider the power of aesthetic evidence, especially working in conjunction with moral arguments, for God's existence.

By Kant's lights, we can and should look at the world in more than one way. From the perspective of understanding, we can see the world simply as a web of causal relations; but from the point of view of practical reason, we can apprehend free agency volitionally obedient to the laws of reason. As Roger Scruton puts it, "These two points of view are incommensurable: that is to say, we cannot derive from one of them a description of the world as seen from the other"(Scruton 2014, p. 35). Again, when it comes to the evidential significance of beauty, the suggestion has been that there may be discernible a kind of appeal whose force is not reducible to a propositional argument. There is something essentially, ineliminably experiential about it; for those who cultivate a taste for it, an openness and attentiveness to it, and the eyes with which to see it, the result may well be a more expansive perception of what is real. This possibility is one that this essay has gestured at, albeit in a preliminary sort of way; there is good work to be done here.

Scruton puts it like this in a suggestive passage, with which we will draw this exploratory essay to a close:

> It is helpful . . . to register a protest against what Mary Midgley calls "nothing buttery". There is a widespread habit of declaring emergent realities to be "nothing but" the things in which we perceive them. The human person is "nothing but" the human animal; law is "nothing but" relations of social power; sexual love is "nothing but" the urge to procreation; altruism is "nothing but" the dominant genetic strategy described by Maynard Smith; the *Mona Lisa* is "nothing but" the spread of pigments on a canvas; the Ninth Symphony is "nothing but" a sequence of pitched sounds of varying timbre [sic]. And so on. Getting rid of this habit is, to my mind, the true goal of philosophy. And if we get rid of it when dealing with the small things—symphonies, pictures, people—we might get rid of it when dealing with the large things too: notably, when dealing with the world as a whole. And then we might conclude that it is just as absurd to say that the world is nothing but the order of nature, as physics describes it, as to say that the *Mona Lisa* is nothing but a smear of pigments. Drawing that conclusion is the first step in the search for God (Scruton 2014, pp. 39–40).[19]

Funding: This research received no external funding.

Institutional Review Board Statement: Not applicable.

Informed Consent Statement: Not applicable.

Data Availability Statement: Not applicable.

Conflicts of Interest: The author declares no conflict of interest.

Notes

[1] The arguments in question typically assume or assert that the relevant phenomenological experiences put us in touch with objective realities, either aesthetic or moral ones. But sometimes the inferences appeal merely to those aesthetic or moral experiences themselves while bracketing the issue of whether they put us in touch with objective realities. For example, see (Ashbach 2019, 2021).

[2] This paragraph provides a perspicacious summation: "Further, if our judgment of all aesthetic value is free of governing concepts, purposeless, and disinterested, we can sense why those who follow after could see aesthetic value as useless and thus an unnecessary consideration for theodicy. While the beautiful, *according to* Kant, may be the mascot of morality, so to speak, it cannot play on the team. This means that a Kantian framework will likely inhibit its usefulness in theodicy. Theodicy seeks to find order and purpose in a world disrupted by evil, but, as Jeremy Begbie writes, for Kant a 'judgment of taste does not add to our stock of knowledge about the world; it is not a claim to knowledge; it never asserts that there is order and purpose in the world.' If this is the case, then aesthetic judgment must be irrelevant in making judgments about God's goodness. Nor can

we look to the aesthetic with an eye for its application to religious concerns, as such desires would cancel out our capacity for disinterested judgment. Thus, though Kantian aesthetics and the modern attitude it influences may perhaps be able to give a *coherent* account of judgment, its nature and structure prevent *cooperation* with theodicy's task".

3   Palmquist's excellent worth is well worth considering more than we can here; to mention just a few examples: See his (Palmquist 2009), which discusses a possible "religious argument" for God's existence in Kant's *Religion*. Focusing on moral/transcendental arguments that have an aesthetic element, Palmquist reads Kant's theory of religion as a sequel to the *Third Critique*, not the *Second*, so he seems to be claiming that Kant had some kind of aesthetic version of the moral argument in mind here. As such, it sets out to synthesize moral considerations with aesthetic ones (such as the cohesiveness of a religious community) in a way that seems to bolster the argument being defended in this paper. In addition, a paper Palmquist delivered at the 12th International Kant Congress in 2015 was published in the proceedings of that Congress, under the title "Creative Genius: The Aesthetic Basis for a Kantian Symbolic Theology". One last article to mention for now is his (Palmquist 1992).

4   Interestingly, providence is a crucial category in Tallon's effort to build an aesthetic theodicy, and this is one more way in which Kant's help might be enlisted and their projects parallel.

5   Note later that this is in line with Ameriks' notion that the aesthetic argument, if Kant provides it, is not altogether independent.

6   Hare spends quite a bit of time discussing not just beauty, but also the sublime, in Kant's aesthetics. His take is quite different from that of David Bentley Hart as we find in the latter's (Hart 2003).

7   Even if we were to grant that Kant gave an aesthetic argument and that it is transcendental in nature, what would be needed is something supersensible; it is unclear whether what is needed is that this supersensible object be God.

8   Consider these words from G. H. Hardy's *Mathematician's Apology* as but one example: "The mathematician's patterns, like the painter's or the poet's, must be *beautiful*; the ideas, like the colours or the words, must fit together in a harmonious way. Beauty is the first test: there is no permanent place in the world for ugly mathematics".

9   Nicholas Wolterstorff dubs a similar approach "Anselmian" in this specific sense: "Anselm assumed the acceptability of engaging in a practice of reflection that presupposes the existence of God without first having proved the existence of God". This is Wolterstorff's modus operandi in (Wolterstorff 2008).

.0   This bears some resemblance, too, to Eleonore Stump's effort through the use of Franciscan (rather than Dominican) second-person knowledge to make the case that in, say, Job there is a sort of answer to the problem of evil provided, though it speaks to the believer more so than the unbeliever. Some of this is reminiscent, too, of C. S. Lewis's *Til We Have Faces*. See (Stump 2012; Baggett and Baggett 2022). There is a relevant distinction in this vicinity, of course, between unbelievers having *less* of an ability to glean the relevant insights and having *none*.

11   In this *NDPR* analysis of Murphy's relevant work (*God and Moral Law: On the Theistic Explanation of Morality*), Mike Almeida writes, "If an explanans driven approach has no apologetic value in the sense Murphy describes, then it is hard to see how taking such an approach could, as described above, move us ultimately to a theistic account of morality. If consideration of the distinctive features of God in relation to morality does not at least increase the likelihood of the hypothetical explanans, then the explanans driven approach is not particularly well-suited to at least one goal (admittedly, not the most pronounced goal) of the book. But further, if Murphy is right about the lack of apologetic value in the explanans driven approach, then presumably there would be no corresponding decrease in the likelihood of the hypothetical explanans even if the distinctive features of God in relation to morality yielded a moral picture broadly and deeply inconsistent with the moral explananda. But then the explanans driven approach so described would amount to an odd exercise in determining what morality might look like under the assumption of a hypothetical explanans whose nature makes it an essential explainer of morality. I think it is good news for the project that Murphy is probably mistaken about the apologetic value of the explanans driven approach. There is really no reason not to believe that consideration of the distinctive features of God in relation to morality either increases or decreases the likelihood of the hypothetical explanans". See https://ndpr.nd.edu/reviews/god-and-moral-law-on-the-theistic-explanation-of-morality/ (accessed on 25 March 2023.)

12   From Swinburne's *The Existence of God*: An argument is C-inductive just in case $P(h/e\&K) > P(h/K)$, which means some evidence (e) increases the probability of a particular hypothesis to a higher level than it would otherwise be given our background knowledge. Whereas an argument is P-inductive IFF $P(h/e\&K) > 1/2$, which means some evidence (e) increases the probability of a particular hypothesis to over 50%, rendering the conclusion likely true. See (Swinburne 2004).

13   Some might assert that this sort of appeal is an example of a problematic "God of the gaps" argument, but God here is not an explanation in lieu of a scientific one, but rather the ground of any explanations at all, including scientific ones—at least if Hare's appeal to the need for a supersensible author is right. But to make this case requires careful attentiveness to the full array and rich significance of the aesthetic evidence rather than an a priori insistence on their domestication and deflation.

14   Of course, this is also ironic because the pains Kant took to point out the subjective elements of aesthetics (and morality) is exactly why some have misread him as denying their objectivity.

15   A smattering of resources on arguments from beauty and beauty as theodicy include (Moreland 2004; Swinburne 2004; Viney 1985; Wynn 1999; Tennant 1930; Dubay 1999; Wiker and Witt 2006; Swinburne 1998; Pruss 2004; Williams 2001; Stump 2007; Zemach 1997); Jim Spiegel has some good thoughts on the argument from beauty in a series of posts entitled, "An Anti-Naturalist

16 Argument from Beauty" and "Why Beauty is an Objective Quality in the World" (Howell 2007; Tallon 2008). Balthasar's first seven volumes in his sixteen-volume "trilogy" focus on the beautiful.

16 Kant's notion of beauty as *disinterested* arguably allows room for morally neutral expressions of it (or worse), leaving space for something of an apparent fragmentation among the transcendentals. That there could in principle be such postmodern phenomena as "immoral beauty" or "ugly virtue" (or "ugly truth" for that matter) might be thought to represent counterexamples or defeaters to the notion that they are ontologically on par or necessarily congruent with one another. But canonical teaching among (say) the great monotheistic traditions that such fragmentation is not normative and that, in a world redeemed, it will no longer be so, can make sense of our visceral intuition that such possibilities are not reflective of how reality ought to be.

17 In the *Septuagint*, too, God's original creation was dubbed *good* for being an expression of God's ordered beauty.

18 Error theorist J. L. Mackie largely put ethical and aesthetic judgments in the same proverbial boat, thinking the same sort of analysis applies, but he admitted a disanalogy. We have, he argued, fewer social reasons to objectify aesthetics than we do ethics, which is why, he thought, an error theory of aesthetics is, of the two, the more readily accepted. See his (Mackie 1977).

19 Thanks to two excellent anonymous reviewers at *Religions*.

References

Adams, Marilyn McCord. 1999. *Horrendous Evils and the Goodness of God*. Ithaca: Cornell University Press.

Ameriks, Karl. Forthcoming. The Retrieval of Objectivist Aesthetics in Kant, Beethoven, and John Hare: 'Diesen Kuß der ganzen Welt'. Unpublished.

Ashbach, Jonathan. 2019. The Phenomenological Moral Argument: A New Formulation of a Classic Theistic Defense. *Philosophia Christi* 21: 135–51.

Ashbach, Jonathan. 2021. Rediscovering the Aesthetic Argument. *Philosophia Christi* 23: 291–312.

Ayer, A. J. 1952. *Language, Truth, and Logic*. New York: Dover Publications.

Baggett, David, and Marybeth Baggett. 2022. Self-Knowledge, Who God Is, and a Cure for Our Deepest Shame: A Few Reflections on *Till We Have Faces*. *Perichoresis* 20: 3–20.

Dubay, Thomas. 1999. *The Evidential Power of Beauty: Science and Theology Meet*. San Francisco: Ignatius.

Evans, Stephen C. 2010. *Natural Signs and Knowledge of God: A New Look at Theistic Arguments*. Oxford: Oxford University Press.

Gadamer, Hans Georg. 2004. *Truth and Method*, 2nd ed. Translated by Joel Weinsheimer, and Donald G. Marshall. New York: Continuum.

Hare, John E. 2023. *Unity and the Holy Spirit*. Oxford: Oxford University Press.

Hart, David Bentley. 2003. *Beauty of the Infinite: The Aesthetics of Christian Truth*. Grand Rapids: Eerdmans.

Howell, Russell. 2007. Does Mathematical Beauty Pose Problem for Naturalism? *Christian Scholar's Review* 35: 493.

Lippard, Lucy R. 1990. The Spirit and the Letter. *Art in America* 80: 238–45.

Mackie, John. 1977. *Ethics: Inventing Right and Wrong*. New York: Penguin Books.

McCain, Kevin, and Ted Poston, eds. 2018. *Best Explanations: New Essays on Inference to the Best Explanation*. Oxford: Oxford University Press.

Moreland, James Porter. 2004. *Scaling the Secular City*. Ada: Baker.

Murdoch, Iris. 1989. *The Sovereignty of the Good*. London: Routledge.

O'Connor, Timothy. 2002. The Problem of Evil: An Introduction. In *Philosophy of Religion: A Reader and Guide*. Edited by William Lane Craig. Edinburgh: Edinburgh University Press.

Palmquist, Stephen. 1992. Does Kant Reduce Religion to Morality? *Kant-Studien* 83: 129–48. [CrossRef]

Palmquist, Stephen R. 2009. Kant's Religious Argument for the Existence of God. *Faith and Philosophy* 26: 3–22. [CrossRef]

Penulhum, Terence. 1992. Divine Goodness and the Problem of Evil. In *The Problem of Evil*. Edited by Marilyn McCord Adams and Robert Merrihew Adams. Oxford: Oxford University Press, pp. 69–83.

Plantinga, Alvin. 2011. *Where the Conflict Really Lies: Science, Religion, and Naturalism*. Oxford: Oxford University Press.

Pruss, Alexander. 2004. The Cosmos as a Work of Art. Available online: https://www.google.com.hk/url?sa=t&rct=j&q=&esrc=s&sou rce=web&cd=&cad=rja&uact=8&ved=2ahUKEwjG06zuosqAAxWDbfUHHcRuDDcQFnoECBEQAQ&url=http%3A%2F%2Fal exanderpruss.com%2Fpapers%2FCosmosAsArt.html&usg=AOvVaw1bSflDMPWXMilnDPZ73wJF&opi=89978449 (accessed on 25 March 2023).

Quinn, Philip L. 1992. God, Moral Perfection, and Possible Worlds. In *The Problem of Evil: Selected Readings*. Edited by Michael L. Peterson. Notre Dame: Notre Dame University Press.

Scruton, Roger. 2014. *The Soul of the World*. Princeton: Princeton University Press.

Sorley, William. 1935. *Moral Values and the Idea of God: The Gifford Lectures Delivered in the University of Aberdeen in 1914 and 1915*, 3rd ed. London: Cambridge University Press.

Stump, Eleonore. 1985. The Problem of Evil. *Faith and Philosophy* 2: 417. [CrossRef]

Stump, Eleonore. 2007. Beauty as a Road to God. *Sacred Music* 134: 11–24.

Stump, Eleonore. 2012. *Wandering in Darkness: Narrative and the Problem of Suffering*. Oxford: Oxford University Press.

Swinburne, Richard. 1998. *Providence and the Problem of Evil*. Oxford: OUP Oxford.

Swinburne, Richard. 2004. *The Existence of God*, 2nd ed. Oxford: Clarendon.

Tallon, Philip. 2008. The Mozart Argument and the Argument from Enjoyment. In *Two Dozen (or so) Arguments for God: The Plantinga Project*. Edited by Jerry L. Walls and Trent Dougherty. Oxford: Oxford University Press.

Tallon, Philip. 2012. *The Poetics of Evil: Toward an Aesthetic Theodicy*. Oxford: Oxford University Press.

Tennant, Frederick Robert. 1930. *Philosophical Theology*. Cambridge: CUP Archive, vol. 2.

Viney, Donald Wayne. 1985. The Aesthetic Argument. In *Charles Hartshorne and the Existence of God*. Albany: SUNY, chp. 9, pp. 119–28.

von Balthasar, Hans Urs. 1982. *The Glory of the Lord: A Theological Aesthetics*. Edinburgh: T & T Clark, vol. 1, p. 38.

Wiker, Benjamin, and Jonathan Witt. 2006. *A Meaningful World: How the Arts and Sciences Reveal the Genius of Nature*. Westmont: IVP.

Williams, Peter. 2001. Aesthetic Arguments for the Existence of God. *Quodlibet Journal* 3: 1–13.

Wolterstorff, Nicholas. 2008. *Justice: Rights and Wrongs*. Princeton: Princeton University Press.

Wynn, Mark. 1999. Providence and Beauty. In *God and Goodness: A Natural Theological Perspective*. Milton Park: Routledge, chp. 1, pp. 11–36.

Zemach, Eddy. 1997. *Real Beauty*. University Park: Penn State Press.

 *religions*

Article

A Christological Critique of Divine Command Theory

Martin Jakobsen

Department of Theology, Ansgar University College, 4635 Kristiansand, Norway; jakobsen@ansgarskolen.no

Abstract: This paper presents a theological critique of divine command theory, a metaethical theory stating that moral wrongness is constituted by God's command. First, I argue that this theory does not qualify as a Christian moral theory because it lacks connections to central parts of Christian theology, such as Christology. This argument does not imply that the theory is wrong nor that it is inconsistent with Christianity—only that it is not Christian as such. Second, I argue that divine command theory does not fit well with the New Testament's vision of the moral life, in which being conformed to the image of Christ has primacy over adherence to law. This argument implies that the Christian ethicist should look elsewhere for a metaethical theory. I next argue in favour of a moral theory of imitation, in which the moral life consists of imitating God, the prime exemplar of goodness, which is made possible through an imitation of Christ.

Keywords: divine command theory; imitation; Christian ethics; Robert Adams; metaethics

1. Introduction

Divine command theory states that morality depends on God's command. Proponents of divine command theory formulate this dependent relation differently. Moral obligations may, for instance, be caused by, grounded by, identical to, or constituted by God's command (Lee and Evans 2022, p. 94). However, they all agree that an act is morally wrong if God has forbidden it and obligatory if God has commanded it (Hare 2022). There are many strengths to a divine command theory of morality. It explains the objectivity, universality, and normativity of morality (Lee and Evans 2022). For this article, the most important strength is that it also provides a tight connection between God and morality.

Critiques of divine command theory have mainly been philosophical[1]. In this paper, I present a theological critique of divine command theory, arguing that although the theory provides a tight connection between God and morality, it does not cohere very well with central parts of Christian theology. I consider the divine command theory formulated by Christian moral philosopher Robert Adams along with perspectives from John Hare, Stephen C. Evans, and Philip Quinn—whom are all recognised as the leading contemporary defenders of divine command theory (Lee and Evans 2022, p. 94; Hare 2019).

At the beginning of his *Finite and Infinite Goods*, Adams presents a theistic theory of value. He argues that there is one intrinsic good—one prime exemplar of goodness—and that this intrinsic good is God (Adams 1999, pp. 14, 28). All good things derive their goodness from God. This means that something is good only insofar as it resembles God. For instance, it is good for humans to be compassionate because this resembles God. Furthermore, Adams develops a theory of moral wrongness, a theory of what makes an act morally obligatory or morally wrong. He argues in favour of a divine command theory in which moral wrongness is constituted by the commands of a loving God.

To prepare for my critique of divine command theory, let me draw attention to how philosopher Linda Zagzebski distinguishes between two ideas of morality (Zagzebski 2004, p. xi). She writes that some ethical theories arise from the idea that morality compels, and some ethical theories arise from the idea that morality attracts. From the idea that morality compels follows a conception of ethics that focuses on law. One example of this is Kant's theory in which ethics is the law of reason. This conception of ethics has since

Citation: Jakobsen, Martin. 2023. A Christological Critique of Divine Command Theory. *Religions* 14: 558. https://doi.org/10.3390/rel14040558

Academic Editor: David Baggett

Received: 27 March 2023
Accepted: 19 April 2023
Published: 21 April 2023

been dominant in Western theological ethics, or at least argues Elizabeth Anscombe in the classical paper "Modern Moral Philosophy" (Anscombe 1958). However, theological ethics do not need to be seen as an ethics of compelling law. Morality can be seen as attracting rather than compelling. The idea that morality attracts is found in Plato, where the good has an almost magnetic force. This is the conception of ethics that Zagzebski recommends.

This distinction between two ideas of morality shows how Adams's moral theory is simultaneously Platonic and Kantian. Adams's value theory is very much inspired by Plato's treatment of the good, while his theory of moral rightness and wrongness is essentially an ethics of law. What I call for is to wholeheartedly embrace the idea that morality attracts—not only when it comes to value theory, but also when it comes to our understanding of rightness and wrongness. I argue that Christian ethics should not be seen as primarily an ethics of law in which morality flows from God's commands; rather, it should be conceived of in terms of imitating the divine.

My argument consists of two parts. First, I consider the place of Christ in Christian ethics. Second, I consider a New Testament vision of a good life, especially the Pauline imagery of being "in Christ." These two factors, I argue, suggest that the moral life does not consist of following divine commands but of imitating God.

2. What Makes a Moral Theory Christian?

What is it that qualifies a moral theory as a Christian moral theory? If a moral theory is to be called Christian, it is not enough that the theory is consistent with Christian theology. Immanuel Kant's ethical theory is admittedly consistent with Christian theology (Hare 1996), but it would not be correct to describe it as Christian ethics. For ethics to qualify as Christian ethics, it must be integrated into Christian theology.

Some might argue that the interesting question is not whether a certain moral theory can be labelled Christian, but whether it is true. I do not oppose this at all. When evaluating philosophical or theological theories and determining whether the theory is true, I hold that coherence is the best method. And the philosophical notion of coherence is precisely what I have in mind when I state that Christian ethics must be integrated into Christian theology[2]. For two theories to cohere (such as ethics and theology), it is not enough that they are consistent; they must also be connected. Both the number of connections and the strength of connections are relevant (Olsson 2012; Rescher 1973, pp. 168–75). The connection would be stronger if elements in two theories logically entail one another rather than merely suggesting one another, if the connection pertains to central parts of the theory rather than peripheral parts, and if the connection is fine-grained rather than coarse-grained—that is, if it is detailed and specific rather than vague (Søvik 2016, pp. 38–39).

Because consistency is a matter of either/or and connectedness is required, there are some clear cases for whether a moral theory qualifies as Christian. A moral theory that is inconsistent with Christian theology will not qualify; a moral theory that is consistent but not connected will not qualify. However, because connectedness is a matter of degree, there will also be some borderline cases. Take John Finnis's natural law approach to ethics (Finnis 2011). The theory is consistent with Christian theology and has some connections, so it cannot be ruled out immediately as "not Christian ethics". However, the connections are few; the theory Is connected to creation theology but few other parts of Christian theology. Moreover, the connections are vague; although the theory has a few connections to theology, the connections lack the detail and precision that would specifically connect it to Christian theology. For instance, the theory does not connect to a specific Christian conception of God but to a vague conception of a benevolent God. This is not to say that Finnis's project fails. After all, he does not try to justify his ethic as Christian ethics. It is merely questionable whether a moral theory with few and weak connections to Christian theology qualifies as a Christian moral theory.

An advantage of this approach to the question of what makes a moral theory Christian is that the approach leaves open exactly how a moral theory integrates into Christian theology. Approaches that specify exactly how morality and theology are to be connected risk restricting the field of Christian ethics. For instance, stating that Christian ethics must "arise from the gospel of Jesus Christ" (O'Donovan 1986, p. 11) might be a bit too restrictive because it rules out approaches to ethics that arise from conceptions of the spirit or the church[3]. Stating that Christian ethics must be "governed by the whole [salvation] story" (Biggar 2011, p. 3) is a more open criterion, but it might omit approaches to Christian ethics that for theological reasons—such as certain views on the fall and sin—omit parts of the whole salvation story, such as not letting creation theology govern Christian ethics.

Although I do not specify exactly how Christian ethics must integrate into Christian theology, I give some direction by stating that a strong connection must be precise and connected to central rather than peripheral parts of Christian theology. Because the most central part of Christian theology is Christ, a moral theory that is not connected to Christ has a weak connection to Christian theology and hardly qualifies as a Christian moral theory. If a moral theory integrates a conception of God but not a specific Christian conception, the theory qualifies as theistic ethics rather than Christian ethics. Therefore, although it is too strong of a statement to say that Christian ethics must arise from the gospel of Jesus Christ, Christian ethics must at least be connected to Christ.

One could argue that my criterion—that Christian ethics must be integrated into Christian theology—would not be met by Jesus or his early disciples whose ethics were entirely Jewish, suggesting that something is wrong with the criterion[4]. Although it is correct that Jesus and his followers saw it as crucial to remain faithful to the God and the covenant of the Old Testament, it is also true that central to the disciples' and the New Testament writers' thinking about God (theology) and about human behaviour (ethics) is the life and teaching of Jesus Christ (Witherington 2016b, vol. 2, pp. 10, 30). In some cases, the life and teaching of Jesus overlapped with Old Testament ethics, or dismissed previous requirements (some food laws and sabbath requirements), or intensified them (marriage and divorce), or gave new content to what the people of God directed their lives toward (eschatology and the kingdom of God) (Witherington 2016b, vol. 2, p. 430). Therefore, although the early followers of Jesus did not integrate their moral thinking into a fully-fledged Christian systematic theology, their moral thinking has a strong connection to Christ, and in that sense, their moral thinking is integrated into (the early stages of a) Christian theology.

Consider the case of divine command theory. This moral theory has no obvious inconsistencies with Christian theology, and it has important connections. The conception of a good God who cares for humanity is essential to Adams's divine command theory, as is the conception of a God who is willing and able to communicate his will (Adams 1999, p. 263). A divine command theory also uses biblical imagery of God as king, ruler, and judge who issues his decrees. Although these theological features are not exclusive to Christian theology, thereby not entailing Christian theology, they are not peripheral. However, Christ—who is essential to Christian theology—is not essential to this moral theory. Christ is not necessary; all that is necessary is a legislative God issuing commands. In Adams's 400 pages on God and morality, Christ is rarely mentioned, and he is never made relevant to Adams's moral theory. Not only does this mean that Adams—who is a Christian—is missing out on all the resources of Christian theology that derive from the life, death, and resurrection of Christ when he develops this ethical theory, it also means that the theory does not qualify as a Christian moral theory because of the lack of a specific connection to central elements in Christian theology, such as Christology.

How might a divine command theorist respond to this? One way could simply be to say that I am stating the obvious because divine command theory was never meant to be a Christian conception of morality but rather a theistic conception that could include religious traditions other than Christianity. Adams (Adams 1999, p. 6) as well as other proponents of divine command theory (Hare 2015, p. vii; Jeffrey 2019, pp. 1–2; Evans 2013) have answered along these lines. Another response could be to argue that although a divine command theory may not need Christology, it could include it. This is the possible response I pursue.

One way divine command theory could connect with the life and teaching of Christ is to suggest that Christ gives content to the divine commands. Both Karl Barth and John Hare take this route. According to Barth, ethics is an aid to hearing God's voice, hearing what God commands. Where do we hear God's voice? In the Word of God, that is, in Jesus Christ (Barth 1957b, vol. II.2, p. 559). When Barth structures his *Ethics* in a trinitarian manner—writing about the commands of God the creator, the redeemer, and the reconciler— the commands of God the reconciler form the material heart of Barth's divine command theory, making Christology central to his applied ethics (Barth 1961, vol. III.4, pp. 24–25; 2013; Biggar 1993, p. 48). Hare has a similar approach, arguing that God's commands are revealed in the Bible and Jesus Christ. Hare asks us to imagine a situation in which we did not have the life of Christ as a moral example: "Would we know simply from analyzing human nature that we should love our enemies, and forgive seventy times seven times, and take on the role of becoming each other's servants?"(Hare 2011, p. 151). No, says Hare. The moral law cannot be deduced from creation (Hare 2011, p. 150; 2015, chap. 4). We need something transcendent to tell us what fulfilment to seek and what not to seek. Moral theories that attempt to deduce morality from human nature fail to hear at least some of God's commands and also risk "losing God as a person who speaks to us"(Hare 2015, p. 250). Although Hare writes this to argue against a natural law approach to ethics, his insistence on Christ as an indispensable moral example shows how central Christ is to the material content of Hare's ethics.

The divine command theories of Barth and Hare show that this ethical theory can be connected to Jesus Christ because Christ gives content to the divine commands. However, I argue that this is not sufficient for divine command ethics to qualify as Christian ethics. Consider the distinction between metaethics, normative ethics, and applied ethics. Metaethics considers the nature of morality (what are moral obligations?), normative ethics considers how and by what criteria we judge what we should morally do (consequences? duties?), and applied ethics applies this moral evaluation to concrete practical moral problems (for example, how should we think about euthanasia?). Hare and Barth show that divine command ethics can be combined with theological convictions on how to discern the will of God, which might lead to a normative ethics and an applied ethics connected to the life and teachings of Christ. However, divine command theory is a metaethical theory on the nature of moral obligations. Because Hare and Barth do not connect the metaethical theory to Christ, they have not shown that divine command theory qualifies as a Christian moral theory.

Some might object here, arguing that there is no need to demand that a metaethical theory must be Christian, just as there is no need to construct a Christian cosmology or a Christian microbiology. I agree that there is no need to construct a Christian microbiology because Christian beliefs do not contribute to the production of knowledge in this field. Regarding metaethics, I believe that things are different. Christian beliefs about who God is might be useful when considering the question of how morality is grounded in God. If morality depends on God, knowledge of God might reveal how this dependence relation should be formulated. Some may prefer to formulate a metaethics that is theistic rather than Christian, arguing that morality is grounded in God without using a specific Christian notion of God (see Jeffrey 2019, pp. 1–2). An advantage with what can be called a thin description of God—in which God is described as the God of the Abrahamic traditions or as omnipotent, omniscient, and omnibenevolent—is that it grants a theistic metaethics that may be accepted by a variety of religious and philosophical traditions. A disadvantage with a thin description of God is that it omits the features that are distinct in a Christian conception of God, leaving out resources that might be useful when describing the relationship between God and morality. I suggest that the Christian philosopher ask herself: If the Christian description of God is correct, what follows from this? A distinctive Christian view of God, which includes the incarnation, might make a difference in the metaethical description of how morality depends on God (Jeffrey 2019, pp. 63–64). As such, the question of whether a metaethical theory qualify as a Christian moral theory is more than a discussion on semantics. It is a question that might affect how we formulate a metaethical theory.

Another similar objection might be as follows: it is the material content of a moral theory that matters, not the metaethical structure. In that case, what is needed for an ethical theory to qualify as Christian is that the theological material is made relevant to the moral life—that is, to the level of normative and applied ethics (Biggar 2011, p. 2). To this, I say that the metaethical structure matters for the other branches of ethics. Metaethics matters for how the moral life is described, perceived, and communicated. Metaethical theories will often influence the discourse on applied ethics (Stephen 2006). As such, it is not indifferent to Christian theology how the metaethical theories are formulated.

Second, I say that divine command theory is a metaethical theory, and the problem at hand is whether this metaethical theory qualifies as Christian. To say that the metaethical theory can lead to an applied ethics that is integrated into Christian theology does not suffice. Consider Barth's ethics again. Regarding the construction of a Christian metaethics, Barth's approach to ethics is somewhat un-Barthian. He insists that theology "as a whole and in all its parts" must be Christologically determined (Barth 1956, vol. I.2, p. 123). Although his normative and applied ethics are Christologically determined, his metaethics is not. Barth's metaethics is not without connections to Christian theology. Barth is a divine-command theorist, holding that God's command constitutes what is a right and wrong action[5]. This metaethical position is theologically grounded in various ways. First, it is grounded in the view that God is sovereign. Ethics, then, is always subject to God's decision. Moreover, the position is grounded in the view that the human creature is a sinner—a creature that "does not find the divine good in himself"(Barth 1957a, vol. II.1, p. 554). Because the human creature does not manage to will or do the good, morality comes as a bidding from outside—a commanded law imposed on a reluctant nature (Biggar 1993, p. 15). Although Barth makes connections to Christian theology, they are not connections to central parts of Christian theology, such as Christology, which Barth believes should determine all parts of his theological thinking. The strongest contender for such a connection comes when Barth connects ethics to the belief that God is a God who reveals himself: because God is a God who reveals himself and his will for humanity, the moral life is understood as a life "addressed by God"(Barth 1957b, vol. II.2, p. 547). The goodness of actions and the obligatoriness depend on "what God says"—God's command (Barth 1957b, vol. II.2, p. 547; McKenny 2021, p. 57). The question, then, is how strong these connections are to central parts of Christian theology. I say that they are not very strong. First, the connection to Christian theology is not precise. Connecting ethics to the belief that God is a God who reveals himself is not a fine-grained connection to God's revelation in Christ but a connection to the more coarse-grained belief that God reveals himself. Second, the connection to divine command ethics is not precise. The theological convictions that God reveals his will and that man is fallen and in need of God's guidance entail that God communicates moral rightness and wrongness. However, these convictions neither suggest nor entail, but merely fit with, the view that moral wrongness is constituted by God's command—which is the view of divine command ethics.

3. Imitation in the New Testament

In the New Testament, ethical prescripts are found in the form of commands. In the Gospel of John, Jesus says, "this is my commandment, that you love one another" (John 15:12)[6]. The question I have at hand is not whether biblical texts or Jesus himself expresses commands but whether the biblical material suggests that moral obligations are constituted by commands, as divine command theory holds. I argue that the vision of the moral life found in the New Testament as well as the commands expressed by Jesus suggest that moral obligations are not constituted by God's commands but rather by God's nature.

First, consider some of Jesus's commands, such as to be perfect and be merciful: "Be perfect, therefore, as your heavenly Father is perfect" (Mathew 5:48) and "be merciful, just as your Father is merciful" (Luke 6:36). Here, Jesus points back to God both to explain why we have a certain duty and to give content to the duty. He does the same in his command to love. Jesus says that he imitates the Father's love and that his followers in turn should imitate the love of Jesus: "Just as I have loved you, you also should love one another" (John 13:34). The same is the case in Jesus's teaching on forgiveness. In Matthew 18, Jesus tells a parable to illustrate that there is no limit on how many times we should forgive. Why is there no limit? Because there is no limit to God's forgiveness[7]. Therefore, because God forgives, humans should forgive. In addition, because God loves, humans should love. The same structure is present in the Old Testament imperative "be holy". Why should God's people be holy? Because "I, the Lord your God, am holy"(Leviticus 19:2). These expressions of command suggest a deeper reason for upholding a certain duty than the command itself: that humans should uphold a certain duty not because God says so, but because God is so (Linville 2012, pp. 156–58). In other words, humans should imitate God. Now, Jesus is not recorded using the word "imitation" (Greek: μιμέομαι). However, the theme of imitation is present when Jesus urges people to "follow me" and to learn from his example (Mark 1:17, Matthew 11:29).

The theme of imitation is central in Paul's writings. Here, the heart of the moral life is the imitation of God after the model of Christ (Grenz 1997, pp. 119–20, 267–68; Witherington 2016a, vol. 1, p. 244). When urging his fellow Christians to live a moral life, Paul tells them to be "imitators of God" (Ephesians 5:1)[8]. Moreover, he lets the exemplar of Christ determine the content of moral prescriptions. Paul urges his readers to have the same mindset as Jesus Christ (Philippians 2:5); he writes that a husband should love his wife just as Christ loved the church and gave himself up for her (Ephesians 5:25) and that people should forgive one another "as God in Christ has forgiven you" (Ephesians 4:32.). Although the term "imitation" appears in Paul's writings, he tells his readers only three times to imitate Christ[9]. A more central term in Pauline theology is that of being "in Christ" (Dunn 1998, p. 391)[10]. New Testament scholar James Dunn identifies three ways in which Paul uses this term (Dunn 1998, pp. 397–99). There is an objective usage that refers to the redemptive act that has happened or will happen in Christ (e.g., Romans 3:24). A subjective usage refers to the believers' existential participation in the new reality brought about in Christ (e.g., Romans 12:5). Finally, there is an active usage in which Paul urges his readers to adopt a particular attitude or action. These three categories overlap. Dunn's point is not to construct clear categories but simply to show how deeply integrated the notion of being in Christ is to Pauline theology. I want to draw attention to Paul's active usage of the term "in Christ". This usage shows how Pauline theology at its core connects the notion of union with Christ with the moral life. Union with Christ entails a Christ-like life, and a Christ-like life means a life of imitation[11]. To borrow the words of another New Testament writer: whoever claims to live in him must live as Jesus did (1 John 2:6).

Imitatio Dei

Jesus's grounding of commands and Paul's theme of imitation strongly suggest a metaethics in which moral obligations depend on God's nature and not God's commands. An alternative metaethical view of divine command theory could be, in the words of Christian philosopher Linda Zagzebski, a "moral doctrine of Imitatio Dei" (Zagzebski 2004, p. 190). Zagzebski argues that God is the paradigmatically good person, that all value derives from God, and that human virtues are those traits that imitate God (Zagzebski 2005, p. 358). She also specifies the aspects of God we are to imitate: the emotions that motivate God to act should also motivate us. For this article, there is no need to commit to a specific view of what aspect of God we are to imitate. It might be God's emotion, attitudes, intentions, or virtues. I want to draw on the notion of "imitation"—that God is the paradigmatically good exemplar for imitation.

To describe morality in terms of imitation is not new. Imitation is key in Plato's value theory. It is also central to Aristotle's normative ethics where we learn to live virtuous lives by imitating someone's example (Aristotle 1932, p. 1448b; 1934, p. 1115b). Several Church fathers describe the moral life in terms of imitation; however, contrary to Aristotle, they specify the exemplar we are to imitate (Athanasius 1885, chap. 9; Origen 1885, sec. 4.1.31; Irenaeus 1885, vol. 1). As Clement writes, "our instructor Jesus should draw for us the model of the true life"(Clement 1885, sec. 1.12).

The moral doctrine of Imitatio Dei works better inside a Christian framework than outside. However, this is not to say that Imitatio Dei works only in a Christian framework. The moral significance of human likeness to God can be found in many traditions, such as Judaism (Leviticus 19:2; Sotah 14a) as well as Stoicism and Platonism (Russell 2004). When I say that Imitatio Dei works better in a Christian framework, I mean that Christian theology solves some epistemological problems that other philosophical or religious frameworks might not resolve. First, if one attempts to imitate the divine, one must have some knowledge of the divine. One needs to give an account of how humans, mere immanent creatures, can come to know the transcendent. The next task is even more difficult. One needs to describe what on Earth a life of imitating the divine would look like. The difficulty lies in the vast distance between human nature and divine nature; God is wholly other. These two issues might be difficult to resolve but not that difficult within a Christian framework. According to Christian theology, God has revealed himself through Jesus Christ. In Jesus, humans can imitate a person who combines the divine nature with human nature. This means that it is possible to describe what it would be for a human to imitate the divine: by learning how Jesus responded to certain situations and by learning how Jesus was motivated by certain ideals, goals, and purposes, we can learn what a life of imitation looks like (Zagzebski 2004, p. 233). Therefore, one can say that Imitatio Christi facilitates Imitatio Dei.

Imitatio Dei is well integrated into Christian theology because it has strong connections to central parts of Christian theology. It shows the importance of Christology in ethics. It is Christologically determined in its material aspect because the content of the imitation is spelled out by stories of the life of Christ[12]. Imitatio Dei is Christologically determined in its formal aspect as Christ is the essential centre of the moral theory: Christ is not just a good exemplar for imitation but the defining exemplar of the good life. To imitate Christ is not merely to imitate a being who happens to instantiate a set of general principles or virtues so that someone else could equally well have filled the role of exemplar by instantiating a set of virtues. Rather, the imitation is essentially tied to the person of Christ, the Incarnate one.

There is a difference in how a divine command theory and a theory of imitation connect to various themes in Christian theology. Consider how these theories connect the Christian moral life to the goal of the Christian life. A common theological conception is to take the goal of human life to be a loving union with God. Not everyone agrees that this is the goal of human life, but divine command theorists such as Karl Barth, John Hare, and Stephen C. Evans at least agree. They take union with God, becoming co-lovers or friends with God, as the human goal (Barth 1957b, vol. II.2, p. 549; Hare 2001, p. 53; 2011, p. 210; Evans 2013, p. 31). A divine command theory connects the moral life and its goal through obedience and covenant. The theory describes the moral life as obedience to God's law. Obedience to God's law is then seen as facilitating a relationship with God, that is, becoming God's people through obedience (Hare 2015, p. 39). A theory of imitation draws a different connection because both the moral life and its goal can be described as a life in Christ, being conformed to the image of Christ and united with him. This, I will say, gives a more direct connection between the Christian moral life to the goal of the Christian life. The way divine command theory connects the Christian life with its goal corresponds more with an Old Testament Covenant theory in which obedience to the law facilitates a life with God. A theory of imitation connects through Christology, where a life in Christ facilitates union with God.

Because a theory of imitation connects to such a central part of Christian theology—a central part that is connected to other theological themes—numerous connections to Christian theology exist. For instance, the theory of imitation connects to the theological theme of sanctification. The Christian life does not consist of conformity to law but rather of being conformed to the image of Christ. A moral theory of imitation, as any moral theory, recognises the importance of doing what is right. We can imitate how Jesus acts. However, the primary emphasis lies on the moral agent's character, on becoming the sort of person who does what is right—on becoming the person God intends each of us to be. In this sense, a theory of imitation is a type of virtue theory because the moral properties of persons (virtues) are more basic than the moral properties of acts and outcomes. A moral theory that does not primarily draws attention to what a person does (follows commands) but rather the person's character (trying to resemble the character of God) fits better with how sanctification involves transformation. Moreover, it connects to the Christian view of revelation. God ultimately revealed himself in the person of Jesus. This means that since the Incarnation, the will of God is both perfectly expressed and perfectly fulfilled in Jesus Christ—not in a set of commands. Because a divine command theory does not connect to such a central part of Christian theology as Christology, it will not have the same number of connections to other theological themes.

4. Possible Objection: Christ Commands Us to Love

A divine command ethicist might argue that there are some key connections between divine command theory and Christian theology. Philip Quinn, for instance, argues that a divine command theory should be the preferred ethical theory for Christian moral philosophers (Quinn 1992, p. 493). He argues this by making two points: that the commandment to love one another is central to Christian ethics and that it is vital that this is expressed in the form of a command (Quinn 1992, p. 504). I grant Quinn his first point. Quinn presents two reasons in favour of the second point that are based on the claim that the specific love commanded by God is unnatural for humans in their present condition[13]. He points to Kierkegaard's distinction between (1) erotic love and friendship and (2) the Christian love of the neighbour. With erotic love and friendship, humans choose a favourite based on preferences; someone is loved in contrast to the rest of the world (Kierkegaard 1995, pp. 19/IX, 23). However, the kind of love that Jesus speaks of is a kind of love that does not choose individuals at the expense of others. It is a love that extends to all people, equally (Kierkegaard 1995, pp. 21/IX, 25). This means that the love Jesus speaks of will place every human—including one's beloved, one's friend, and one's very self—at the same distance from oneself as one's worst enemy or billions of people with whom one has had no contact. It may be easy to imagine a God who loves all people equally, says Quinn, but it is difficult to see how it could be either desirable or feasible for humans to respond to one another in this way. If this love were optional, most of us would not pursue it (Quinn 1992, pp. 504–506). Therefore, Quinn's first reason for why this love needs to be a command is that only a dutiful love can embrace everyone without distinction. A natural love based on our preferences will extend only to some people; it will oppose a universal extension. After all, humans would normally prefer not to love their enemies. Therefore, it needs to be issued as a command. The second reason is that only a dutiful love can be safeguarded from alterations in its object. Quinn writes that if the beloved loses the traits that made them erotically attractive, the erotic love will change. A natural love based on our preferences will in that sense be unstable. Only when it is a duty to love—when the love is not contingent upon certain features of its object—is love secured (Kierkegaard 1995, p. 39/XI42; Quinn 1992, p. 507).

Although Quinn's argument may show that neighbour love should be regarded as a duty, the argument does not show that neighbour love is constituted by a divine command. To be convinced that this duty is something that in the end depends on a divine command, one must be convinced that moral duties are best understood as divine commands. That is, we must already be convinced of what the argument attempts to prove (Wainwright 2013, p. 134). As Quinn writes, the fact that a Christian ethics of love *can* be put in terms of commands does not imply that it *must* be formulated or is *best* formulated in such terms (Quinn 1992, p. 504). I grant that divine command theory can explain the distinction between good acts that are obligatory (duties) and good acts that are not and does so more straightforwardly and elegantly than most theories. However, divine command theory is not the only way to make sense of obligation (see, for instance, Jakobsen 2020, vol. 67, pp. 236–42).

Quinn's reasoning can be interpreted as a way to integrate divine command ethics and Christian theology because it is key to his argument that Jesus commands us to love. Jesus has the role of an ethical authority over his people. In a similar way, Hare proposes a connection between divine command theory and Christian theology by starting from the notion of how a king or a lord has authority over his people[14]. The first of the Ten Commandments states, "I am the Lord your God, who brought you out of Egypt, out of the land of slavery. You shall have no other gods before me" (Deuteronomy 5:6–7). This commandment expresses a particular relationship between God and the Israelites; God is their Lord, and they are his people. The commandments, then, express the obligations God establishes within this covenant relation (Hare 2015, p. 148). This reasoning can also be formulated Christologically. Jesus is lord; we are his people. To proclaim that Jesus is lord is to proclaim that Jesus has authority over his people and that this relationship between Jesus and his people is expressed, on our side, by obedience (Hare 2015, p. 39). Having Christ as lord, then, entails obedience to his commands. As Jesus says, "if anyone loves me, he will obey my teaching" (John 14: 23–4).

Both Quinn and Hare connect divine commands to Christ, either by arguing that Christ is lord with authority to command or by stating that Christ's command to love must be understood as a command. Both these lines of reasoning connect well to central parts of Christian theology, but their connection to divine command theory is not that strong. Although Hare's argument may show that God's people should obey the lord, it does not show that the commands constitute wrongness—only that it would be wrong not to do as commanded.

Some might worry that divine commands are made irrelevant to ethics if one rejects a divine command theory. Others could make a stronger claim: that such a moral theory cannot incorporate commands, so the theory would be falsified if, for instance, God issues a command—which, according to the Bible, God surely has (Harrison 2018, p. 19)[15]. However, a theory of imitation can incorporate divine commands and grant them great normative force. I suggest the following conception of divine commands: God's commands do not constitute moral wrongness; they communicate moral wrongness. To understand God's commands as communicating moral wrongness is a departure from a divine command theory. However, the main elements of the theory can still be maintained. One may hold that God's commands guide us and that God's commands have such great normative force that they make acts obligatory. Moreover, one might still hold that God's commands are sufficient for something to be obligatory. Hare writes that for "a Christian who is a divine command theorist, the Golden Rule gives us obligation not because we know the reason for it in our reason, but because Jesus commanded" (Hare 2015, p. 230). However, one does not need to be a divine command theorist to hold that Jesus commanding something is reason enough to act accordingly; one does not need to hold that divine commands constitute moral duties to believe this, it is sufficient to hold that divine commands communicate moral wrongness. Therefore, God's commands are not made irrelevant when one rejects a divine command theory. Even though God's commands are not seen as constituting moral wrongness, they can be seen as communicating moral wrongness.

5. Conclusions

My theological critique of divine command theory does not suggest that divine command theory is false, only that it is not well integrated into Christian theology and as such does not qualify as a Christian theory of morality. My critique has two parts. First, I argue that this theory is not a Christian moral theory because the metaethical theory lacks connections to central parts of Christian theology, such as Christology. Second, I argue that divine command theory does not fit well with the New Testament's vision of the moral life. In New Testament ethics, the deepest reason for doing what is required of us is not that God says so but that God is so. Seeing the moral life as a life of imitating Christ integrates into Christian theology better than divine command ethics does and can still incorporate the ethical relevance of divine commands.

Funding: This research received no external funding.

Data Availability Statement: Not applicable.

Conflicts of Interest: The author declares no conflict of interest.

Notes

[1]   See, for instance, (Antony 2008; Koons 2012; Morriston 2009; Sullivan 1993; Joyce 2002; Craig et al. 2020; Jordan 2012; Murphy 2002, 2011; Wielenberg 2020, 2022). A consequence of the fact that most critiques are philosophical is that books defending divine command ethics—such as *God and Moral Obligation* by Evans, *Finite and Infinite Goods* by Adams, and *God's Call* by Hare—mainly deal with philosophical rather than theological critique.

[2]   Some might worry whether this allows for some timeless truths. The metaethical theory that is true today would presumably also be true in the days of Moses, but it certainly could not be labelled as Christian in those days because there was no Christian theology into which to integrate it. Now, it is entirely possible to hold that there are some timeless truths and also hold that coherence is a good method of pursuing truth. Consider our capability of knowing God. Because God's self-disclosure has occurred over time—culminating in God's self-revelation in Jesus Christ—we are in a better position today to know who God is than in the days of Moses. Therefore, in the same way that God is always the same but we are in an epistemologically better position to know who God is after the incarnation, God's grounding of morality is always the same but we are in a better position to reveal this after the Incarnation. So, using coherence as a method for pursuing truth—especially when combined with a view of progressive revelation—implies that some people at a certain time and place will be in a better situation to discover some (timeless) truths.

[3]   O'Donovan is not as restrictive in *Self, World, and Time* (O'Donovan 2013). Because *Resurrection and Moral Order* is "an outline for evangelical ethics", it would be more to the point to say that evangelical ethics must arise from the gospel of Jesus Christ.

[4]   Thank you to an anonymous referee for this objection.

[5]   As opposed to the other divine command theorists mentioned in this article, Barth also holds that what is good for humans is constituted by God's command (Barth 1957b, vol. II.2, p. 547; McKenny 2021, p. 54).

[6]   NRSV is used unless otherwise stated.

[7]   Zagzebski makes this point (Zagzebski 2004, p. 240).

[8]   See also 1 Thessalonians 1:6; 1 Corinthians 11:1.

[9]   Ephesians 5:1, 1 Thessalonians 1:6, and 1 Corinthians 11:1. There are also other cases in which Paul urges his readers to imitate himself (1 Corinthians 4:16) or other churches (1 Thessalonians 2:14) who are in Christ.

[10]   See also (Sanders 1977, pp. 502–508). The phrase "in Christ" or "in the Lord" occurs 130 times in the Pauline Corpus.

[11]   Paul holds that it is not our imitation but the work of Christ that bring us into union with Christ (Dunn 1998, pp. 410–11). This is to say that moral life is a consequence of the union with Christ rather than a precondition. See, for instance, Romans 6, where Paul first elaborates on the "in Christ" motif (6:1–11) and then draws the ethical consequences (6:12–14).

[12]   The theological question of the relationship between the historical Jesus and the Christ is important one but is not addressed here.

[13]   What Quinn seems to have in mind here is the traditional Christian thought of the human condition as fallen (Quinn 1992, p. 508).

[14]   I am grateful to Hare for making this point at the *God and Morality* conference at Aix-Marseille Université, 2021.

[15]   Harrison critiques a theory that, similar to mine, grounds morality in God but not in God's command (Jordan 2012). Harrison's critique is connected to his view on the relationship between normative reasons and commands. He argues that some normative reasons (presumably obligations) are identical to commands. I argue that a command gives rise to a reason and that God's command gives rise to an overriding reason, that is, an obligation (Jakobsen 2020).

References

Adams, Robert Merrihew. 1999. *Finite and Infinite Goods: A Framework for Ethics*. Oxford: Oxford University Press.

Anscombe, Gertrude E. M. 1958. Modern Moral Philosophy. *Philosophy* 33: 1–19. [CrossRef]

Antony, Louise. 2008. Atheism as Perfect Piety. In *Is Goodness without God Good Enough?: A Debate on Faith, Secularism, and Ethics*. Edited by Nathan King and Robert Garcia. Lanham: Rowman & Littlefield Publishers, pp. 67–84.

Aristotle. 1932. *Poetics*. Translated by William H. Fyfe. Cambridge: Harvard University Press, vol. 23, Aristotle in 23 Volumes.

Aristotle. 1934. *Nicomachean Ethics*. Translated by Harris Rackham. Cambridge: Harvard University Press.

Athanasius. 1885. On the Incarnation. In *Ante-Nicene Fathers*. Edited by Alexander Roberts, James Donaldson and Arthur Cleveland Coxe. Buffalo: Christian Literature Publishing Co.

Barth, Karl. 1956. *Church Dogmatics, Volume I.2*. Peabody: Hendrickson Publishers.

Barth, Karl. 1957a. *Church Dogmatics, Volume II.1*. Peabody: Hendrickson Publishers.

Barth, Karl. 1957b. *Church Dogmatics, Volume II.2*. Peabody: Hendrickson Publishers.
Barth, Karl. 1961. *Church Dogmatics, Volume III.4*. Peabody: Hendrickson Publishers.
Barth, Karl. 2013. *Ethics*. Eugene: Wipf & Stock Publishers.
Biggar, Nigel. 1993. *The Hastening That Waits: Karl Barth's Ethics*. Oxford: Clarendon Press.
Biggar, Nigel. 2011. *Behaving in Public: How to Do Christian Ethics*. Grand Rapids: W. B. Eerdmans.
Clement. 1885. The Instructor. In *Ante-Nicene Fathers*. Edited by Alexander Roberts, James Donaldson and Arthur Cleveland Coxe. Buffalo: Christian Literature Publishing Co.
Craig, William Lane, Erik J. Wielenberg, and Adam Lloyd Johnson. 2020. *A Debate on God and Morality: What Is the Best Account of Objective Moral Values and Duties?* New York: Routledge.
Dunn, James D. G. 1998. *The Theology of Paul the Apostle*. Grand Rapids: W. B. Eerdmans Pub.
Evans, C. Stephen. 2013. *God and Moral Obligation*. Oxford: OUP.
Finnis, John. 2011. *Natural Law and Natural Rights*, 2nd ed. Clarendon Law Series; Oxford: Oxford University Press.
Grenz, Stanley J. 1997. *The Moral Quest*. Downers Grove: InterVarsity Press.
Hare, John E. 1996. *The Moral Gap: Kantian Ethics, Human Limits, and God's Assistance*. Oxford: Clarendon Press.
Hare, John E. 2001. *God's Call: Moral Realism, God's Commands, and Human Autonomy*. Grand Rapids: W. B. Eerdmans.
Hare, John E. 2011. *Why Bother Being Good? The Place of God in the Moral Life*. Eugene: Wipf and Stock Publishers.
Hare, John E. 2015. God's Command. In *Oxford Studies in Theological Ethics*, 1st ed. Oxford: Oxford University Press.
Hare, John E. 2019. Religion and Morality. In *The Stanford Encyclopedia of Philosophy*, 2019th ed. Edited by Edward N. Zalta. Available online: https://plato.stanford.edu/entries/religion-morality (accessed on 16 March 2023).
Hare, John E. 2022. God and Morality. In *Encyclopedia of Religious Ethics*. Edited by William Schweiker. Hoboken: Wiley-Blackwell, pp. 41–47. [CrossRef]
Harrison, Gerald. 2018. Normative Reasons and Theism. In *Palgrave Frontiers in Philosophy of Religion*. Cham: Springer International Publishing.
Irenaeus. 1885. Against Heresies. In *Ante-Nicene Fathers*. Edited by Alexander Roberts, James Donaldson and Arthur Cleveland Coxe. Buffalo: Christian Literature Publishing Co.
Jakobsen, Martin. 2020. Moral Realism and the Existence of God: Improving Parfit's Metaethics. In *Studies in Philosophical Theology*. Leuven: Peeters Publishers, vol. 67. [CrossRef]
Jeffrey, Anne. 2019. *God and Morality*, 1st ed. Cambridge: Cambridge University Press. [CrossRef]
Jordan, Matthew Carey. 2012. Divine Attitudes, Divine Commands, and the Modal Status of Moral Truths. *Religious Studies* 48: 45–60. [CrossRef]
Joyce, Richard. 2002. Theistic Ethics and the Euthyphro Dilemma. *Journal of Religious Ethics* 30: 49–75. [CrossRef]
Kierkegaard, Søren. 1995. *Works of Love*. Translated by Howard V. Hong, and Edna H. Hong. Princeton: Princeton University Press.
Koons, Jeremy. 2012. Can God's Goodness Save the Divine Command Theory from Euthyphro? *European Journal for Philosophy of Religion* 4: 177–95. [CrossRef]
Lee, J. Harrison, and C. Stephen Evans. 2022. Divine Command Theories of Moral Obligations. In *Encyclopedia of Religious Ethics*. Edited by William Schweiker. Hoboken: Wiley-Blackwell, pp. 94–103. [CrossRef]
Linville, Mark D. 2012. Moral Particularism. In *God and Morality: Four Views*. Edited by R. Keith Loftin. Downers Grove: InterVarsity Press, pp. 135–58.
McKenny, Gerald. 2021. Karl Barth's Moral Thought. In *Oxford Studies in Theological Ethics*. Oxford: Oxford University Press.
Morriston, Wes. 2009. What If God Commanded Something Terrible? A Worry for Divine-Command Meta-Ethics. *Religious Studies* 45: 249–67. [CrossRef]
Murphy, Mark C. 2002. A Trilemma for Divine Command Theory. *Faith and Philosophy* 19: 22–31. [CrossRef]
Murphy, Mark C. 2011. *God and Moral Law: On the Theistic Explanation of Morality*. Oxford: Oxford University Press.
O'Donovan, Oliver. 1986. *Resurrection and Moral Order: An Outline for Evangelical Ethics*. Leicester: IVP.
O'Donovan, Oliver. 2013. Self, World, and Time. In *Ethics as Theology*. Grand Rapids: William B. Eerdmans Publishing Company, vol. 1.
Olsson, Erik. 2012. Coherentist Theories of Epistemic Justification. In *The Stanford Encyclopedia of Philosophy*. Edited by Edward N. Zalta. New York: Springer. Available online: http://plato.stanford.edu/archives/spr2014/entries/justep-coherence/ (accessed on 11 December 2022).
Origen. 1885. De Principiis. In *Ante-Nicene Fathers*. Edited by Alexander Roberts, James Donaldson and Arthur Cleveland Coxe. Buffalo: Christian Literature Publishing Co.
Quinn, Philip L. 1992. The Primacy of God's Will in Christian Ethics. *Philosophical Perspectives* 6: 493–513. [CrossRef]
Rescher, Nicholas. 1973. *The Coherence Theory of Truth*. Oxford: Clarendon Press.
Russell, Daniel C. 2004. Virtue as "Likeness to God" in Plato and Seneca. *Journal of the History of Philosophy* 42: 241–60. [CrossRef]
Sanders, Ed P. 1977. *Paul and Palestinian Judaism: A Comparison of Patterns of Religion*. London: SCM Press.
Søvik, Atle Ottesen. 2016. A Theoretical Framework for Talking Seriously About God. In *Talking Seriously about God: Philosophy of Religion in the Dispute Between Theism and Atheism*. Edited by Atle Ottesen Søvik and Asle Eikrem. Wien: LIT Verlag, pp. 55–76.
Stephen, Darwall. 2006. How Should Ethics Relate to (the Rest of) Philosophy? Moore's Legacy. In *Metaethics after Moore*. Edited by Mark Timmons and Terry Horgan. Oxford: Clarendon Press, pp. 17–38.

Sullivan, Stephen J. 1993. Arbitrariness, Divine Commands, and Morality. *International Journal for Philosophy of Religion* 33: 33–45. [CrossRef]

Wainwright, William J. 2013. *Religion and Morality*. Ashgate Philosophy of Religion Series; London: Routledge.

Wielenberg, Erik J. 2020. Divine Command Theory and Psychopathy. *Religious Studies* 56: 542–57. [CrossRef]

Wielenberg, Erik J. 2022. Divine Commands Are Unnecessary for Moral Obligation. *Journal of Ethics and Social Philosophy* 21: 142–49. [CrossRef]

Witherington, Ben. 2016a. *New Testament Theology and Ethics, Volume 1*. Downers Grove: IVP Academic.

Witherington, Ben. 2016b. *New Testament Theology and Ethics, Volume 2*. Downers Grove: IVP Academic.

Zagzebski, Linda Trinkaus. 2004. *Divine Motivation Theory*. Cambridge: Cambridge University Press.

Zagzebski, Linda Trinkaus. 2005. Morality and Religion. In *The Oxford Handbook of Philosophy of Religion*. Edited by William J. Wainwright. Oxford Handbooks in Philosophy. Oxford: Oxford University Press, pp. 344–65.

Article

Normative Reasons, Epistemic Autonomy, and Accountability to God

Brandon Rickabaugh

Graduate Department of Philosophy of Religion, Palm Beach Atlantic University, West Palm Beach, FL 33401, USA; brandon_rickabaugh@pba.edu

Abstract: According to many, human autonomy is necessary for moral action and yet incompatible with being morally accountable to God's divine commands. By issuing commands that ground normative facts, God demands our accountability without understanding our normative reasons for moral action, which crushes human autonomy. Call this the *Autonomy Objection to Theism* (AOT). There is an unexplored connection between models of normative reason and AOT. I argue that any plausible AOT must be stated in terms of an adequate model of normative reason. There are two broad metaethical categories for models of normative reason: anti-realist or realist views. I defend the thesis that both anti-realism and realism about normative reasons fail to support AOT by means of a dilemma. If the AOT defender adopts anti-realism about normative reasons (subjectivism and constructivism), AOT loses its force. However, if the AOT defender adopts moral realism, they face the same problem as the theist, as normative fact constrains autonomy. Consequently, AOT is a problem for all moral realists, including non-theists, such as Russ Shafer-Landau, David Enoch, and Erik Wielenberg, among others.

Keywords: divine command theory; normative reasons; moral realism; moral knowledge; autonomy; constitutionalism; subjectivism; theistic metaethics

Citation: Rickabaugh, Brandon. 2023. Normative Reasons, Epistemic Autonomy, and Accountability to God. *Religions* 14: 662. https://doi.org/10.3390/rel14050662

Academic Editor: David Baggett

Received: 20 April 2023
Revised: 5 May 2023
Accepted: 10 May 2023
Published: 16 May 2023

Copyright: © 2023 by the author. Licensee MDPI, Basel, Switzerland. This article is an open access article distributed under the terms and conditions of the Creative Commons Attribution (CC BY) license (https://creativecommons.org/licenses/by/4.0/).

1. Introduction

We can enjoy morally significant autonomy or theism, but not both. So says a long-standing Kant-inspired object, that any version of theism according to which we are accountable to God by divine command.[1] This objection is based on two claims: (1) human autonomy is necessary for moral action, and (2) human autonomy is incompatible with the standard theistic claim that humans are morally accountable to God apart from understanding their reasons for obeying God. Call this line of reasoning the *Autonomy Objection to Theism* (AOT).[2]

Among the many replies to AOT, none explore the connection between the nature of normative reason (reasons for moral action) and AOT. Exploring this connection sets up a new way of answering AOT. I show that any plausible AOT must be stated in terms of an adequate model of normative reason. There are two broad metaethical categories for models of normative reason: anti-realist or realist views. I defend the thesis that both anti-realism and realism about normative reasons fail to support AOT by means of a dilemma:

The AOT Dilemma: If the AOT defender adopts anti-realism about normative reasons (subjectivism and constructivism), AOT loses its force. But, if the AOT defender adopts moral realism, they face the same problem as the theist, as normative fact constrains autonomy.

If correct, a surprising thesis is revealed: AOT is not a problem unique to theism but for all moral realists. This would be a serious problem as several non-theists embrace realism. For example, Michael Huemer writes, "I would say the objectivity of morality has nothing to do with God. As to "how" it is objective, it is objective by not constitutively depending on the attitudes of observers" (Huemer 2021, pp. 156; see also Huemer 2013). In explaining the thesis of his book, Wielenberg writes:

> I accept moral realism yet I believe that God does not exist. I also find it unsatisfying, perhaps even "lame" as Mackie would have it, to posit mysterious, quasi-mystical cognitive faculties that are somehow able to make contact with causally inert moral features of the world and provide us with knowledge of them. The central goal of this book is to defend the plausibility of a robust brand of moral realism without appealing to God or any weird cognitive faculties. (Wielenberg 2014, p. ix)

The AOT Dilemma, if correct, poses a serious problem, especially for those AOT defenders who adopt moral realism. So why think the *AOT Dilemma* is defensible?

2. Autonomy Objections to Theism

2.1. Divine Command Theory

AOT targets divine command theory, according to which at least some normative facts depend on or are grounded in facts about God's commands.[3] Following Robert Adams and C. Stephen Evans, I will limit the scope to moral obligations as follows (Adams 1987; Evans 2013).

> *Divine Command Theory* (DCT): At least some normative facts—facts about moral obligation—are grounded in facts about God and God's commands.[4]

The fact that any action, φ, is morally wrong is grounded in facts about φ being contrary to facts about God and God's commands. The obligation and wrongdoing statements of DCT are compatible with, if not consequent of, each other. If one has an obligation to φ, then bringing about φ is morally right or good, while failing to φ is morally wrong.

I understand divine commands as communications from God regarding our collective and individual accountability to God for action and cultivating virtues to live a particular kind of life (perhaps one like Jesus's) and become a particular kind of person (perhaps like Jesus). One might think that in following God's commands that one cultivates the virtue of accountability to God. This virtue is a trait of those who are rightfully held accountable, who welcome and embrace being accountable and thereby show a sensitivity to what the relation requires (Evans and Rickabaugh 2022; Evans 2023). A sincere theist (notably Jews, Muslims, and Christians) might seek to cultivate the virtue of accountability to God, as they are accountable to God for their lives as a whole. Of course, the fact that one has a moral obligation to cultivate the virtue of accountability to God is grounded in facts about God and God's commands.

2.2. Two Versions of the Autonomy Objection to Theism

It is worth distinguishing AOT from a related objection. Jean-Paul Sartre argued that if God created us, we would be mere objects, like a "paper knife", unable to form a meaningful life by creating ourselves (Sartre [1946] 2007, pp. 20–23). Similarly, according to Kurt Baier, God is "a kind of superman . . . a sort of playwright-cum-legislator-cum-judge-cum-executioner" (Baier [1957] 2008, p. 83). These objections from self-creative autonomy are far weaker than AOT. For one thing, full self-creative autonomy does not guarantee a meaningful life. Plausibly, only the kind of autonomy God allows is necessary for a meaningful life (see e.g., Penner (2015)). Secondly, God could overcome any degradation of human life by bringing about a much more significant meaning to life overall (see e.g., Kraay and Dragos (2013)).

AOT requires a substantive notion of autonomy, a theory of normative reasons, and the relation between the two. To clarify these concepts, I will consider the autonomy objections of Nowell-Smith and James Rachels, as they are the most developed and discussed.

2.2.1. The Infantilizing Argument

The first version of AOT is what I will call the *infantilizing argument* (Nowell-Smith [1961] 1999). Nowell-Smith's infantilizing argument employs Jean Piaget's theory of moral development, especially the second developmental stage, where children (ages 5–9) obey their parent's normative commands as unbreakable authoritative directives. Understanding what these moral rules are for or what makes them worth following does not guide the child's obedience. In this respect, they are infantile. Children become autonomous in the third developmental stage by evaluating the reasons for obeying normative commands. The child's non-autonomous infantilizing obedience dissolves as they gain an equal footing with adults (Piaget 1965).

According to Nowell-Smith, the stage two parent/child relationship is analogous to the God/human relationship. Just as the normative authority of the parent infantilizes the child, the normative authority of God infantilizes the human person.[5] Similarly, Walter Sinnott-Armstrong points to cognitive science studies showing that raising children to obey God's commands simply because God commanded them undermines their moral development (Sinnott-Armstrong 2009, p. 110). "Religious morality", says Nowell-Smith, "is infantile" (Nowell-Smith [1961] 1999, p. 403). If DCT is true, so the objection goes, all are infantilized by God, subjugating us to the psychological development of children in Piaget's second stage.

2.2.2. The Worship Argument

The argument defended by Rachels, what I will call the *worship argument*, attempts to show that the moral duty to worship God destroys human dignity. Kant's words are often conjured for this point: "Kneeling down or prostrating oneself on the ground, even to show your veneration for heavenly objects, is contrary to the dignity of humanity…" (Kant [1797] 1996, p. 437).[6] According to Rachels, to acknowledge God is to recognize God's unlimited authority and our ultimate accountability to worship God. "That God is not to be judged, challenged, defied, or disobeyed", writes Rachels, "is at bottom a truth of logic; to do any of these things is incompatible with taking him as One to be worshiped" (Rachels 1971, p. 333). Why think this is true? According to Rachels, this conception of God is self-evident and self-explanatory.[7] The fact that God exists, if it is a fact, entails that we are accountable to God in such a way that we cannot come to know apart from God why we are so accountable. We are not autonomous in gaining moral knowledge about our accountability to God.

2.2.3. The Nature of Autonomy in AOT

Defining 'autonomy' is notoriously difficult. After surveying numerous notions of autonomy, often used interchangeably, Gerald Dworkin concludes that conceptions of autonomy are so diverse that they share only two traits: "autonomy is a feature of persons and that it is a desirable quality to have" (Dworkin 1988, p. 3). Some thirty-three years later, this problem remains.[8]

For my purposes, I need only consider the aspects of autonomy employed by defenders of the autonomy objection. Consider the claim of autonomy objector Robin Le Poidevin:

> The truly moral agent is one who wishes to be his own master, not the instrument of some other power, and not to trust the deliverances of some supposed authority, but to work out for themselves the rightness of certain kinds of behavior. (Le Poidevin 1996, p. 84)

Poidevin echoes Kant's definition of autonomy as "the property of the will by which it is a law to itself (independently of any property of the objects of volition)" (Kant [1785] 1997, p. 440). Autonomy objectors also endorse Kant's thesis that self-legislation and self-government are necessary for autonomy and human dignity (Ibid., pp. 435–36). Although, AOT does not reduce the ability to self-legislate or self-govern regarding the freedom to choose to φ or not to φ. One can be free to φ or not to φ and make one's choice irrationally, yet not self-governing in any relevant way. Likewise, not being externally controlled or coerced to φ does not entail that one acts autonomously. Freedom is necessary but not sufficient for autonomy.

AOT also requires that insofar as one is autonomous, one must be able to step back from one's desires and assess moral actions rationally. In conjunction with the freedom requirement, the rationality requirement allows us to act intentionally. This tracks with the standard (procedural) view of autonomy in bioethics, according to which an agent is autonomous concerning an action if it is performed intentionally, with understanding, and without determining influences.

Taken together, we get the following thesis:

Personal Autonomy: An agent *S* has personal autonomy, *iff*, *S*'s actions are performed intentionally, with understanding, and without conditions that determine *S*'s actions.

The autonomy objector might agree that the features of personal autonomy are necessary conditions for human autonomy in general, yet insufficient for the *infantilizing* and *worship* arguments. A child in Piaget's second developmental stage can act intentionally, undetermined, and with understanding, for example, that her parent knows more than she does. So, if one is infantilized, it is not for a mere lack of personal autonomy.

AOT is concerned with a more specific thesis than *Personal Autonomy*. It requires epistemic autonomy or what Robert Adams calls *total inner directedness*: the power to rely exclusively on one's reasoning or feelings in adopting moral principles, values, and priorities (Adams 1999, p. 271). More precisely:

Epistemic Autonomy: An agent *S* has epistemic autonomy, *iff*, *S* is able to form *S*'s beliefs by *S*'s cognitive resources, and *S*'s actions are performed intentionally, with understanding, and without conditions that determine *S*'s actions.

We can distinguish this from epistemic interdependence, the ability to think with and consult other agents as external cognitive resources. An important aspect of intellectual autonomy is that it provides an ideal context for forming true beliefs and gaining understanding and knowledge.

The autonomy objector does not require that one have epistemic autonomy *tout court*. As Elizabeth Fricker has shown, an ideal autonomous knower, someone who only believes what she can find out through her cognitive resources, without the testimony of another, does not exist (Fricker 2006). One cannot gain knowledge apart from the cognitive resources of experts. Fortunately, for the autonomy objector, AOT only requires epistemic autonomy regarding accountability to God.

2.3. Epistemic Autonomy and Normative Reasons

AOT requires that one's reasons for moral action, one's normative reason, must be adopted as a consequence of one's *Epistemic Autonomy*. I understand the nature of normative reason as follows:[9]

Normative Reason: An agent *S* has a normative reason to *φ* at time *t*, *iff*, some fact about *φ* (concerning *S*'s situation at *t*) plays a particular role in explaining what *S* ought to do at *t*.

Accordingly, the explanation of what one ought to do at *t* supervenes on one's reasons for and against the available courses of action at *t*. To seek out an explanation for why one should obey God is to seek out one's normative reasons for obeying God. When free to do so, one has the following kind of autonomy:

Normative Reasons Autonomy: An agent *S* has normative reason autonomy with respect to *φ* at time *t*, *iff*, *S* decides to *φ* at *t* because *S* has a normative reason to *φ* at *t*, and *S* comes to know *S*'s normative reason with *Epistemic Autonomy*.

Accordingly, one is autonomous with respect to obeying God just in case one decides to obey God in light of one's normative reasons for doing so. One comes to know those reasons through one's cognitive resources intentionally, with understanding and without determining conditions.

Normative reasons autonomy is the point of contention in the *infantilizing* and *worship arguments*. Consider Kai Neilson's rhetorical question:

> Is it really hubris or arrogance or sin on our part to wish for a life where we make our own decisions, where we follow the rules we do because we see the point of them and where we need not crucify our intellects by believing in some transcendent purpose whose very intelligibility is seriously in question? Perhaps by saying this I am only exhibiting my own hubris, my own corruption of soul, but I cannot believe that to ask this question is to exhibit such arrogance. (Nielson 1991, p. 22)

The autonomy objector claims that if DCT is true, then seeking to understand one's normative reasons for obeying God entails that one disobeys God. The thought is that to seek one's normative reasons to obey God requires refraining from obeying God until those normative reasons are found. Withholding obedience to God, even for the sake of understanding one's normative reasons for doing so, is to judge, challenge, and defy God. Thus, DCT entails the impossibility of possessing the autonomy necessary for coming to know (with one's cognitive resources alone) one's normative reasons for obeying God and not disobeying God. That is, exercising one's *Normative Reasons Autonomy* by seeking to know one's normative reasons for obeying God is itself an act of disobedience to God. Without *Normative Reasons Autonomy*, we are infantilized and degraded by the inability to discover our normative reason for obeying God. AOT, therefore, depends on the nature of normative reason, especially the close connection between normative reason and autonomy.

3. Anti-Realist Models of Normative Reason and Varieties of AOT

AOT is a thesis about normative reasons, namely, that God should provide the autonomy necessary for us to seek and discover what normative reasons we have to be accountable to God, to live according to his divine commands. In order to know the kind of autonomy necessary for seeking and discovering these normative reasons, at least two things must be clarified: (a) the nature of normative reasons and (b) the relationship between normative reason and autonomy. Thus, the AOT advocate must posit a model of normative reason that is capable of supporting AOT. Moreover, the posited model of normative reasons must be closely linked to autonomy in such a way that God must provide this autonomy for the sake of our seeking and discovering the normative reasons for obeying God. Advocates of AOT have not clarified (a), and therefore have not clarified (b). In what follows, I will explore the most popular anti-realist models of *Normative Reason* in order to clarify (a) and (b). In doing so, I will argue that both models fail to support AOT.

3.1. Subjectivism about Normative Reasons Autonomy

Subjectivism about normative reason is a desire-fulfillment theory, grounding facts about normative reasons in facts about specific mental states: desires, attitudes, or aims. More precisely:

> *Normative Reasons Subjectivism*: The fact that an agent S has a normative reason to φ at time t is grounded in facts about S's desires.

What explains the fact that one has a normative reason to φ is the fact that φ-ing will satisfy one's attitudes or desires. So, Hume was correct: "Reason alone can never be a motive to any action of the will", and reason alone "can never oppose passion in the direction of the will" (Hume [1739] 1967, 2.3, p. 413). Put more famously, "Reason is, and ought only to be the slave of the passions and can never pretend to any other office than to serve and obey them" (Ibid. p. 415).

Prima facie, normative reason subjectivism seems to champion autonomy. Normative reason is only an instrument. The direction of explanation is from desire to reasons for action (Sobel 2021, p. 307). Facts about one's desire, not any authority, divine or otherwise, grounds facts about one's normative reasons. More specifically:

> *Subjectivist Normative Reasons Autonomy* (SNR-Autonomy): An agent S is autonomous with respect to φ at time t, *iff*, the fact that S has a normative reason to φ at time t is grounded in facts about S's desires.

Consequently, one is autonomously accountable to God just in case one decides to obey God because one is in the mental <desiring to obey God>. On *SNR-Autonomy*, what one ought to do at t supervenes on one's desire(s) at t. Therefore, one's normative autonomy can go only where one's desires allow it.

SNR-Autonomy is certainly at odds with divine command theory. According to DCT, facts about one's accountability to God and the facts that ground one's normative reasons to obey God have nothing to do with one's desires. Normative facts are iconoclastic with respect to one's desires as they are grounded in facts about God and God's commands.

A Problem for Subjectivist Normative Reasons Autonomy

As previously explained, AOT requires a close connection between autonomy and normative reasons. On *SNR-Autonomy*, however, it is not clear why normative reason should be closely related to autonomy. It may make more sense to identify autonomy with the ability to realize one's preferences. In most subjectivist views (especially Humeanism), the weight or justificatory force of a normative reason covaries with the strength of one's desire for x and the likelihood that S's φ-ing will realize S's desire for x.[10] Thus, facts about normative reasons are always grounded in facts about one's desires, although facts about one's normative reasons autonomy are grounded in facts about desires in conjunction with facts about the likelihood of an action fulfilling one's desire. However, now, paradoxically, a person's autonomy is a function of external circumstances not totally within the person's control, violating the non-determined condition of personal autonomy. Moreover, it is not clear how much, if any, autonomy one has when reason is a slave of one's passion. If reason only obeys desires, normative reasons are disconnected from personal or normative reason autonomy.

Perhaps the subjectivist can modify their thesis to avoid these aforementioned problems. Some subjectivists (e.g., David Hume and Henry Sidgwick) limit the scope of relevant desires to *informed* desires that reveal one's true concern (see e.g., Hume ([1739] 1967, p. 460), and Sidgwick ([1907] 1981, pp. 111–12)). Some characterize an informed desire as a second-order Frankfurt desire, that is, what we desire to desire within the context of our life projects (Frankfurt 1971). Others hold that facts about an ideal agent's desires, not an agent's actual desires, ground facts about normative reasons. If any of these restrictions hold, one might argue that *Normative Reason Autonomy* requires only that normative reasons are determined by informed desires, which are not determined by anything outside the agent. Perhaps one's desire for x is a function of external factors, although their second-order desire, their desire-to-desire x, is not a function of external factors.

This move will not work for at least two reasons. First, plausibly, this reply assumes compatibilism. The second-order desires are autonomous (within one's control) by being internal mental states, while the first-order desires are not within one's control but a function of external circumstances. However, compatibilism is disputed, and therefore not difficult to avoid for incompatibilists and determinists. Second, Mark Murphy has persuasively argued that a desire-based theory is rightly understood as a simple unrestricted subjectivism according to which, if one desires x, then one has a normative reason to act to satisfy one's desire for x, as there is no adequate rationale for informed desire limitations (Murphy 2001).

Even if subjectivism can be limited to informed desires, the same problem arises. Suppose informed desires are second-order desires. In this case, one is autonomously accountable to God just in case one obeys God because one has a second-order desire: to have the desire to obey God. Nevertheless, there still exists a gulf between autonomy and normative reason. If one is led by second-order desires, then what role does reason have to play?

Alternatively, suppose that the fact that S has a normative reason to φ is grounded in facts about an idealized version of S, S_1. Consequently, one is autonomously accountable to God just in case they decide to obey God because an idealized version of them would desire to obey God. The same problem as before arises: any desire of S_1 is a function of factors external to S. One decides to obey God, not because of their desire, but because an idealized version of them would desire to obey God. However, one is never in control of the desire that an idealized version of them would have. This fact undermines personal autonomy and, thus, normative reason autonomy. Therefore, the autonomy objector must reject *SNR-Autonomy* for an alternative model of normative reason.

Lastly, consider the assumption that one should pursue Epistemic Autonomy, without which AOT cannot get off the ground. On subjectivism (SNR-Autonomy), one has a normative reason for pursuing Epistemic Autonomy just in case one is fulfilling their mental state 'desiring to pursue Epistemic Autonomy.' How does this motivate a conflict between DCT and Epistemic Autonomy? What follows from the fact that God's commands conflict with one's desire to have Epistemic Autonomy? That one's desire is frustrated by normative facts grounded in facts about the normativity of God and his commands does not entail that one has a right to fulfilling one's desires, including one's desire for Epistemic Autonomy. The use of desire in *Normative Reasons Subjectivism* deflates AOT to a mere desire-based objection. However, that one desires *Epistemic Autonomy* to seek one's normative reasons for obeying God does not entail or make plausible that one ought to fulfill that desire or that one has a right to disobey God's commands. The connection between Normative Reason and Epistemic Autonomy required by AOT is not secured by Normative Reasons Constructivism. It provides no reason for which God must provide Epistemic Autonomy for the sake of our seeking and discovering the normative reasons for obeying God. Therefore, Normative Reasons Subjectivism is incapable of supporting AOT.

3.2. Constructivism about Normative Reasons Autonomy

Like subjectivists, constructivists hold that normative facts *originate* in certain mental states (attitudes or desires) (see e.g., Markovits 2014; and Street 2009). Unlike subjectivism, the fact that S has a particular mental state attitude does not by itself ground the fact that S has a normative reason to φ. Instead, for a normative reason to be correct is, in the words of Sharon Street, "for it to stand up to the specified sort of reflective scrutiny; the normative judgment's correctness is constituted by the fact that it withstands this scrutiny" (Street 2008, p. 209). More precisely:

> *Normative Reasons Constructivism*: The fact that an agent S has a normative reason to φ at time t is grounded in facts about the rational evaluation of the attitudes and activities of S or S's community toward φ at time t.

The constructivist model grounds facts about normative reasons in facts about the rational responses of one or more human beings. In this way, the standards of normative reasons are procedurally self-authenticating.

The relationship between constructivism about normative reason and autonomy seems straightforward.

> *Constructivist Normative Reasons Autonomy*: (CNR-Autonomy): An agent S is autonomous with respect to φ at time t, *iff*, the fact that S has a normative reason to φ at time t is grounded in facts about the rational evaluation of the attitudes and activities of S or S's community toward φ at time t.

On *CNR-Autonomy*, what one ought to do at t supervenes on the rational evaluation of one's attitudes or those of one's community at t. This includes whether or not one ought to pursue *Epistemic Autonomy*.

At this point, one might reply that constructivism is not committed to a specific theory of autonomy, much less one that ties normative reasons to autonomy. However, I am concerned with the conjunction of constructivism about normative reason and the autonomy objection, which requires a close connection between normative reason and autonomy.

Problems for Constructivist Normative Reasons Autonomy

Constructivism comes in two forms: social and individual. *Social constructivists* see normative facts as grounded in facts about the attitudes and activities, the values of society, and facts about society's circumstances, both of which are determined by the rational decision procedure of a society. Consequently, one is autonomously accountable to God just in case one decides to obey God because one's society has determined that it values obedience to God by their chosen rational decision procedure.

It is not clear how social constructivism is compatible with *Normative Reasons Autonomy*. Normative reasons grounded in procedural produced agreements are binding only on those participating in the agreement. However, suppose facts about normative reason are grounded in facts about one's mental state and attitude toward agreeing to socially constructed normative facts. In that case, we are back to a subjectivist view.

Alternatively, if the aforementioned is not the case, that is, if facts about normative reasons are binding because they are constructed by society, then personal autonomy and normative reasons autonomy are lost. What one ought to do, and the normative reasons one has for doing so are determined not by the individual but by one's society. For example, in defending social constructivism, David Copp recognizes that "in some cases, cultural or social acceptance is needed for a person to have a sense of self-respect, and in different cultures, different things contribute to social acceptance."[11] These "background facts" are imposed on the individual by their society. Thus, like subjectivism, there is no close connection between normative reasons and autonomy.

However, will not the constructivist say one can rationally reflect on the societal agreement and judge that one should keep it? Therefore, the agreement comes from others, but normative reason tells one that they ought to keep it. This will not evade the problem altogether. Suppose morality holds because one ought to agree to live by the socially constructed agreement. In that case, at least one normative fact precedes the agreement, one that is not constructed; namely, that one ought to keep the agreement, which contradicts social constructivism (Copp 1995, p. 167).

Alternatively, *individual constructivists* see normativity as created by each person, perhaps to avoid the previous problem. Some follow Kant's view that normative reason is a formal principle—a categorical imperative—allowing us to govern our inclinations, deciding which must be followed, which must not be followed, and which are permissible but not required, which apply without reference to adopting any ends or goal for ourselves. One evaluates proposed principles of action by discerning which can rationally be willed as universal. In this way, normative facts arise from a free rational will standing under the categorical imperative. However, whether such a formal principle can provide concrete guidance is unclear. Can one will a universal law that she should not step on sidewalk cracks? Probably not, but only because we recognize no value in such a principle. Formal reason itself does not tell us this.

Alternatively, Christine Korsgaard proposes that individual constructivists supplement Kant's categorical imperative by adding to it a principle of personal identity. We must choose what she calls *the moral law*—what Kant calls a kingdom of ends—a maxim *we must give ourselves* regarded as a law according to which we act only on maxims that "all rational beings could agree to act on together in a workable cooperative system"(Korsgaard 1996b, p. 99; see also Kant [1785] 1997, 4: 433). Facts about the principles that one can rationally will as a universal law are partially grounded in facts about one's sense of who they are. Korsgaard explains:

> But part of the normative force of those reasons springs from the value we place on ourselves as human beings who need such identities. In this way, all value depends on the value of humanity; other forms of practical identity matter in part because humanity requires them. Moral identity and the obligations it carries with it are therefore inescapable and pervasive. (Korsgaard 1996b, pp. 21–22)

Therefore, normative reason is constructed. Facts about normative reason are grounded in facts about the value of humanity, and facts about the value of humanity are grounded in facts about our assignment of value regarding our individual sense of identity. However, this makes morality subjective since people have wildly different senses of identity. Think, for example, of the differences between the white nationalist and the individual whose life is rooted in opposition to racism.

Korsgaard tries to limit the subjectivity. Constructivists typically characterize their view as entailing *qualified anti-realism* or what Christine Korsgaard calls *procedural realism*: "values are constructed by a procedure, the procedure of making laws for ourselves" (Korsgaard 1996b, p. 112). As Julia Markovits and Kenneth Walden explain, normative facts exist, but they do not exist independently of the parts of which they are constructed (Markovits and Walden 2021, p. 318). Normative facts are, therefore, not sui generis. In agreement with realists, constructivism affirms that there are normative facts, properties, and relations and that normative facts can be known. This is compatible with subjectivism. Moral facts are determined by mental states—desires—and one can know moral facts by knowing one's desires. However, like the subjectivist, the constructivist denies that normative facts are mind-independent. As Sharon Street explains:

> Normative truth, according to the constructivist, does not outrun what follows from within the evaluative standpoint, but rather consists in whatever is entailed from within it. (Street 2010, p. 371)

Still, Korsgaard tries to limit the subjectivity of constructivism by arguing that every reasonable person's identity should include recognizing the value of every human person. Thus, according to Korsgaard, if one is to value one's humanity, one must value the humanity of all human persons. However, this implies that humans have an objective, mind-independent value independent of normative constructions, which contradicts constructivism.

At the same time, Korsgaard tries to avoid positing an objective value for human persons. In her view, one necessarily values one's self. So to be rationally consistent, one should value others like one's self. But why be rationally consistent? In Korsgaard's view, the will must have a law, but it is its own law, so "nothing determines what that law must be. All that it has to be is a law" (Korsgaard 1996b, p. 98). Thus, no one should be rationally consistent in an objective sense. The collapse into subjectivism is unavoidable.

Moreover, in Korsgaard's view, autonomy is the source of all normativity (Ibid., p. 91; Korsgaard 1996a). However, if autonomy is the source of all normative value, then the autonomy objector cannot explain why human autonomy is valuable in the first place.[12] The autonomy objection cannot be defended or even motivated by constructivism. Consider the AOT assumption that one ought to pursue *Epistemic Autonomy*. On *Normative Reasons Constructivism*, one has a normative reason for pursuing *Epistemic Autonomy* just in case the rational evaluation of the attitudes and activities of one's community decides so. *Normative Reasons Constructivism*, therefore, deflates AOT to an objection from the normative constructions of a community. However, that one's community constructs normative reasons that presumably conflict with God's normative commands does not entail that one's community and its citizens have the right to secure *Epistemic Autonomy*. That is, *Normative Reasons Constructivism* provides no reason for which God must provide Epistemic Autonomy for the sake of our seeking and discovering the normative reasons for obeying God. Therefore, *Normative Reasons Constructivism* is incapable of supporting AOT.

4. The Real Issue: Realism about Normative Reasons

Now I will argue that the real issue driving AOT is moral realism, specifically realism about normative reasons. This shows that moral realism about normative reason motivates AOT. Therefore, what was thought to be a problem for divine command theory is a problem for all moral realist theories or, at least, all realist theories about normative reasons.

4.1. Moral Realism

According to *Moral Realism*: Facts about normativity are (a) grounded in objective, mind-independent facts and (b) apply universally (to rational beings). *Moral Anti-Realism* rejects (a) and (b). Ralph Wedgwood points out that the fundamental questions about normative reason concern the dispute between the realist or what he calls the "recognitional" view and the constructivist. On realism, normative reasoning "fundamentally consists in attempting to figure out what is a good thing to do and what is not and then choosing accordingly" (Wedgwood 2002, p. 139).

Applied to normative reasons, we get the following:

Normative Reason Realism: Facts about *S*'s normative reason to φ at *t* are (a) grounded in objective, mind-independent facts and (b) apply universally (to rational beings).

Normative Reason Anti-Realism: Facts about *S*'s normative reason to φ at *t* are not (a) grounded in objective, mind-independent facts and (b) do not apply universally (to rational beings).

Normative reasons, on a realist view, are grounded in normative facts, while on an anti-realist view, they are grounded in procedural facts (constructivism) or desire facts (subjectivism).

It must be understood that moral realism does not stand at odds with autonomy but is only a theory of autonomy, according to which facts about the value of autonomy are grounded in mind-dependent facts. The self-referential aspect of autonomy and authenticity, in the words of Charles Taylor, "doesn't mean that on another level the content must be self-referential: that my goals must express or fulfill my desires or aspirations, as against something that stands beyond these" (Taylor 1991, p. 82). Failure to understand this, in the words of Taylor, "lends legitimacy to the worst forms of subjectivism" (Ibid.)

4.2. Why Moral Realism Is the Actual Problem

I have argued that the most popular anti-realist models of normative reason cannot plausibly support AOT. Formally, these anti-realist views appear to support AOT insofar as they view normative rationality and autonomy as merely instrumental; no facts about authority, divine or otherwise, ground facts about one's normative reasons. However, as I argued in Section 2, in their specified material form (for example, subjectivist and constitutive models), the anti-realist views fail. Consequently, realist models of normative reason are all that remain to formulate AOT. This is enough to raise the *AOT Dilemma*. However, first, I want to raise two further points that show why *Moral Realism* is the actual problem.

4.2.1. Virtual Reality, the Simulation Hypothesis, and Accountability to God

Here is another way to clarify my point. I want to argue that David Chalmers's argument about the worship-worthiness of a virtual god shows that AOT is likewise a debate that assumes moral realism. Chalmers offers the following as one reason for his atheism:

Even if the Abrahamic God exists, with all those godlike qualities of perfection, I will respect, admire, and even be in awe of him, but I won't feel bound to worship him ... I don't think any qualities can make a being worthy of worship. As a result, we never have good reason to worship any being. No possible being is worthy of worship. (Chalmers 2022, p. 144)

Setting aside the claim that no qualities can make a being worthy of worship, I will focus on the metaethical theories working behind the scenes in Chalmers's reasoning.

Now, Chalmers's argument is couched within *virtual realism* and *simulation realism*, that is, his view that virtual reality and the objects of a computer simulation are just as real as non-virtual or physical reality and non-virtual objects.[13] He provides five criteria for *x* being real: *x* exists, has causal powers, is mind-independent, is non-illusory, and is a genuine *x*. However, if the virtual is not real, then the simulation is not worthy of worship because things that are not real are not worthy of worship. Without that assumption, the question about worshiping a simulator god is not relevantly different from the question about worshiping God.

More to the point, Chalmers's argument assumes that facts about one's normative reasons (specifically concerning worshiping a simulator god) are, at least partially, grounded in facts about reality and the qualities that would make a being worthy of worship. According to Chalmers, one has no normative reason to worship a simulator god because no qualities could make any being worthy of worship. Of course, if a simulation is not real, it could have constructed anti-realist or subjectivist normative facts. However, in that case, Chalmers's argument will not succeed. I take this to show that debates about normative reasons regarding virtual reality are analogous to debates about normative reasons concerning DCT. Both bottom out in the debate over realism and anti-realism.

4.2.2. Realism and Normative Constraints, and Normative Reasons Autonomy

"The object of systems of morality", writes Matthew Arnold, "is to take possession of human life" (Arnold [1865] 1902, p. 344). The reality of objective moral truths constrains human autonomy insofar as one cannot determine (subjectively or constructively) the structure of normative reasons or the conditions under which one rightly seeks and obtains knowledge of one's normative reasons. We are born into this situation. We come into the world without consent to the nature of normative reasons and without knowing our normative reasons. Facts about normative reasons and the nature and attainment of moral knowledge are not grounded in facts about one's mind or the construction of cooperating minds. As with DCT, moral realism entails that moral knowledge, including knowledge of our normative reasons, requires submission to how normative facts present themselves in reality.[14]

The ethical demand of reality captured by moral realism entails significant constraints on the normative status of human autonomy. Constructivist Sharon Street understands this well. Street rightly criticizes non-theistic moral realism as resting on "nothing more than an unreasoned faith, with realism about reasons and value, thus becoming a rather odd form of religion" (Street 2016, p. 299). Street understands that it is not theism or DCT alone that places limits on human autonomy but moral realism itself.

5. Conclusions: The Real Dilemma

AOT is not a problem unique to theism but a problem for all moral realists. Moreover, as pointed out in the Introduction, there are plenty of atheists who are moral realists. The following are a few more. Similarly, Russ Shafer-Landau writes:

> The laws of logic and rationality are normative. They tell us what we ought to do. But no one invented them. If you have excellent evidence for one claim, and this entails a second claim, then you ought to believe that second claim. If you are faced with contradictory propositions, and know that one of them is false, then you must accept the other ... If you are an atheist, you'll deny that God made up such principles. If any principals are objective, these are. So we have here objective, authorless, normative laws. (Shafer-Landau 2004, pp. 77–78)[15]

In explaining the objectivity of morality (moral realism), Walter Sinnott-Armstrong writes:

> If what makes an aggressive war morally wrong is that it hurts innocent people, then whether it is wrong does not depend on my desires, such as whether I want to harm those people. It also does not depend on my beliefs, such as whether I believe that the war will hurt those people ... Thus, atheists and agnostics can hold not only that there are moral facts but also that these moral facts are objective rather than subjective. (Sinnott-Armstrong 2009, p. 75)

Consider also how David Enoch explains one's epistemic access to the correlation between normative truths and normative judgments from a moral realist view:

> I argue that the correlation that needs to be explained is not as striking as it seems, and that whatever by way of correlation does need explaining can be explained consistently with Robust Realism, by a godless (and so speculative evolutionary) pre-established harmony kind of explanation. (Enoch 2011, p. 13)[16]

Clearly, at least some atheists embrace moral realism.[17]

Here is a final word from Wielenberg: "The foundation of morality is a set of axiomatic necessary moral truths. No being, natural or supernatural, is responsible for the truth of or has control over these ethical truths" (Wielenberg 2005, p. 66; see also, Wielenberg 2009). The autonomy restrictions on normative reasons are, according to Wielenberg, etched into the necessary moral truths of reality. Thus, the non-theistic moral realists find themselves, just as the theist does, in a universe iconoclastic to our normative reasons autonomy.

The *AOT Dilemma* remains. If one is to advance AOT, the most plausible models of normative reason are anti-realist, that is, subjectivism and constructivism. Yet, as I argued in Section 2, these anti-realist theories are too weak and inadequate to link autonomy to normative reason, much less in a way that supports AOT. However, as I argued in Section 3, if the autonomy objector adopts moral realism about normative reasons, they face a nearly identical problem as the theist, as normative fact constrains autonomy. Therefore, one can preserve normative facts and lose AOT or keep AOT and lose the objective goodness of autonomy and a place to press AOT. Either way, the *Autonomy Objection to Theism (AOT)* collapses.

Funding: This article was made possible by a generous grant from the Templeton Religion Trust. The opinions expressed in this publication reflect the views of the authors and do not necessarily reflect the views of the Templeton Religion Trust. For more information on this grant see www. livingaccountably.com. I would like to thank my research team for the Accountability as a Virtue project: C. Stephen Evans, Charlotte VanOyen-Witvliet, Byron Johnson, Sung Joon Jang, John Peteet, Robert C. Roberts, Andrew Torrance, Brendan Case, Matthew Bradshaw, and Joseph Leman.

Institutional Review Board Statement: Not applicable.

Informed Consent Statement: Not applicable.

Data Availability Statement: Not applicable.

Acknowledgments: I would like to thank C. Stephen Evans for providing very helpful feedback on an earlier draft of this paper, as well as Anna Ruth, Lucas Merritt, Sheki Lafanzio and an anonymous referee for helpful suggestions.

Conflicts of Interest: The author declares no conflict of interest.

Notes

[1] It is often overlooked that elsewhere Kant affirms that all moral laws are divine commands. See, Kant ([1788] 2015, p. 129); Hare (2000); and Hare (1992, p. 30).

[2] To be clear, by 'autonomy objection,' some mean debates about treating religious views as irrelevant to issues in moral philosophy. See (MacIntyre 1959, pp. 103–9). Others have in mind the debate about any conflict between the normative value of autonomy and religious ethics, especially divine command theory. I have in mind only the latter.

[3] Some classify divine command theory as a type of *theological voluntarism*, where normative facts depend on divine acts or intentions. However, there are good reasons to reject this classification. See, e.g., Evans (2022).

[4] Adams states DCT with respect to wrongdoing rather than obligation: "[A]n act is wrong if and only if it is contrary to God's will or commands (assuming God loves us)" (Adams 1987, p. 121). Adams also endorses the stronger modal thesis: necessarily, for any action, *a*; if *a* is ethically wrong, then *a* is contrary to the commands of a loving God. (Ibid., p. 132). For my purposes, I do not need the stronger modal thesis.

[5] However, the parent/child relationship is not clearly analogous to the God/human relationship. While the parent/child relationship is one of degree where the child develops into an adult and, in some cases, into a parent. The same is not true of the God/human relationship. Although humans mature, they do not develop into anything close to God. Part of what motivates the autonomy argument is the intuition that as children mature into adulthood, they not only search for themselves, but become selves in a way that dissolves the accountability relationship between parent and child. However, if God has legitimate permanent authority, the same is not true of the God/human relationship, and our accountability to God never dissolves.

[6] It is not clear that Kant is chastising the worship of God, but only the veneration of idols. Still, some take Kant to hold that worshiping God is at odds with human autonomy.

[7] Notice that Rachel's objection is not stated in terms of DCT. However, we can understand the normative requirement of worshiping God as a divine command grounded in God's nature or being. Moreover, as many divine command theorists hold

that divine commands are grounded in God's nature or being, Rachels's worship argument is a species of the autonomy objection against DCT.

Nomy Arpaly, for example, untangles eight distinct notions of autonomy commonly conflated in recent contemporary work. See Arpaly (2003, pp. 117–48).

This is an adaptation of Ralph Wedgwood's notion of a reason for action. See (Wedgwood 2009).

Mark Schroeder is the primary subjectivist who rejects this thesis. See (Schroeder 2007). For a subjectivist response to Schroder, see (Sobel 2017, chp. 15).

This is one reason why social constructivists, such as Copp, hold that normative reasons are morally neutral and "self-grounded" in facts about a society's nature that is constructed by that society. See (Copp 1995, p. 173).

This argument is similar to Hegel's objection that Kant's notion of autonomous will removes the normative content of practical/normative reason. See (Hegel [1820] 2011, scts. 133–37).

See Chalmers (2022), Chapter 6. Chalmers provides five criteria for what counts as real. For my purposes, I need not indicate those details.

For a brilliant treatment of moral knowledge, see Dallas Willard (2018).

See also, Shafer-Landau (2003).

See also, Enoch (2014, pp. 208–21).

For another example, see FitzPatrick (2008).

References

Adams, Robert. 1987. *The Virtue of Faith and Other Essays in Philosophical Theology*. Oxford: Oxford University Press.

Adams, Robert. 1999. *Finite and Infinite Goods: A Framework for Ethics*. New York: Oxford University Press.

Arnold, Matthew. 1902. *Essays in Criticism*. Oxford: Clarendon Press. First published 1865.

Arpaly, Nomy. 2003. *Unprincipled Virtue: An Inquiry into Moral Agency*. Oxford: Oxford University Press.

Baier, Kurt. 2008. The Meaning of Life. In *The Meaning of Life*. Edited by Elmer Daniel Klemke and Steven M. Cahn. Oxford: Oxford University Press. First published 1957.

Chalmers, David. 2022. *Reality+*. New York: W. W. Norton.

Copp, David. 1995. *Morality, Normativity, and Society*. New York: Oxford University Press.

Dworkin, Gerald. 1988. *The Theory and Practice of Autonomy*. Cambridge: Cambridge University Press.

Enoch, David. 2011. *Taking Morality Seriously: A Defense of Robust Realism*. Oxford: Oxford University Press.

Enoch, David. 2014. Why I am an Objectivist about Ethics (and Why You Are, Too). In *The Ethical Life*, 4th ed. Edited by Russ Shafer Landau. Oxford: Oxford University Press, pp. 208–21.

Evans, C. Stephen. 2013. *God and Moral Obligation*. Oxford: Oxford University Press.

Evans, C. Stephen. 2022. Could a Divine-Command Theory of Moral Obligations Justify Horrible Acts? Some Kierkegaardian Reflections. *The Monist* 105: 388–407. [CrossRef]

Evans, C. Stephen. 2023. *Living Accountably: Accountability as a Virtue*. Oxford: Oxford University Press.

Evans, C. Stephen, and Brandon Rickabaugh. 2022. Living Accountably: Accountability as a Virtue. *International Philosophical Quarterly* 62: 41–64. [CrossRef]

FitzPatrick, William Joseph. 2008. Robust Ethical Realism, Non-Naturalism, and Normativity. *Oxford Studies in Metaethics* 3: 159–205.

Frankfurt, Harry. 1971. Freedom of the Will and the Concept of a Person. *Journal of Philosophy* 68: 5–20. [CrossRef]

Fricker, Elizabeth. 2006. Testimony and Epistemic Autonomy. In *The Epistemology of Testimony*. Edited by Jenifer Lackey and Ernest Sosa. Oxford: Oxford University Press, pp. 225–50.

Hare, John. 2000. Kant on Recognizing our Duties as God's Commands. *Faith and Philosophy* 17: 459–78. [CrossRef]

Hare, Richard Mervyn. 1992. The Simple Believer. In *Essays on Religion and Education*. Reprinted in Richard Mervyn Hare. Oxford: Clarendon Press.

Hegel, Georg Wilhelm Friedrich. 2011. *Elements of the Philosophy of Right*. Translated by H. B. Nisbet. Cambridge: Cambridge University Press. First published 1820.

Huemer, Michael. 2013. An Ontological Proof of Moral Realism. *Social Philosophy and Policy* 30: 259–79. [CrossRef]

Huemer, Michael. 2021. Groundless Morals. In *A Debate on God and Morality*. Edited by Adam Lloyd Johnson, William Lane Craig and Erik J. Wielenberg. New York: Routledge.

Hume, David. 1967. *A Treatise of Human Nature*. Edited by L. A. Shelby-Bigge. Oxford: Oxford University Press. First published 1739.

Kant, Immanuel. 1996. *The Metaphysics of Morals*. Translated and Edited by Mary Gregor. Cambridge: Cambridge University Press. First published 1797.

Kant, Immanuel. 1997. *Groundwork of the Metaphysics of Morals*. Translated by Mary Gregor. Cambridge: Cambridge University Press. First published 1785.

Kant, Immanuel. 2015. *Critique of Practical Reason*. revised edition translated and edited by Mary Gregor. Cambridge: Cambridge University Press. First published 1788.

Korsgaard, Christine M. 1996a. *Creating the Kingdom of Ends*. Cambridge: Cambridge University Press.

Korsgaard, Christine M. 1996b. *The Sources of Normativity*. Cambridge: Cambridge University Press.

Kraay, Klaas J., and Chris Dragos. 2013. On Preferring God's Non-Existence. *Canadian Journal of Philosophy* 43: 157–78. [CrossRef]

Le Poidevin, Robin. 1996. *Arguing for Atheism: An Introduction to the Philosophy of Religion*. New York: Routledge.

MacIntyre, Alasdair. 1959. *Difficulties in Christian Belief*. London: SCM Press.

Markovits, Julia. 2014. *Moral Reason*. Oxford: Oxford University Press.

Markovits, Julia, and Kenneth Walden. 2021. Kantian Constructivism. In *The Routledge Handbook of Practical Reason*. Edited by Ruth Chang and Kurt Sylvan. New York: Routledge, pp. 318–35.

Murphy, Mark C. 2001. *Natural Law and Practical Rationality*. Cambridge: Cambridge University Press.

Nielson, Kai. 1991. *God and the Grounding of Morality*. Ottawa: University of Ottawa Press.

Nowell-Smith, Patrick. 1999. Morality: Religious and Secular. In *Philosophy of Religion: The Big Questions*. Edited by Eleonore Stump and Michael J. Murray. Malden: Blackwell, pp. 403–11. First published 1961 in *The Rationalist Annual*.

Penner, Myron. 2015. Personal Anti-Theism and the Meaningful Life Argument. *Faith and Philosophy* 32: 336–37. [CrossRef]

Piaget, Jean. 1965. *The Moral Judgement of the Child*. Translated by Marjorie Gabain. New York: Free Press.

Rachels, James. 1971. God and Human Attitudes. *Religious Studies* 7: 325–37. [CrossRef]

Sartre, Jean-Paul. 2007. *Existentialism Is a Humanism*. Translated by Carol Macomber. New Haven: Yale University Press. First published 1946.

Schroeder, Mark. 2007. *Slaves of the Passions*. Oxford: Oxford University Press.

Shafer-Landau, Russ. 2003. *Moral Realism: A Defence*. Oxford: Oxford University Press.

Shafer-Landau, Russ. 2004. *What Ever Happened to Good and Evil?* Oxford: Oxford University Press.

Sidgwick, Henry. 1981. *The Methods of Ethics*, 7th ed. Indianapolis: Hackett. First published 1907.

Sinnott-Armstrong, Walter. 2009. *Morality without God?* Oxford: Oxford University Press.

Sobel, David. 2017. *From Valuing to Value*. Oxford: Oxford University Press.

Sobel, David. 2021. How to Be a Subjectivist. In *The Routledge Handbook of Practical Reason*. Edited by Ruth Chang and Kurt Sylvan. New York: Routledge.

Street, Sharon. 2008. Constructivism about Reasons. In *Oxford Studies in Metaethics*. Edited by Russ Shafer-Landau. Oxford: Oxford University Press, vol. 3.

Street, Sharon. 2009. In Defense of Future Tuesday Indifference: Ideally Coherent Eccentrics and the Contingency of What Matters. *Philosophical Issues* 19: 273–98. [CrossRef]

Street, Sharon. 2010. What is Constructivism in Ethics and Metaethics? *Philosophy Compass* 5: 363–84. [CrossRef]

Street, Sharon. 2016. Objectivity and Truth: You'd Better Rethink It. In *Oxford Studies in Metaethics*. Edited by Russ Shafer-Landau. Oxford: Oxford University Press, vol. 11.

Taylor, Charles. 1991. *The Ethics of Authenticity*. Cambridge: Harvard University Press.

Wedgwood, Ralph. 2002. Practical Reasoning as Figuring Out What is Best: Against Constructivism. *Topoi* 21: 139–52. [CrossRef]

Wedgwood, Ralph. 2009. Intrinsic Values and Reasons for Action. *Philosophical Issues* 19: 321–42. [CrossRef]

Wielenberg, Erik J. 2005. *Value and Virtue in a Godless Universe*. Cambridge: Cambridge University.

Wielenberg, Erik J. 2009. In Defense of Non-Natural, Non-Theistic Moral Realism. *Faith and Philosophy* 26: 23–41. [CrossRef]

Wielenberg, Erik J. 2014. *Robust Ethics: The Metaphysics and Epistemology of Godless Normative Realism*. Oxford: Oxford University Press.

Willard, Dallas. 2018. *The Disappearance of Moral Knowledge*. New York: Routledge.

MDPI

St. Alban-Anlage 66

4052 Basel

Switzerland

www.mdpi.com

Religions Editorial Office

E-mail: religions@mdpi.com

www.mdpi.com/journal/religions

Printed in the USA
CPSIA information can be obtained
at www.ICGtesting.com
LVHW062037231123
764661LV00013B/1254